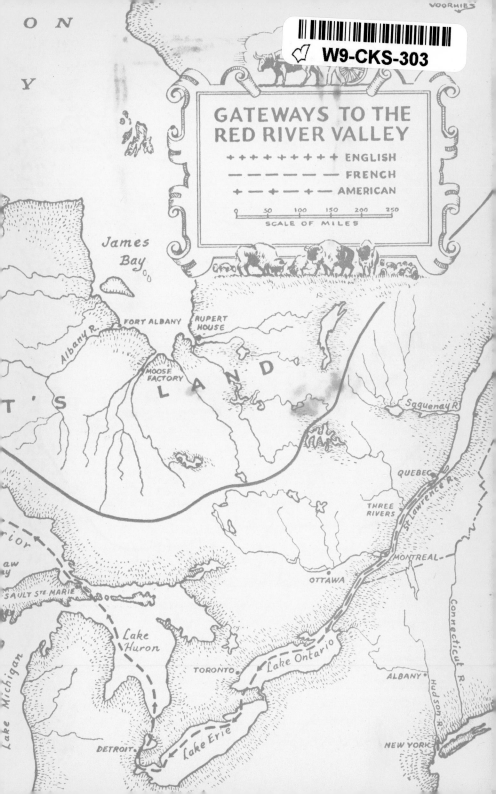

GATEWAYS TO THE
RED RIVER VALLEY

+ + + + + + + + ENGLISH
— — — — — — FRENCH
+ — + — + — + — AMERICAN

SCALE OF MILES
50   100   150   200   250

Red River Runs North!

Red River Runs North!

by

VERA KELSEY

HARPER & BROTHERS PUBLISHERS

New York

RED RIVER RUNS NORTH!

WITH PLEASURE, APPRECIATION, AND GRATITUDE,
THIS BOOK IS DEDICATED

To the scores, if not hundreds, of men and women in Red River Valley and beyond its borders, who so generously contributed time, knowledge, and understanding to its preparation.

Acknowledgments

To the many contributors to the making of *Red River Runs North!* this book most gratefully has been dedicated. But all books which require wide research in many fields gradually assemble a Without Which Department to whose members acknowledgment is doubly due.

In that sense, this one is more deeply indebted than can be said here to Dr. and Mrs. Bruce Chown, Mrs. J. H. McDonald, Mr. J. H. Johnston, librarian, Provincial Library, Parliament Building, and Mr. Clifford P. Wilson, editor, *The Beaver,* in Winnipeg; to Dr. H. L. Walster, Dean of the School of Agriculture and Director of the North Dakota Agricultural Experiment Station, in Fargo, North Dakota; to Miss Lora Crouch, librarian, Carnegie Public Library, and Mr. Herbert Krause, novelist, in Sioux Falls, South Dakota; and in Minneapolis, to the staff of the Minneapolis Public Library, and, above all, to its tirelessly able Reference Librarian, Miss Elizabeth Bond.

To these must be added, for their assistance in special fields:

Mr. C. H. Attwood, former Director of Water Resources, Province of Manitoba, Winnipeg.

Mr. James Baccus, North Dakota Farm Bureau, Fargo

Mr. and Mrs. Harold W. Bangert, Fargo

Mr. and Mrs. Philip R. Bangs, Grand Forks

Mr. and Mrs. O. J. Barnes, Grand Forks

Mr. and Mrs. Clifford Billingsley, Grand Forks

Mr. M. L. E. Brownell, editor, *National Home Monthly,* Winnipeg

Miss Vera Bollinger, Dean of Women, State Teachers College, Valley City, North Dakota

Dr. and Mrs. R. D. Campbell, Grand Forks

Mr. and Mrs. John S. Dalrymple, Minneapolis

The Reverend Father d'Eschambault, St. Boniface Historical Society, Genthon, Manitoba

Professor and Mrs. Richard M. Elliott, St. Paul

Professor J. H. Ellis, Department of Soils, University of Manitoba, Winnipeg

Miss Donna Forkner, Wahpeton, North Dakota

Mr. Hjalmar Rued Holand, Ephraim, Wisconsin

Mr. Harry Harm, East Grand Forks, Minnesota

Miss Clara Holmes, Public Relations Officer, Women's Division, Canadian Pacific Railway Company, Winnipeg

Mr. G. R. Jacobi, Glendale, California

Mr. Frederick Stevens Kittson, Philadelphia

Mr. and Mrs. Harold C. Knox, Winnipeg

Mrs. Douglas McKay, Winnipeg

Mr. Donald A. McKenzie, editor and publisher, *The Crookston Daily Times,* Crookston, Minnesota

The Honorable Mr. R. F. McWilliams, Lieutenant Governor of Manitoba, Winnipeg

Miss Grace Lee Nute, Minnesota Historical Library, St. Paul

Mr. M. M. Oppegard, editor and publisher, *Grand Forks Herald*

Mr. H. D. Paulson, editor, *Fargo Forum*

Mr. J. R. Pratt, Greater North Dakota Association, Fargo

Mr. Osborn Scott, manager (now retired), Canadian National Railways, Winnipeg

Mr. and Mrs. A. E. Selby, Minneapolis

Mr. Frank Sherlocke, East Grand Forks

Mr. and Mrs. J. B. Shirk, Minneapolis

Mr. Vilhjalmur Stefansson, New York City

Mrs. Edith Thompson, society editor, *Grand Forks Herald*

Mr. J. Ronald Todd, librarian, Northwest Library, University of Washington, Seattle

Judge and Mrs. Charles Vogel, Fargo

Miss Irma Walker, librarian (now retired), Carnegie Public Library, Grand Forks

Colonel W. K. Wilson, Jr., District Engineer, Corps of Engineers, St. Paul District

CONTENTS

MAPS

Necessary Words

Years before *Red River Runs North!* ever was thought of, it fell to my lot to guide an American VIP through the protocol of being received by Brazilian VIP's in Rio de Janeiro's intellectual circles. Most Americans, meeting on foreign soil, immediately ask one another, "Where are you from?" but this one said to me, "Where did you grow up?"

With no idea that he'd be much the wiser, I told him, "In North Dakota."

A neon light flashed on in his eyes. "And how's the raging Red?"

"Red River?" I said. "Oh, he's the same quiet, wriggling stream he always was."

"Quiet, nothing! In flood, he's one of the most dangerous and destructive rivers in North America."

"You must be thinking of one of the Red Rivers in the South," I suggested, and for emphasis, repeated, "I grew up right on his banks in Grand Forks, North Dakota."

"I'm thinking of Red River of the North," said he, "and I grew up right on his banks in East Grand Forks, Minnesota."

The VIP had lived there before 1900, during a period when Red River rose in two of the most destructive floods of his career. I hadn't come along until the next century when the River was resting up for the floods of the 1930's and '40's which finally brought Canadian and American Governments into action to control him.

Because Red River's variety of mood is matched only by the variety of his Valley's history, *Red River Runs North!* resembles the one-seventh of an iceberg that rises from untold depths into view. To tell the complete story of discovery and exploration, of the fur trade; of the people, particularly of the *Métis* or half-breeds, born of the meeting of pioneer white men with the Valley's Indian tribes; of religion, education, politics; of the dual pioneer British-Protestant and French-Catholic regimes north of the Boundary; above all, to tell of agriculture, and of the scores of men[1] who gave color and

[1] From the beginning, Red River's domain was—and still is—a man's world.

direction to Red River history, would fill the well-known bookshelf.

Accordingly, to meet the arbitrary limits of one volume, *Red River Runs North!* has been curtailed in some more familiar areas to permit expansion in others less well or un- known but more important. Incidental features, like the dog sledge and stagecoach, for example, are but lightly mentioned to give space to Red River Cart, the steamboat, and the railroad, which assumed the heavy roles in its unfolding drama.

Especially has it been expanded to permit detailed accounts of the buffalo hunting, of the Prairie Sioux, of the phenomenon of a million-dollar Red River Trade, emerging like a hidden river from the Wilderness of a century ago, to open both the Canadian and American Northwests and to bracket Canada and the United States as continental nations between Atlantic and Pacific Oceans. Strangely, the economic, political, and social significance of these three Valley factors never has been noted, locally or abroad, much less appraised and appreciated.

Thanks to the uniform innocence of the Valley's residents, including my own, concerning their physical, historical and cultural background, the long task of writing this book has not been without its lighter moments. Still startling to recall is the transformation of a gentle old descendant of the original Red River colony of 1812 into a fire-eating defender of the British Empire. To her suggestion that I make copious note of some obscure historical landmark, I had replied that because I was telling the story of the American as well as the Canadian Valley, I must leave such recording to local pens. Rearing back, she demanded, *"Do you mean to tell me those Americans are claiming Red River?"* She was far from the only Canadian resident of the Valley I encountered who was certain Red River of the North rose somewhere north of the International Boundary.

From Seattle, Washington, to Hartford, Connecticut, Americans wrote, telegraphed or telephoned me about some living or recently departed relative who was, authentically, "the first white child born in Red River Valley." Similarly sincere and generously intentioned citizens offered me interviews on the ground that, having arrived in the Valley of 1892 or '93, they could give me its story in a firsthand nutshell. Speaking before all manner of intellectual, social and economic groups from south to north of its boundaries,

I quickly learned to state with my first breath where Red River rose and where he went, the extent and location of his Valley proper. Otherwise, hoary-headed residents, born and reared within range of the River, would interrupt to ask.

Local innocence of Red River of the North and his Valley is only surpassed by that of Americans and Canadians at large. The briefest glance at any map shows Red River to be the dividing line between Minnesota and North Dakota. Yet recently the *Saturday Evening Post* informed its readers that Red River flows into the Mississippi. James Truslow Adams, in the book of maps he prepared to clarify their geography for Americans, not once but *nine* times pictures Red River as rising in South Dakota to streak like a homing pigeon for Lake Winnipeg. And so one could continue to vertigo through modern Canadian and American literatures.

Because the Valley is in a transitional stage that only the future can interpret, *Red River Runs North!*, with the exception of certain modern aspects whose roots predate 1890, brought itself to a natural conclusion with that year. Winnipeg, agricultural capital of the Canadian half, now revels in the throes of a changeover to agricultural-industrial, with a long view toward industrial. In the American section, King Wheat which seventy-five years ago received its kingdom on a salver and took no thought for the morrow, today is forced to stand aside while aggressive heirs apparent—Potato, Sugar Beet, and Barley—seize and hold more and more of its acres, and the national trend toward decentralization of industry brings more and more allied mills and factories to others.

The beginning of flood control; electrification of even most outlying areas; the rise of bus, truck, and commercial plane as transport; the family automobile and private plane, which now enable residents of rural districts to live in towns—all are affecting and changing Valley life and objectives.

Fargo, until yesterday second to Grand Forks in importance, has leaped far out in front to lead in population and functions as distributing, transportation and industrial center. Quiet villages suddenly are alive with ambitions and plans of city proportions. Everywhere the chain store, as it replaces with its impersonal branches the blocks of privately owned businesses on their Main Streets, is making its mark. Whether for good or ill, the years to come must tell.

Though by no means the ugly duckling of the Valley, Northwest Minnesota until recently, because of certain original ideas of social and political economy, has been the retarded duckling. Today, it is so sleek with enterprise and prosperity that Minnesota towns far to the east, to share in its reflected glory, post great signs along the highways to proclaim themselves, "Gateway to Red River Valley."

Beneath all local explanations for the changing times rests the fact that both the United States and Canada are growing up, to integrate their hundreds of independent regions, their thousands of distinctive types of citizens, into a common land, culture, and nationality. Until 1890, Red River Valley was a highly independent and colorful individual, with its own traits, good and bad. Since then, those great levelers and unifiers, the school, the automobile with its trailing highways, the motion picture, radio, telephone, national magazine, newspaper, and inexpensive book reprints, have had their sway. Today, except for three regional characteristics, there is little to distinguish residents of Red River Valley from those of the Mohawk, Okanogan, Ottawa, Columbia or any other North American river's valley. No longer are they Red Riverites; they are Americans and Canadians.

Two of these regional characteristics are clearly visible to the naked eye. The first is a tremendous and hardly repressed vitality that even in a room of quietly listening people, fairly bends the walls outward. In pioneer days, only the fit could survive; these are their descendants. The second is mobility.

Until day before yesterday, earliest arrivals, to go anywhere at all, had first to travel fifteen hundred miles to find a point of departure; until yesterday, from one to three hundred. Today's Red Riverites think nothing of running up to Winnipeg for dinner, a hockey game, or shopping, or to Minneapolis for an evening at the Ice Follies, the spring engagement of the Metropolitan Opera Company, a football game, or more shopping. Of setting off at a moment's notice for a few days in California, Florida, northern Canada or some Caribbean Isle. Naturally, if a visit to the Orient, Africa or South America seems indicated, they allow a little more time. Because so many of the older generations are but briefly removed from some European "Old Country," commuting by ship or, modernly, by plane, is an old Red River custom.

Perennially, members of the younger generation, their formative years spent on prairies that in many respects so resemble the sea, are lured to investigate what lies just over the unbroken, always receding horizon. Scratch an engineer, agronomist, geologist, or other -ist, in Tibet, Rhodesia, Matto Grosso, on South or North Pole expedition, and you'll find a son—sometimes, these days, a daughter —of Red River Valley.

This vitality and mobility, however, united with the general assumption that Red River of the North and his Valley have no long, deep-rooted history, culture, traditions of their own, have bred into large numbers of every generation the third and tragic Valley characteristic. Dimly or vividly they feel as untied, unfilled, and unrelated to their native soil as a drifting toy balloon. Older heads turn to study clubs, book clubs, music clubs; crowd to listen to outside speakers and entertainers, however dubious their offerings; travel the world. And, incidentally, in their trips to Winnipeg, Minneapolis, Chicago, and in the artist and symphony series they bring to their home towns, they probably hear more and better music during a year than all but the most dedicated music lovers in New York or other large cities.

Particularly on the younger generations, the so-called "older" East and West Coasts and the South, whose histories and literature they may know though they do not know their own, and ancient, distant lands exert an irresistible attraction. With pitiful—if often, justifiable—optimism, they learn foreign languages to fit themselves for trade, consular, engineering or teaching posts abroad. Or, wrapping their green-as-lettuce talents in a shiny new B.A., they set off for New York. The annual loss to Red River Valley is greater than any ever caused by flood, drought, or grasshopper.

It is the hope of this book, simplified melody of the richly chorded song of Red River though it is, that in its pages, Red River's own, as well as Canadians and Americans everywhere, may find that they share in the soil of this little-known Valley a culture and tradition, first rooted by men, events, and Red River of the North two hundred centuries ago.

To readers of *Red River Runs North!* three final words of explanation are due. Today the region covered in its pages is known as the *Old* Northwest. Until the 1890's, however, it was *the* Northwest. So Northwest it remains here.

To the warning in the Bibliography about the authenticity of the source material must be added a supplementary caution. Although the fewest possible statistics have been used, those few are suggestive only. In their casual attitudes toward the tiresome things, the three different sections of the Valley during pioneer days were as one. Later, the United States and Canada took census figures and other data at different times by different techniques for different purposes. Even today there is no sure way of correlating them.

To name the bewildering number of small settlements concerned, because of the nature of the Valley's economy and of its political divisions to east and west of Red River and north and south of the Boundary, would serve no other purpose than confusion. Accordingly, the name of the original nucleus about which others grew has been chosen to represent various districts. Thus, Red River Settlement, now Winnipeg, includes most of the Canadian Valley; Pembina, the northern American Valley; Grand Forks, Fargo, Breckenridge, other sections as one travels south. And St. Paul embraces the sundry Minnesota towns that, as way stations on Red River Trails and stagecoach routes, contributed to the travail or progress of Red River Valley.

VERA KELSEY

Red River Runs North!

One Month West of Sundown

Ninety million years ago a vast sea rolled between the Rocky Mountains and the Archean Hills of Minnesota. Then the earth inhaled a long, deep breath. Slowly, through millennium after millennium, the sea's bed rose. In time, as great plains, it linked land masses, east, west, and south, into the North American Continent.

Over the rising plains for long, inconceivably long eras, a temperate climate breathed. Vegetation, lush and low, came to them then, and small beasts to feed on it, and fantastically large reptiles. Erosion came, too. Nibbling continuously, winds, rains, rivers, shaped the soft new land into hills, plateaus, and odd formations.

Softest of all was the very heart of the continent. Here, equidistant from Arctic, Atlantic, and Pacific Oceans and, to the south, from the Gulf of Mexico, continuing erosion carved a primitive design for a valley. A valley three hundred miles long. About one hundred miles wide. Shallow at its southern end, it deepened steadily toward the north.

Through dateless prehistoric time, while this valley was little more than a dimple in the surface of the earth, a sheet of ice and snow, similar to those now covering Antarctica and interior Greenland, formed over northern Europe and America. In North America, it lengthened southward, crept over the high, young plains.

Approximately where the International Boundary lies invisible between Canada and Minnesota-Dakota, this continental icecap, thousands of feet deep, incalculably heavy, slowed to a halt. Over neighboring areas it spread raggedly, but into the primitive valley, it thrust a deep-probing finger—Red River Glacier.

Under centuries of summer suns and winter cold, Red River Glacier alternately melted—and paused. Melted—and paused. As it melted, a lake formed in the valley. Hills and ridges enclosed it on all sides but the north. There the retreating icecap provided an impassable but mobile wall.

1

The wall retreated ever northward. The lake grew larger, overflowed the little valley. North, east and west it rippled shallowly, but in the valley it ranged in depth from two hundred feet at the south to six hundred at the north. Finally, seven hundred miles long, some forty to fifty miles wide, its waters surpassed in extent the combined areas of the five Great Lakes.

For a thousand years waves of this glacial sea rolled over the valley. As they rolled, they cast up sand and rocks to east and west as beaches. Rock and loam they crushed, compressed, and sank to form a firm, smooth bed, fifty to one hundred and more feet deep on the valley floor. This they covered and covered and covered again with pure silt, black as ebony, heavy as lead, fine as face powder.

And to the south, in their eternal urge to reach the sea, the waters cut a channel through a height of land into the bed of a still more ancient watercourse, the "glacial river Warren." This bed they widened and deepened as they rushed southeast, then northeast, in a great 250-mile V, to shape the bed of today's Minnesota River, then join the Mississippi below what is now Minneapolis.

Centuries later, the young northern plains, unable longer to support the weight of the withdrawing icecap, dropped. Now the escaping waters could not flow south. Turning, they hurried away to Hudson Bay. Finally only vestiges of the great sea remained. Lake Manitoba! Lake Winnipegosis! Lake Winnipeg!

So eight or ten thousand years ago, this inland sea departed, unseen, unsung, and—until 1879—unnamed. Then, to honor the first internationally known scientist to declare that glacial ice created the soil the sea had laved, it was christened Lake Agassiz.

Where Red River Glacier had been, Red River Valley remained, *a newborn piece of this earth.*

Straight as an arrow for 315 miles, it lies between Lake Traverse in the northeast corner of South Dakota and Lake Winnipeg in Canada's Manitoba. To an air age, 315 miles may seem a bagatelle. But compared with many better-known areas, Red River Valley's proportions are impressive. They equal those of the Genesee and Shenandoah Valleys, are twice those of the Mohawk's. New Hampshire plus Vermont equal Red River Valley.

Yet to its residents it is a valley in name only. Sloping down imperceptibly to the north, sloping up almost as imperceptibly to east and west, its contours are so smooth and even that its lands are classified as prairies. From the air, however, its valley outline can be traced. To the south by low ridges. Midway, by hills and knolls. And, to the north, by what historic man, nostalgic for the rugged terrain from which he came, called mountains.

Half in the United States, half in Canada, Turtle Mountains at their highest rise no more than three hundred feet. Manitoba Escarpment and Pembina Mountain are but two units of the tremendous ridge that extends from Canada's Saskatchewan Valley through North Dakota into Minnesota. Because crystals in its venerable shales sparkle under sun and moon, Indians early christened it the Mountains of Shining Stones, a title later appropriated by the Rockies. In Stony Mountain, a few miles northwest of Winnipeg, the Valley boasts still a third summit. A hoary peak of some 400,000,000 years, it soars to a height of sixty feet.

Once as capes and headlands, these ancient elevations looked down on the inland sea that washed their feet. Today, historic landmarks, they continue to look down on a sea of luxuriant grains and grasses that in green and golden waves ripple from horizon to horizon.

From the moment the waters of glacial Lake Agassiz began to withdraw, began, too, the long drama in which Red River Valley assumed many roles. First and foremost has been its role as warroad and battlefield. Between grass and forest. Between man and beast. Between man and beast versus the elements and their tireless allies, isolation and loneliness. Between red man and red man. Red man and white. White man and *Métis*, the native Valley half-breed in whose veins the blood of white man warred with that of red. Between culture and culture. Hunting versus fur trade. Fur trade versus agriculture. And today, as Act III builds toward its climax, it foreshadows in Act IV a new and unexpected struggle between agriculture and industry.

For untold centuries the Valley has been a two-way highway. Following Red River from south to north, buffalo on their annual migrations cut the first deep trails. Following the buffalo came the Indian, on foot, accompanied by dog then pony travois. Behind him, white man and *Métis* in summer guided growing thousands of that creaking phenomenon, Red River Cart; in winter, adopted the Indian's gaily harnessed dog teams and sledges. Over their ruts trundled stagecoach and wagon express. Where they led, highway and railway followed, and now, the plane.

Because of this constant ambulation, Red River Valley has an unbroken tradition of itinerant settlements, and a pattern for them, whether permanent or temporary. On their buffalo hunts, Red River tribes erected immense circular camps about a central, ceremonial enclosure. Borrowing tribal wisdom for their own hunts, white men and *Métis* found it so effective that they employed the circular design for trading post and fort, for their fortified, one-night camps on Red River Cart Trails, and, finally, for pioneer villages built about that trademark of the prairies, the towering red elevator.

From the advent of the white man, Red River Valley has been a continental gateway, from east to west, from south to north. French and British explorers knew it as the "shortest route (due west from Red River) to the Western Sea." Modern railroads, highways and airways have proved them right. Because of the 1,500-mile wall of waterways, rock, bog and forest that marks the International Boundary from Atlantic Coast to North Dakota, its level prairies, as the first land crossing between United States and Canada, early assumed international political and economic importance.

Further enriched by the bones and flesh of thousands of generations of vegetation, hundreds of generations of beast and bird, the soil Red River Glacier laid down has proved a cornucopia of inexhaustible fertility. Only the Valley of the Nile can equal it, and that Egyptian land must be renewed each year with freshly silted waters.

Droughts, floods, grasshoppers, depressions, every natural and man-made catastrophe, have harried one section or another. From time to time its residents cruelly have exploited and abused it. Yet never in its known history has the soil from end to end of the Valley recorded total failure.

In turn, during the century preceding 1890, Niagaras of furs, pemmican, and No. 1 Hard Wheat have poured from this cornucopia. Ever since, a diversified Niagara of everything agricultural, from grains, sugar beets, potatoes, cattle, dairy products, to sunflower seeds, continuing to flow, has endowed its people with the highest income per capita in the world.[1]

[1] Because of the difficulty of correlating Canadian and American census and other statistics (for 1945), the difference between Canadian and American property values, and the fact that Valley boundaries and county lines, the unit

But this is not a book about agriculture. Interesting, and profitable, as its modern riches are, they represent historically but a few paragraphs in the richer story of the Valley, of the men it made and of the men who made it.

Why then is a valley, so productive, so strategically located at the very heart of the continent, almost unknown today, even to its own people?

For one reason: because not until late in the nineteenth century was it defined and identified as Red River Valley. Long before the white man ever saw it, wide-ranging Indian tribes, noting that the thundering herds preferred its deep sea of grass above all other stamping grounds, christened it "Buffalo Country." To colonial explorers and fur traders that title located it exactly. For France's and Britain's Atlantic colonies it was merely a part of the Great Beyond west of Lake Superior. As late as 1850, to place it in relation to St. Paul, a traveler described it as "one month's hard march at 20 miles a day west of sundown."

But there are much more important reasons for its obscurity in comparison with smaller, poorer, yet widely known valleys. At the head of the list stands the fact that *Red River Runs North!* Due to this vagary, his Valley was no part of the Louisiana Purchase, had no place in the program Thomas Jefferson launched to open the American Northwest. Contrary to the east-to-west course of migrating peoples throughout history, its first European settlers came from the north, by way of Hudson Bay. Until less than a century ago, residents on both sides of the Boundary faced north. And, taking a leaf from the book of their contrary River, they never did anything the easy way if a hard way could be found.

Not only is the Valley halved, roughly, by the Boundary. Like poor old Gaul, it is divided, politically and, again roughly, *in partes tres.* As a result of the first division, its people live under two flags, with all that means in tariffs, Customs, immigration and other barriers. The transcontinental railways, highways and airways that carry them east and west carry also their interests, ideas, trade, al-

---

on which figures are based, do not synchronize, exact figures cannot be given. Approximately and conservatively, however, it is estimated that if Red River Valley's half million people ever gave a thought to totaling *annually* the value of property and products, they would find themselves in possession of more than one billion dollars in wealth.

legiance. North-south services and interchange, in comparison, are
meager.

As a result of the second, the Canadian section is known as Southern Manitoba or simply included in the valley of Lake Winnipeg as
often as it is identified with Red River. The quarter south of the
Boundary and east of Red River categorically is designated as Northwest Minnesota. Only North Dakota's quarter, west of the River,
ever and always has borne its own name.

Yet unknown or little known, merely by existing the Valley has
affected, even determined, the destiny of great enterprises and nations far beyond its own borders. Red River washed the cornerstone
from beneath Colonial France; laid the cornerstone on which the
Dominion of Canada rose. Three transcontinental railroads, a dozen
cities north and south of the Boundary owe their founding, their
impetus, or both, to the Valley and its people. Without some knowledge of Red River Valley, it is as impossible to know the history of
either Canada or the United States as to complete a jigsaw puzzle
with one piece missing.

Similarly, men and events operating far from Red River wrote
whole chapters of the Valley's history while the Valley itself lay fal-
low and waiting. During Revolutionary times and immediately after,
white men may have ranged along Red River—say, one to every
25,000 of the 110,000 square miles his waters drain. No matter. John
Paul Jones, harrying the British Isles, Napoleon with his schemes to
do likewise, Benjamin Franklin, the feudal lords of Highland Scotland, all were shaping shadows of events to come. And when they
came, they shaped the substance of many an eminent career—Verendrye, Lord Selkirk, John Jacob Astor, Sir George Simpson, James J.
Hill, Lord Strathcona, many, many more. Others, like Peter Pond
and Jay Cooke, rose through contact with the Valley, only to fall
when they lost touch with it.

But who shall say that any man or woman who crossed the seas by
sailing ship, descended from Hudson Bay by open York boat, or
crossed the continent, afoot, by canoe or horseback, later by wagon,
prairie schooner, immigrant train, was not as great in spirit and in
deed? With little more than courage and a hoe, they broke virgin
prairie soil. They withstood bitter cold and storm, hunger, loneliness, Indian and fur trader, terrorizing prairie fires, plagues of grasshoppers, mice, and flood. Yet somehow they found time and zest

for singing and dancing, for reading and writing, for keeping faith in and with God, for learning to share with others what little they had.

As they disciplined soil and River to their will, soil and River disciplined them. As soil and River abundantly rewarded them, they rewarded the Valley by creating a new life in its great lone land. Simple men and women though they were, the exigencies of time and place, requiring more than they had, forced them to endure and surmount, to devise and create. With the precious seed they dropped in their jagged furrows, they sowed this new creative spirit. Not during Act III, perhaps, but certainly in Act IV, the Valley must reap in music, literature, all the arts and sciences, a richer harvest than any ever grown from wheat kernels.

But these men and women form the cast of Act II—from 1812, when the first European colonists descended from Hudson Bay to form the first permanent settlement in Red River Valley, to 1890, when in the view of their successors, the Valley was ready to enter its modern era.

It was not entirely coincidence that brought the handful of Scotch and Irish peasants to the forks of Red and Assiniboine Rivers while, on the Atlantic Coast, Great Britain and the United States were at war. It definitely was no coincidence that the Civil War's aftermath of ruin and depression and the embattled conditions in Europe peopled the American Valley in one great tidal wave between 1879 and 1885. The Valley's soil proved a powerful sounding board for the Goddess of Liberty's lifted cry, "Give me your huddled masses, yearning to breathe free." Both migrations were in keeping with the Valley's own tradition of unceasing struggle and combat.

By 1890, from Lake Traverse to Lake Winnipeg, almost 300,000 people had taken root. Railroads webbed it from south to north, east to west. Along their gleaming steel, tens of thousands of farms, hundreds of hamlets, villages and towns, checked in like corn every five or ten miles, throbbed with pride, enterprise and wealth.

In Winnipeg, at the forks of Red and Assiniboine Rivers, lots valued on Monday at $1,000 resold before Saturday for $10,000. At the junction of Red and Red Lake Rivers, Grand Forks, gateway to the northern Valley; at the junction of Red and Sheyenne Rivers, Fargo, gateway to the southern, rode on rising tides of dollars. As the *Minneapolis Tribune,* eyes on Minnesota flour mills and merchants waxing fat on Valley products and trade, editorialized on the American half of the Valley:

> The people of Red River Valley are going to have so much money this winter they will hardly know what to do with it. Their wheat crop alone brought them $180,000,000.[2]

Ah, but they did—as will be seen later.

Subtracting quickly—1812 from 1890 leaves seventy-eight years; 1879 from 1890, but eleven! Is Red River Valley then a land of miracles that in less than a century can turn a remote river fork into the metropolis of central Canada, transform bearded farmers, ex-fur traders, ex-steamboat captains into American gentlemen in white tie and tails within a decade?

No.

Because the cast of Act II inherited and developed another tradition, colorful, enduring, resourceful, adventurous. A tradition founded by the long procession of heroic peoples and individuals who during Red River Valley's Act I gambled their lives against great odds for great stakes.

---

[2] There were times during the writing of this book when it would have been acute pleasure to boil dear little children in oil, but it is not as an alternative to that relief that these pages remain unpeppered with asterisks and tiny numerals referring readers to the back of the book for the source of each quotation. In the honest belief that only Kipling's One Man in a Thousand pads back and forth between statement and source, such "Notes" have been omitted. Almost without exception, it can be assumed that the quotations are taken from autobiographies, biographies, historical records, and first hand accounts listed in the Bibliography. A few owe their origin to treasured letters, diaries, and other personal documents in private hands.

PART I

Outside the Door of History

1. A RIVER IS BORN

While east, west and south, North America was peopled, and even in the north men traveled well-worn trails, this newest, richest valley remained unknown, unsought. Though earliest European explorers and traders followed rivers and lakes inland and three mighty waterways provided entrance to Red River Valley, first nature, then man, fought to keep it secret.

The St. Lawrence, Red River's eastern doorway, is well known. Familiar, too, is the saga of explorers and traders powering fragile canoes up 1,000 miles of its majestic waters to traverse the even greater grandeur of Lakes Huron and Superior.

But between Lake Superior and Red River of the North lay the Wilderness; 500 miles of Great Beyond, or Laurentian Shield, as it is mapped today. Here lake after lake, a necklace of liquid sapphires, alternated with swamps and bogs. Here river after river swirled round hostile rocks or tumbled in rapids and waterfalls. Here awful supernatural monsters, howling for the blood of mortal man, roamed trackless virgin forests. Tried by this miscellany of perils, earliest explorers had to thread a passage through spider-bodied Rainy Lake, through Rainy River's falls and rapids, Lake of the Wood's 13,000 isles, into Winnipeg River.

A maverick artery, Winnipeg River issues from Lake of the Woods in numerous tortuous channels, only to reassemble in one recalcitrant course to charge across 165 miles of open prairie. Now it descends 349 feet in a succession of wild cataracts, every variety of cascade, treacherous eddy, and wave on wave rising in green masses to break over hidden rocks. Now it swells into large, deep lakes full of islands bounded by precipitous cliffs or rounded, granite hills. In a final burst it joins its waters with Lake Winnipeg's.

Lake Winnipeg, in turn, set up new hazards. More than 250 miles long, at times 25 to 65 miles wide, this glacial vestige is one and one-half times larger than "Great" Lake Ontario. A treacherous sheet, it spreads over more than 8,500 square miles. Far out of sight of land, its depth may be no more than six or seven feet. On a moment's

11

notice, it can whip up a storm. Islands litter its surface. Neither their
shores nor those of the mainland offer many havens. Out of bitter
experience, Indians named it *Quinipeg*—Nasty Ocean Lake.

Northern entrance to Red River Valley is north-flowing Nelson
River. Named for a British sailing master who lies buried at its
mouth, it more exactly fulfills its Indian title, *Kawerinagawa*—
Wicked River. Before its portlike mouth could be entered, head-
winds and storms, fog and icebergs of North Atlantic and Hudson
Bay had to be surmounted. Almost from its source in Lake Winnipeg,
it breaks into heavy falls and rapids. Unsheltered by highlands, its
channel is always at the mercy of wind, rain, snow, and sun. On
its shores, black flies, "bulldogs" or horseflies, and mosquitoes breed.
Only the last 90 of its 400-mile course to Hudson Bay are navigable.

The Mississippi, Red River Valley's southern entrance, however,
was all that could be desired. Its broad, navigable highway could be
entered anywhere from the Gulf of Mexico to its junction with the
Minnesota River some thousand miles north. And the Minnesota
River, flowing through a valley so rich and gentle it frequently is
referred to as the Garden of Eden, offered 250 miles of peaceful
paddling to its source in Big Stone Lake. Minnesota—"sky-tinted
waters"—the very name was peaceful, safe.

From Big Stone Lake a mile and a half portage across the
meadowland of Brown's Valley leads directly north into Lake Traverse and so to Red River of the North.

Yet when finally forced to penetrate the great beyond, pioneer
explorers and traders ignored this hazardless southern approach, to
embrace perils and hardships of eastern and northern. And with
good reason. Upper Mississippi and Minnesota Rivers, to say nothing of Red River Valley itself, lay within the domain of the American Indian feared and hated above all others—the Forest and Prairie
Sioux.

To Hiawatha and his wife, Minnehaha, a child was born. She was
so lovely and full of promise they gave her the most beautiful name
they knew. *Itasca*, meaning breast.[1]

As a maiden, lovelier still, Itasca filled Chebiabo, ruler of the

---

[1] According to factual minds, it was Henry Rowe Schoolcraft who, in 1832,
devised the word Itasca from the Latin phrase, *verITAS CAput*, to proclaim
Lake Itasca the "true head" of the Mississippi River.

BEFORE VERENDRYE, 1734. British and French conceptions of the Red River Country both claimed but knew nothing about.

Above: Detail from *Map of New France* in Gueudeville's *Atlas Historique*, Vol. 6, 1732

Right: Detail from *Map of the British Empire in America* by Henry Popple, 1733

spirits of the dead, with desire. But Itasca refused to leave her land of gentle hills and valleys, bright with sun. Her refusal so enraged Chebiabo that he uprooted the hills, split the heavens with lightning. Then, while thunder deafened the ears of her trembling people to her cries, he carried his unwilling bride to his home in the depths of the earth.

Never was Itasca reconciled. To this day she weeps and mourns. And her tears, welling, keep fresh and full the springs and rivulets that, trickling into lakes, form the ultimate sources of three great river systems—Mississippi, St. Lawrence, and Red River of the North.

As far as Red River and Mississippi were concerned, the St. Lawrence was simply a neighboring youth who went east to engage on a long and honorable career. But because Red River rises only nine feet above the Mississippi and not many more miles away, a curious kinship always has existed between them.

For a time, in fact, the two rivers were in doubt themselves as to which was going to be which. Mississippi, rising south of the heights of land that separate the waters emptying into Hudson Bay from those seeking the Gulf of Mexico, started north. Red River, rising north, started south.

Shortly, a pale-faced youth, Red River was wandering in and out of sometimes hilly, sometimes rolling country, to dally in lake after charming lake. By the time he had expanded under the attentions of eight of them, he was in a most romantic mood. Glimpsing, a mere forty miles to the west, an engaging little brunette, he sped to her side.

This was Bois des Sioux—Sioux Wood—River. Gallantly but ineffectively, the slender little thing was trying to make her way north from her rise in Lake Traverse through the deep, deep loam Lake Agassiz had laid down.

Patiently, tenaciously, he sculptured a channel for her. But now he was a confirmed meanderer. From his (official) origin in Elbow Lake to his exit in Lake Winnipeg, his course, measured in straight lines, is 390 miles. Though never deviating more than five or six miles from his Valley's center, he managed to make it 730.

Long before the arrival of the white man, Chippewa tribes, hunting in the Lower Valley, gave him his name—*Miswagunmewesebee*—because at sunrise and sunset his dirty, clay-toned waters appear rich vermilion. Under French domination, that mouthful shrank to Riviére Rouge. Under British, to Red River. Under American, in deference to southern rivers of the same name, it expanded again to Red River of the North. The Sioux, however, as true lords of the land, called him Ottertail from his rise to his meeting with Bois des Sioux; from there north, *Kitchizibi*—Great River. By whatever name, *never* is he red.

Most rivers are referred to affectionately and gratefully as "she." Not Red River of the North! Centuries of maledictions on his incessant turnings, sluggish apathy, and periodic rages have made his sex unmistakable.

Self-centered, narrow, scarcely more than one hundred feet wide at ordinary, low-water level, Red River reveals his worst traits in American territory. North of the International Boundary, as an almost handsome and benign old Canadian gentleman of generous curves, he moves with assured dignity.

Alas, as he approaches his destination, an immense sea of reeds and rushes impudently intervenes. With a flash of his old American temper, he pushes through. Result: a man-bedeviling delta of six mouths, only one navigable. In this mixture of land, water, and trivial vegetation, his exit into Lake Winnipeg is indescribably lonely.

Before the waters of Lake Agassiz vanished in Hudson Bay, the soil they had laid down in Red River's Valley was welcoming the first seeds. In time, almost 125 different grasses came, almost 2,000 flowering plants, a score of trees, another of vines. Above all, came the prairie rose in such profusion it literally carpeted the Valley with pink, white and red. Highly plumed vetch and other leguminous plants came, too, until the soil was fairly surcharged with nitrogen.

Myriads of waterfowl—wild geese, ducks, herons, pelicans, brown cranes and white—flocked to lakes and standing pools. To the prairies came grouse, partridge, prairie chickens. To the woods that line rivers and lakes, a thousand varieties of birds. Like the tanager, to dazzle sight. Like the meadowlark, to sparkle the air with melody. One, the blackbird, claimed the Valley as his own. His numbers increased until, in flight, they darkened the sun in a swiftly swooping twilight.

Multitudinous small beasts and large found haven here. Most important, the beaver and the buffalo—in thousands, tens, hundreds of thousands.

Only plants disciplined by the ever-blowing winds to send roots deep or widely webbed into the soil, survived. Only birds that devised some plan to ride out storms and cold, only animals that knew to grow thick, warm coats, could remain the year round. Death or departure were the alternatives offered the weak, timid, and unresourceful.

In winter, snows fell steadily, sifting over the Valley floor until a new surface, soft, fine, dry, lay eighteen to thirty inches deep. And occasionally among the chill, dry winds from west and north came the Great Winds. Screaming with cold acquired over ice-capped Rockies or Arctic Circle, plus a thousand miles of frozen plains, they hurled themselves on the Valley to whip and harry snow before them in horizontal hordes. Then for days and nights, howling like a maniac, storm transformed the quiet land from Hudson Bay to Lake Traverse into a savage wilderness of white. Temperatures fell to thirty, forty, fifty below zero. . . .

In summer, veritable Tartars astride massive racing clouds, eastern winds laden with moisture from Great Lakes and small, preyed on the Valley. Green and vicious flares of lightning cracked the skies. Thunder rolled like crashing boulders. Rain—sometimes hail —fell in deluges.

In autumn, fire, wind-fanned and ravenous, fell on the drying grass. Flames leaped to prodigious heights. The air roared with furious clamor. Walls of smoke, bordered with rose by the sun, soared heavenward, to bring night to half the Valley while the rest still knew bright day.

Surviving plants and animals lived and had their being in space and silence as immense and tranquil as the half-universe of sky, domed from an unbroken horizon. Space and a singing silence that absorbed all sound whether the prairies were an ocean of waving green, patterned by wooded tides, or a sea of white, frozen at the very instant its fluid crests foamed to break.

Into this peace came rare natural phenomena to make Red River Valley a wonderland. In summer, dew haloes round sun and moon. Rainbows, duplicate and triplicate, arched and perfect. In winter, sundogs, false moons and suns, the counterfeit as brilliant as the real. Incredible prairie mirages brought clearly into view vistas hidden by the curvature of the earth five to twenty-five miles distant. Fall and winter, aurora borealis shot long columns of pure light across the heavens or, frail and tremulous, fell from terrace to terrace in showers of pastel radiance.

A prairie, says the dictionary, is a level or rolling tract of land covered with grass instead of trees!

2. AND PEOPLES COME AND GO

Perhaps glacial Lake Pelican was thinly frozen over that day, some twenty thousand years ago, when a fourteen-year-old girl ventured out upon it. Or perhaps its waters, whipped to waves by a sudden squall, overturned the rude craft that bore her.

One dismal, mid-June day in 1931, a weary road crew, ripping open a "frost-boil" on a dirt highway along Red River Valley's eastern rim, came to life when the blade of their tractor turned up glistening clamshells. Clamshells, fifteen hundred miles from any sea! Beneath them, twelve feet deep in undisturbed earth, lay the young girl's skeleton.

Archeologists duly measured and classified the first human being known to have entered Red River Valley when it was still but a dimple in the earth. Then in solemn conclave they christened her—the Minnesota Man!

This juvenile representative of the primitive Mongoloids who arrived in ice-free areas of western Minnesota two hundred centuries ago is only one reason why Red River Valley holds a respected place in archeology. Near the channel Lake Agassiz' waters cut into Brown's Valley, the grave of a man buried twelve thousand years ago has been found. Ivory relics uncovered in Agassiz' beaches reveal that a people with an ivory culture once lived and buried their dead there.

In Red River Valley, Mongoloids may have acquired such a taste for glacial conditions that when the icecaps retreated, they followed. Physical characteristics of skeletons buried in Lake Agassiz' bed suggest these Red River pioneers to have been ancestors of the Eskimo.

This much is sure. For four thousand years after glaciers and Mongoloids departed, Red River Valley remained a no man's land.

Inhabitants, however, were on the way. Descendants of the Asiatic migrations that twelve millenniums ago crossed Bering Strait to America, wherever they paused in their long trek over this hemisphere, they erected mounds as graves, religious structures, and fortifications. In Mexico and Central America, Mound Builders evolved the Aztec and Maya cultures. In southwest United States, they founded the Pueblo culture. In Ohio, as the Hopewell peoples, they produced small sculptures that compare with those of Maya and ancient Egyptians. And about the wooded lakes of Upper Mississippi Valley they developed specialized agricultural and industrial skills.

On this descending scale, the bands that wandered into Red River Valley to erect an isolated mound or two as they followed the River north, represented the bottom rung of the ladder. Settling down to rude farming along small, sheltered streams in the Lower Valley, they erected mounds as graves and defensive embankments.

The buffalo seduced them. Why should they sow and harvest, fish and trap, when the migrating herds provided everything necessary for food, clothing, shelter? Turning nomad once too often, Red River's Mound Builders followed the bison into oblivion.

Exactly six centuries before Columbus sighted the West Indies, Erik Thorwaldson, the Norseman, reached Greenland. The year, 892, by virtue of Greenland's geologic union with the Western Hemisphere, therefore, becomes the first authenticated date in the history of the New World. And Erik the Red, the first European known to have set foot on it.

It was, in turn, from the Eastern and Western Settlements Erik founded in Greenland that events derived which may explain the various thirteenth- and fourteenth-century Norse weapons, equipment, and deep-buried camp fires uncovered by plow and flood along Red River's shores.

In 1348, a delegation from Eastern Settlement arrived in Bergen, capital of Norway and Sweden, to spread a sorry tale before the king. Western Settlement had been sacked by Eskimo. Its survivors, abandoning homes and Christianity, had fled to a vast island to the west. Now the ferocious Arctic warriors menaced Eastern Settlement.

The Greenlanders reached the King's ear in the nick of time.

Magnus Erickson, King of Norway and Sweden, was then at the peak of his fanatic zeal to convert mankind to the Roman Catholic faith. Conversion of Russia—his main project—had been stopped short by an outbreak of Black Death among his potential converts. Thus he had on hand funds intended to equip an army large enough to compel the Russians to accept his will.

These funds he now used to fit out an extraordinary expedition. Its purpose was not to save Eastern Settlement from annihilation by the Eskimo. It was to seek out and win back to Christianity the refugees from Western Settlement. As leader of the expedition, King Magnus named Paul Knutson, one of the leading nobles of the Kingdom. And to accompany Knutson, other Norwegian and Swedish nobles, some from the king's own retinue, carefully were chosen. Among them, of course, were priests.

In 1355 the expedition sailed from Bergen. Nine years later it returned.

So says recorded history. The heroic, nine-year Odyssey in America is not completely recorded—yet. But one day it may be. On that day Red River's greatest legend will become one of North American history's greatest chapters. That legend begins when Paul Knutson reached "the vast island to the west."

Charged with restoring Christian worship to the lost Greenlanders, he first had to find them. On the island at that time three regions already were known to the Norsemen of Greenland. *Helluland* (Flat Land Rock), barren and sterile. *Markland* (Nova Scotia), whose thick forests supplied timbers for their building and fuel. *Vinland,* the area about Narragansett Bay discovered in 1003 by Leif Erikson, son of Erik the Red.

In Vinland, the expedition erected a fortified church.[2] About it, as was the custom of the time, Knutson established his base of operations.

Leaving men and a ship or two there, Knutson with forty or more others, on his flagship, *Knorr,* set sail for Markland to spend several seasons searching the north for refugees. Although they found no Greenlanders, they were not discouraged. After all, this wild region was an island. On it somewhere the emigrants must be living. Sailing north to circle it, they entered Hudson Bay.

---

[2] By some authorities believed to be "The Tower," in Newport, R. I.

Not until they encountered Nelson River's fresh waters pouring into the Bay's southwest corner did they realize their error. This was no island. It was a new and immense continent!

All hope of discovering the refugees vanished then. But not all hope of discovery. What an honor to Norway, Sweden and themselves to explore this New World and claim it for their king!

This unanticipated waterway not only would lead them into the New World. It must carry them to an eastbound river which would return them to the Atlantic Ocean and Vinland.

Ships, however, could not ascend the Nelson. Knutson left ten men with the *Knorr* in Hudson Bay to wait a certain time for his return, then sail for Vinland. With twenty-nine others, he embarked in one or more of the ship's small boats.

Via sails and oars, the exploring party sped along, up the Nelson, through Lake Winnipeg. And there, at the lake's end, they found Red River of the North waiting to introduce them to his Valley.

After their circuit of austere and icy Hudson Bay and their passage through bleak northern Canada, what a paradise Red River Valley must have appeared! Green and flowered and fragrant. Warm and brilliant under a summer sun whose course across high blue skies they could follow from dawn to dusk. Alive with game and birds of every kind and color. And if ranges of brown hills moved northward as the buffalo grazed, what awe and fascination, too, must have widened their Nordic eyes.

Only wonder for the richness and beauty of the Valley can explain why they ignored mouth after mouth of Red River's eastern tributaries to sail on and on. Not until Buffalo River offered almost the final exit did they turn left.

But even six centuries ago Buffalo River was only a small stream. It led them through a series of small lakes—perhaps at that time, one long lake—to a dead end. Turning back to a lake, now dry, they followed another small stream to still another dead end in another lake.

From it to Cormorant Lake, however, was an easy 500-foot portage. Now, Red River Valley behind them, they were embedded in forested hills that stretched eastward for hundreds of miles. About the lake, these steep, timbered hills alternated with somnolent swamps, adrone with insects. Yet after days of Herculean labor, the thirty Norsemen had need to rest and replenish their supplies.

On a hillside overlooking the lake, at a point where two rocky islets reminded them of the skerried lakes of Norway, they made camp. Twenty men went out to fish. Ten men remained on shore. When the fishermen returned they found every comrade dead.

No sign or sound from the forests told who the assassins were, whence they came or where they went. Hastily the survivors buried the slain. Then, to escape those dark and sinister forests, they sailed south—into a region that boasts numerous small rivers and more lakes than any other area in the United States.

Pelican River, their first guide, led them into the Ottertail.

So close they were to safety! Not only to safety, but to the honor and glory of being the first Europeans to explore the continent their countryman, Erik the Red, had discovered five centuries before. For Ottertail, of course, is merely another name for Red River of the North. He would have carried them back to his Valley and so to their waiting ship in Hudson Bay.

But in Ottertail's pallid waters the desperate men saw no resemblance to the muddy clay of Red River. And when shortly he began to bear them west, they deserted him for a series of small lakes that led them into Pomme de Terre River.

Vainly they sought a waterway east. River after river flowed south. At last a small stream took them to a small lake circled by stony hills and stunted timber. On the summit of its little island from which they could watch all shores, they camped again. They had something very important to do.

Stronghearted, able and well equipped as they were, they knew now they might never escape this savage and endless land. In this lonely refuge, beset by peril, they felt impelled to leave a written record.

On a large stone they cleaned and shaped to level smoothness, their priest laboriously and exactly engraved in runic characters the tale they had to tell:

> We are 8 Goths [Swedes] and 22 Norwegians
> on an exploration journey from
> Vinland through the West We
> had camp by a lake with 2 skerries one
> day's journey from this stone
> We were out and fished one day   After
> we came home we found 10 of our men red
> with blood and dead   AVE MARIA
> Save us from evil   ·

And on one side of the stone, the priest added a postscript:

> We have 10 of our party by the sea to look
> after our ship 14 days journey
> from this island in the year of our Lord 1362

Inscription completed, stone embedded in the island's soil, the survivors again set out to brave the hazards to come. By lakes, rivers and portages, they reached the Mississippi. Where the city of St. Cloud now stands, the trail of mooring stones, deep and long buried campfires, lost or discarded gear, and the legend end.

Five hundred and thirty-four years later, Olof Ohman undertook to clear the trees from a knoll on his seven-year-old farm near Kensington, Minnesota. Once that knoll had been an island in a small lake. In 1898, it was an elevation surrounded by drying swamp.

Angered by the stubbornness of a single tree, Olof dug away the soil to chop free the roots. The tree was anchored by a heavy flat stone, two surfaces of which were covered with regular and exact "marks." About the stone largest roots had grown in an iron grip.

Thus the Kensington Rune Stone, over which a storm of controversy rages, came to light. Today, at the Smithsonian Institution in Washington, it serves as an enduring symbol that white men, whether or not Knutson and his party, traveled Red River Valley almost six centuries ago.

3. UNTIL THE SIOUX DECIDE TO STAY

Spring in seventeenth-century Red River Valley!

Daily the sun mounts higher, closer to the zenith. In warmth and stillness, prairies shimmer with fresh, tender grasses shot with purple and white violets, red and pink of earliest roses. Even Red River of the North, wide and high with melted snow, shines green-gold in the sun.

But beneath the stillness, the earth vibrates to an inaudible force. Birds rise restlessly from their nest building in the woods along the River. Squirrels scurry to upper branches to chatter anxiously. Small things that live in the ground take deeper refuge.

Diffused at first, like the echo of waves pounding a distant beach, a rumble rolls down the Valley. Gradually, along southern and western horizons a dark line moves between greening earth and forget-me-not blue sky. While the rumble swells to a bellow, a roar of pounding hoofs, clashing horns, the line broadens, thickens.

Buffalo, thousands upon thousands of buffalo, carpet the Valley with a deep, brown nap.

Weeks flow away as they graze steadily northward, following summer to the fertile ranges of the Saskatchewan. There they remain until skies grow gray, and winds, changing from east to northwest, bring chill straight from the snowfields of the Rockies.

The herds begin to move. First frosts find them again in Red River Valley. But now, though Indian Summer blesses the land, they move rapidly. By the time snow lies deep on Lake Traverse, they must be far to the south.

When from the shelter of Minnesota forests that crowd the very rim of old Agassiz' bed, bronzed men, silent, swift as shadows, first marked the rhythm of the annual buffalo migrations, no man can say. Their keen, dark eyes recorded the great beasts' restlessness when the bitter scent of burning grass tinged the breeze, their fear when a fiery glow swept toward them. Noted how ponderously yet swiftly they streamed over the prairie ahead of the leaping flames. How, even though walls of fire barred the way, always in spring they ran north, in autumn south.

Came springs and autumns when many tribesmen waited, on prairie ridges, in ravines, until to either side of the grazing herds, man-guided fire raced toward a converging point. And the buffalo, seeking safety, poured down the narrowing lane exactly as the red men knew they would.

Through clouds of dust and smoke, bone-tipped arrows sped into the terrorized beasts. War clubs, stone knives, stone hatchets rose and fell. Lances darted in and out. When smoke and clamor died away, quiet brown mounds dotted the prairie green.

Now from coulee bottom or river bed appeared a motley procession. Old men and children. Women bent beneath heavy burdens. Dogs dragging rude travois loaded with camp paraphernalia.

On the open prairie a warrior fixed his lance, tipped with scarlet feathers. About it the procession swung in a wide circle until the head of the line moved behind the rear. Around the boundary thus marked, poles rose to form skeleton cones. Over their smooth sides, deer hides were flung. Within minutes, a city functioned there.

Thus Minnesota tribesmen took possession of Red River Valley as the western frontier of the vast circular plain their Great Spirit, *Oanktayhee,* shaped when he first created land and man. The land that included all of today's South Dakota, more than half of Minnesota, eastern North Dakota, and portions of Wisconsin and Iowa. The man who became progenitor of the great *Dacotah*—Alliance of Friends—nation.

To most Dacotah tribes, life in Minnesota forests was good. But increasingly to the buffalo hunting bands, Red River Valley was better. Inevitably came the day when they focused their nomad existence about Lakes Traverse and Big Stone and in the valleys of Bois des Sioux and Red Rivers as far north as the Sheyenne River.

Though this prairie locale demanded an entirely new way of life, it offered everything they desired. Now buffalo meat formed their diet. Buffalo hides covered their teepees, provided their beds, dog harness, lariats. Sinews made strong thread. Bones supplied needles, spoons, and other domestic utensils. Shoulder blades served as hoes to cultivate their maize. Ribs formed arches and clubs for games, runners for sleds. Horns became part of the warrior's headdress. Skulls played a vital role in their communication system; worn over the head, became dancers' masks. Marrow tanned leather, healed wounds. . . .

On the success or failure of the buffalo hunts, the Prairie Dacotahs came to rely so exclusively that Forest Dacotahs and other Indian tribes identified them as the "Nation of the Beef."

During one of these hunts in the early 1600's, while two bands of hunters camped near Lake Traverse, a warrior of one tribe seduced the wife of a warrior of the other. Trying to rescue her, the husband was killed. Ensuing battles between the two bands threatened to embroil the entire Dacotah nation in civil war. The day was saved when the seducer and his tribesmen seceded, but the schism affected Valley history for centuries.

Leaving the land of the Dacotahs, the seceders descended the Valley to ally themselves with the Cree who dwelt at that time between Lower Red River and the Saskatchewan. The Cree gave them land along Red River's principal tributary. From the way the newcomers dropped hot stones into water to boil their buffalo meat, they and the tributary shortly acquired a new name—*Assiniboine,* meaning, "Stone Heaters."

From then on Assiniboines and Cree warred on the Dacotahs and the Dacotahs on them. In time from this unending strife, the Dacotah nation also acquired a new name, *Nadowe-is-iw*—Little Snakes or Adders. *Is-iw,* or Sioux, became the popular name for the Dacotahs, as Chippewa long had been the better-known name for the Ojibways.

Pride and passion for their own domain always had been an outstanding characteristic of the Dacotahs. Now pride in Red River Valley and the never-ceasing warfare against Assiniboines and Cree sharpened the Prairie Sioux's naturally ruthless possessiveness to a ferocity that even excelled that of the Dacotahs of the Forest. When not a warroad along which some hostile band moved, Red River Valley again was a no man's land, feared and avoided by red—later, white—man until less than a century ago.

Now Prairie Sioux chiefs no longer made the annual spring pilgrimage to the sacred cave on the Upper Mississippi to sit in on the solemn Dacotah councils held there. Seldom now did they even attend the councils at Izatys, capital of the Dacotah domain.

Five villages centered about Lake Mille Lacs in northern Minnesota, Izatys was the largest and most permanent settlement of the Dacotah nation. To the chiefs there came news of all the world. Of the failure or abundance of wild rice harvests and buffalo hunts. Of far lands some Sioux band had visited. Of what nations and tribes were at war. On everything they meditated and made decision in the best interest of all their people. Then by swift messenger, news and decisions were communicated to all Sioux tribes, no matter how remote.

And now to the Izatys of the 1650's, reports arrived of the rising power of the Iroquois in the east, of their decimation and conquest of the mighty Huron peoples, of the Ottawas, then the Eries. Later came word that the Iroquois, moving west, were devastating as they moved a domain as large as the Dacotahs' own. That the secret of their power was a new weapon that spit fire.

Izatys chiefs were not disturbed. Even the Iroquois could not boast warriors so strong, fearless, and cunning as the Forest and Prairie Sioux. The Iroquois would not cross *Misi-Sipi,* the Great River.

The Iroquois didn't. But thousands of eastern tribesmen, fleeing before their fury, poured into the region east of the Mississippi.

Among them were Ottawas who possessed not only the weapon
that spit fire, but knives, hatchets and other necessities made of a
new and magic substance.

When word of this reached Izatys, the chiefs, incredulous, despatched envoys to investigate. The envoys found the Ottawas, beheld their iron-barreled muskets, iron knives, hatchets, kettles. And,
believing no mortal man could create such wonders, they lifted
their eyes to the sky and blessed it for guiding Divine Spirits to
this earth.

Humbly they entreated the Ottawas to visit Izatys, share with
the Dacotahs these gifts of the Great Spirit. The Ottawas came. And
when in return for worthless stuff—beaver robes the Sioux wore in
winter, threw away in spring—they gave the Izatys chiefs a few worn
knives, the Dacotahs were more awed and humble still. They and
all their people, they vowed, would hunt beaver throughout the
winter, have quantities of fine new skins to trade if the Divine
Spirits would return in the spring.

In this way, iron, symbol of the white man, though the white man
himself was still half a continent away, came to signal the end of
the Stone Age in the land of the Dacotahs. And historic time approached the very verge of Red River Valley.

Approached, but did not reach it—thanks to the fear and enmity
of Chippewa, Cree, Fox, all the tribes encircling the Sioux domain
to north, east and south. Knowing themselves powerless in battle
against Dacotah warriors, they seized on the newborn fur trade as
an invincible weapon. Only by submissive and extortionate trading
with a "middleman" tribe could the Sioux, now mad for iron, secure
so much as an awl.

More: in exchange for the finest beaver pelts they had to accept
worn, secondhand articles while the middlemen kept the new trade
goods for themselves. Above all, no musket, ball, or powder was
permitted to reach the tribes west of the Mississippi.

This situation endured until 1660, when word reached Izatys that
two iron-creating white gods had descended to the shores of Lake
Superior. Humbly, very humbly, the proud chiefs sent envoys with
gifts of rarest beaver to implore these deities to enter the land of
the Dacotahs.

4. THE "LITTLE PEOPLE"

Among his descriptions of the unrivaled riches and wonders he'd seen during his twenty-one years in the realm of Kublai Khan, Marco Polo inserted a wild guess. The sea that washed the shores of the Orient and the sea that washed the shores of western Europe, said he, were one and the same.

Though published about 1300, his *Travels* did not find a credulous reader until 1490. Two years later Christopher Columbus landed on San Salvador in the West Indies. Convinced he'd reached an outpost to the Orient, he then, and on his later voyages, combed islands and mainland for a passage to the Western Sea.

Nor was he alone in this belief. When at last the Old World conceded a New World had been found, explorers for two centuries hunted a passage through or around it. So sure were they of its existence that they named it in advance, "Strait of Anian."

Portugal's navigators had found gold in tropical Africa, gold, pearls, brocades, in tropical India, rare dyewoods in tropical Brazil. Spain's coffers were bursting with gold and other treasure from Mexico, Central and South America. Burning to enter the ranks of these professional discoverers, England, France, Holland and Denmark scoured Caribbean islands and tropical America's mainland for the Strait of Anian.

Only when unable to emulate the experts did the amateurs turn north. Amateurs, indeed! Somehow all of them managed to sail right by the three gateways to Red River Valley.

Although for generations, perhaps centuries, Portuguese, Basque, English and Breton fishermen had been crossing the dark Atlantic to fish the coastal waters of America from New England to the mouth of the St. Lawrence, not until 1534 could an explorer find that great river's great mouth. Then Jacques Cartier, on fire to discover for France a Northwest Passage to the Orient, entered it.

Cartier was a most reluctant discoverer. On this and later voyages, he followed the river inland for a thousand miles. To an island on which stood a mountain that offered so royal a view it was soon to be known as Montreal. From its summit he beheld the St. Lawrence in all its majesty and the shining web of lesser rivers and lakes flung over its valley. But no waterway that resembled the Strait of Anian. Defeated, he returned to France. Red River's first gateway remained sealed for sixty years.

About twenty years after Cartier departed, English explorers stumbled on Hudson Strait. Their successors entered it to enrich the pageant of Red River history with three memorable scenes.

The first commemorates Henry Hudson's discovery of Hudson Bay in 1610. From a tiny open boat, tossing on the Bay's ice-floed waves, the indomitable explorer, his son, and five loyal men watch with unbelieving eyes their good ship *Discovery* and its mutinous crew abandon them. . . .

London thrilled to the tale of the *Discovery's* mutineers. Henry Hudson had found Northwest Passage! Within a year, Sir Thomas Button weighed anchor for Pekin, via Hudson Bay. With him sailed 160 members of the Company of London Discoverers of Northwest Passage and, as honored guests and guides, two of the mutineers.

Setting for Scene II was the ice-locked mouth of a river flowing into the southwest corner of Hudson Bay. Here Sir Thomas, merchants, and increasingly unhappy mutineers sat out the ten long, bitter, gray months of the winter of 1612-13. And here, when sailing master Nelson died, the river was named to do him honor.

Other fruitless expeditions came and went before the winter of 1631-32 set the stage for Scene III. In the southern arm of Hudson Bay, on another English ship frozen into ice for ten more months, Captain Thomas James recorded trivia of the dreary hours. Of water, water everywhere and not a drop to drink. Of ice that cracked and growled and roared and howled. . . .

The captain's account of the bay that now bears his name did more than inspire Coleridge to write *Rime of the Ancient Mariner.* It convinced England's navigators that Northwest Passage was not to be found by way of Hudson Bay. Red River Valley's northern entrance closed for almost forty years.

Remained the third and most accessible gateway—the broad and shining Mississippi with its blue-green Gulf of Mexico threshold. But Hernando de Soto's discovery of the Lower Mississippi in 1541 had only academic interest for the world. Long before, Spain had claimed all territory in the New World between Florida and Mexico. Now she barred entrance to Red River Valley's southern approach.

A pudgy, forty-pound, unphotogenic animal turned, first French, then English, northward once more. This was the beaver—who provided himself so well against cold that he wore both coat and vest. A coat of long, coarse, shining black hair. A vest so fine, so thick and silky smooth, it excels the finest down.

Between beaver and European, however, stood the Indian.

It was the Indian, using beaver as his coin, who determined the routes by which the white man advanced inland, the extent and boundaries of the territory each Crown might claim, which colonial empire might stand; which must fall. It was the Sioux, specifically, who, barring passage west of the Upper Mississippi, forced exploration and trade to detour north and south of Red River Valley and so kept it secret to the last.

For their part in giving direction to a continent's destiny, both Sioux and Beaver were sacrificed. The Indian's fate was inevitable. Stone was his symbol; iron, the white man's. If a tradition of central Canada's tribes is accepted, Beaver's doom also was decreed. . . .

Anciently, the Beaver were a wise and powerful people who lived like other tribes on dry land. But they scorned fire, did not eat meat, hunt, make war or any other use of their wisdom and power. Angered, the Great Spirit commanded them to become a water people, the prey of man and beast—and thus to die.

As the "Little People," however, Beaver went right on flourishing. In time, all the waters of the northern half of the continent—save only those of the Great Lakes—were occupied by his edifices. Under Beaver rule, the Wilderness between the liquid walls of Lake Superior—Upper Mississippi and Lake Winnipeg—Red River of the North was in danger of becoming the totalitarian state of H_2O.

Angrier still, the Great Spirit conceived another plan. And France, Great Britain, later the United States, in the minor role of Furies, served his will by hunting this befurred defier of the gods to a tragic end.

That doom began when mundane minds in France became avidly curious about the source of beaver robes and pelts trickling into trade by way of Breton fishermen and Jacques Cartier's crews. Let Europe's highborn explorers search for Northwest Passage! Thar was gold in them thar beaver skins! In 1581, a group of merchants sailed for the St. Lawrence Valley to barter for furs themselves. Their success officially launched the fur trade.

Within twenty years so many European competitors were invading St. Lawrence Valley that in 1603 Louis XIV sent Samuel de Champlain over to look around. What he observed determined France to send him back to carry on the fur trade with his left hand and, with his right, to direct the search for Northwest Passage.

While founding Quebec as advance post to the Orient and as a trading post for furs, Champlain discovered that without the friendship of the St. Lawrence's Huron and Algonquin tribes, he could do nothing. The alliance he made with them automatically alienated the still more powerful Iroquois who controlled the region to the south. Thus early, French exploration southward was blocked. Willy-nilly, their approach to Red River Valley became the St. Lawrence.

Champlain also forbade French traders to exchange guns and ammunition with the Indians for pelts. Hurons and Algonquins made no protest. On their own trapping and on the trade they built as middlemen for tribes further west, three trading posts—Quebec, Three Rivers, Montreal—soon flourished along the St. Lawrence.

But the Iroquois, resentful, took their furs south to the Dutch and English who gave them the guns and munition they wanted. By 1650, armed with muskets, they began the campaign of conquest and extermination that drove refugee hordes to the east bank of the Mississippi. For four years the flow of furs ceased. New France faced ruin.

Then, unexpectedly, western tribes gave the Iroquois a stunning defeat. Soon fleets of canoes, deep-riding with pelt-packs, were pouring down the St. Lawrence.

Among the rejoicing French colonists who welcomed the fleets to Three Rivers was a pretty pair of opportunists. Watching those bursting packs unloaded, they formed a partnership on the spot. At that moment the known history of the white man in Red River Valley began.

PART II

The St. Lawrence Brings the French

1. RADISSON AND GROSEILLIERS OUTREACH
THEMSELVES BUT NOT RED RIVER

Seventeen-year-old Esprit Radisson was born for adventure. Already as a cabin boy, he had visited England, Italy, Turkey, learned to speak and read English. Arriving in Three Rivers with his family about 1660, he almost at once had fallen foul of prowling Iroquois who bound him to a stake for slow torture. His audacious genius for persuasion moved them to adopt him instead.

For a year he lived with them in the Mohawk Valley, learning their language and ways. Dutch traders rescued him, sent him to Holland. He had just returned to Three Rivers to find a sister married to stolid, sturdy Medart Chouart when the Indian fleets arrived.

Thirty-two-year-old Chouart had come to New France about 1640 as layman helper to the Jesuit Missions on Lake Huron. But as soon as he learned the Huron and Algonquin languages, their country and customs, he deserted the missions to turn fur trader.

The first act of the new partners was to secure permission—gladly given by the colonial governor in Quebec—to accompany a band of Chippewa west.

Two years later, New France, again for lack of furs, faced ruin. Still fearful of the Iroquois, Indians west and east refused to risk their lives to bring pelts to St. Lawrence trading posts. In the harbor of Quebec, three ships, holds empty, prepared to sail for France.

Tension quickened one morning when score after score of Indian canoes, sides bulwarked with beaver skins, swept down the river. But as they neared the walls of the colonial capital, French flags, waving arms, and shouted greetings proclaimed the arrival of friends.

Radisson and Chouart had returned with a fortune in furs!

Guns of fort and ships roared in salute. For five days Quebec feted the heroes. Chouart, already a sergeant of militia, was promoted to captain. And when the three ships, holds full, sailed for France, the triumphant pair was escorted in state to Three Rivers.

Honors and wealth filled simple Chouart with illusions of

33

grandeur. On some wild, uncleared land, he built a residence, presented himself with the title of *Sieur des Groseilliers* (Sir Gooseberries), in memory of his family's holdings in France, and set himself up as a member of the colonial gentry.

Neither honors nor wealth, however, bedazzled Sir Gooseberries or Radisson to betray the eastern bank of the *Misi-Sipi* as the origin of their furs. Confident they merely had skirted the richer fur region west of the Great River, they were determined to return.

Two years later, the opportunity came. But when they applied for permission to re-enter the interior, a new governor sat in Quebec. He would grant them licenses only on condition that they share their profits with him and take with them two of his own henchmen. By day, Radisson and Groseilliers refused. By night, they slipped away to join a band of westbound Chippewa. The thwarted governor declared them deserters from their military posts and bided his time.

On their first journey west, the partners had followed the Great Lakes to Wisconsin, pushed overland to the Mississippi. This time they passed through Sault Ste Marie into Lake Superior. In its Keeweenaw Bay they found the base of operations they sought.

And there the envoys sent by the Sioux chiefs to invite the two Divine Spirits to Izatys came upon them. Shortly, established on a small lake south of the Sioux capital, the two Frenchmen were watching their savage hosts battle to exchange the finest furs they had ever seen for their tawdry European wares.

Impressed by this and the respect shown them, they forthwith promoted themselves to ambassadors. To initiate their diplomacy, they invited every Sioux and Cree tribe to a great feast to be held in March.

As advance guard for the "Nation of the Beef," thirty assured young warriors were the first guests to arrive. Misled by their simple, brief clothing, the better to take part in games and stag hunts, the ambassadors were unprepared for the advent of the Prairie Sioux:

First came young warriors, bows and arrows in their hands and, on their shoulders, outlined with artificially painted feathers, bucklers on which were represented the sun, moon, and terrestrial figures. Their faces were painted in several colors. Their hair was upturned like a crown and cut—burned rather, for fire is their scissors—very even. The tuft in the center was tied and ornamented with small pearls and Turkey stones [turquoises]. About their throats were necklaces, usually of snakeskin, from which hung several pairs of bears' claws or bits of buffalo horn in an arranged design. Their bodies were oiled with a very thick grease mixed with reddish earth. Their heads were covered with the down of white feathered waterfowl. Earrings of copper wire, shaped in stars and half moons, depended from five pierced holes in their ears.

They were clothed in beaver and deer skins, very light, and each wore at his girdle a [black eagle's] wing. Their stockings were all embroidered with pearls and their very handsome shoes, laced all over, had a piece of buffalo hide sewed to the outside of the heel from which hair trailed half a foot on the snow. They wore swords and knives a foot and a half long, very ingenious hatchets, and clubs like backswords, all these of wood. Tied about their arms were scalplocks of enemies they had slain. And over everything they wore robes of white beaver skins, painted.[1]

Proudly, arrogantly, these braves from Red River Valley marched through the very center of the assembled Forest Sioux and Cree to open a wide aisle. Down this aisle strode the elders, clothed in buffalo robes that hung to the ground. Each carried a handsome red pipestone peacepipe. Last of all came the women under burdens larger than themselves.

Each day of the feasting brought new triumphs to the French diplomats. They won the implacable Dacotahs to become allies of France. They even induced them to make peace with the Cree. And when feasts and ceremonies ended, the oily pair set off with the Prairie Sioux for a six weeks' visit in or near Red River Valley. There they were overwhelmed to find themselves in a camp that could muster seven thousand warriors. Returning to Keeweenaw Bay only long enough to cache the fine pelts they had secured from the Sioux, they crossed to Lake Superior's north shore for a similarly profitable visit with the Cree.

Beaver packs were not the greatest riches they obtained. From both Sioux and Cree they learned about Red River Valley. With members of one or both their hosts, they may even have traveled it. Certainly Radisson's description of the shining stones of Pembina Mountain as "transparent and tender like that of Venice" suggests firsthand knowledge. But the most important item to be recorded was that in the Turtle Mountains were quantities of beaver whose pelts "could not be equalled in the whole world." And from the Cree,

---

[1] From Radisson's *Account of His Travels and Experiences,* here clarified a bit and respelled.

the Frenchmen learned about Lake Winnipeg and that the Nelson and Hayes Rivers emptied into Hudson Bay.

But it was now late June. To cover two thousand canoe-miles to Quebec would take at least three months. Already their accumulated furs required one hundred outsized canoes, manned by five hundred Indians. Reluctantly, the partners started homeward. As they went, they resolved not only to return, but to return by the new route they had learned—*via ship into Hudson Bay, by canoe up the Nelson or Hayes to Lake Winnipeg and so to Red River's Turtle Mountains.*

The venal governor had not bided his time in vain. He threw them into prison, fined them heavily, and confiscated their pelts. Out of more than $300,000 worth of superlative furs, they received but $20,000.

Radisson and Groseilliers had not coped with dangers, obstacles and tribes of half a continent to be cowed by a colonial governor. As soon as they were freed, Sir Gooseberries sailed for France to obtain redress from the king. The simple, weather-beaten man with the homespun title was ridiculed and ignored.

The partners then turned to New England. Twice in Boston ships they tried to reach Hudson Bay. Their persistence attracted the attention of Colonel George Cartwright, in Boston at the time as British commissioner for colonial reorganization. The detailed and vivid account Radisson prepared for him (*see* Bibliography) of their explorations and fur trading successes in turn won the attention of Charles II. A year later the two obscure Frenchmen were escorted through plague-stricken London to the king's retreat at Oxford.

Guests of the king of England, these men whom France had exploited and humiliated opened like morning glories in the sun. They told all they knew, and more. They gave as tested and proved, information about the new route, via Hudson Bay, into the heart of the richest fur country in America. And the English, knowing a great deal more about the Bay than they did, put two and two together.

Their interest quickened by the fact that the Dutch also were bidding for the Frenchmen's services, King Charles and a group of merchants whose patron was adventurous Prince Rupert placed two ships at the partners' disposal. The *Eaglet* and the *Nonsuch* are now to Red River Valley history what Columbus' three little ships are to Spain's.

One early June day in 1669, Radisson on the *Eaglet* and Groseilliers on the *Nonsuch* sailed for Hudson Bay. Storms turned back the *Eaglet,* but the *Nonsuch* won through.

A year later Groseilliers returned to London with a shipload of the choicest pelts brought, up to that time, from America. Counting quickly their thousandfold profits, the merchants hastened to Prince Rupert. Prince Rupert hurried to his cousin, the king. And King Charles, on condition that he receive annually two elk and two black beaver skins, presented the prince with a royal charter.

Originally, to encourage exploration and trade, a royal charter had been granted merchant groups as a form of insurance on ships they equipped to sail western seas. By 1670, this noble document had developed to include not only trade monopolies in known lands, but actual ownership of those lands and the right to exercise in them imperial powers.

But Prince Rupert and his friends formed a most Honorable Company. Their charter, therefore, went far beyond that. It granted "The Governor [Prince Rupert] and Company of Adventurers of England Trading into Hudson Bay" *all known and unknown territory in North America drained by waters that emptied into the Bay.*

This territory—totaling some 1,468,000 square miles—was larger than any European of the time knew existed in the New World. And within this "Prince Rupert's Land," the charter granted:

The whole trade of all those seas, streights, bays, rivers, lakes, creeks and sounds . . . together with all the lands, countries and territories upon the confines of these seas, streights, bays. . . .

By virtue of its north-flowing river, Red River Valley thus, in 1670, came under the domination of the British flag.

2. SIR "DULUTH" ALMOST ATTAINS IT

Indian reports of Groseilliers' arrival in Hudson Bay to set up trading posts for the British galvanized France. Into New France, Louis XIV poured colonists, soldiers, munitions, equipment, money.

A new governor, Louis de Buêde Frontenac, was sped to Quebec to revitalize the colony. He forbade colonial officials to engage in the fur trade, permitted private traders to enter the interior without licenses. He replaced the random system of exploration with organized, determined effort to open up and occupy new territory. And to impress Indians and British alike with the power of French claims and prestige, he devised an elaborate ceremony of annexation.

On a bright June day in 1671, the ceremony's premiere took place on a hilltop near Sault Ste Marie. While a dozen or more impassive Indian chiefs, including several Assiniboine, looked on, a resplendent officer, in the name of the King of France, took formal possession of Lakes Huron and Superior and

all other countries, rivers, lakes and their tributaries contiguous and adjacent thereto, those discovered and those to be discovered, bounded on one side by the Northern and Western Seas and on the other by the South Sea, of all this land in all its length and breadth.

By this blanket extension of New France, Red River Valley in 1671 came under the domination of the French flag.

Two years later, Frontenac sent Louis Joliet and Father Jacques Marquette to explore and annex the Great River, *Misi-Sipi,* which French geographers now declared led straight into the Western Sea. Within four months they returned, shriveled with disappointment, to report that the Mississippi flowed south, straight into Spain's dominions. Fearful of falling into Spanish hands, they had turned back.

Their failure fired Frontenac with determination to know the Mississippi from source to mouth and to establish French sovereignty and trade throughout its valley. It also inspired two very different Frenchmen to find the route to the Orient by way of the Great River. Duluth's expedition was to open a new door to Red River Valley; La Salle's, to slam it in his face.

Daniel Greysolon, Sieur du Lhut, was more or less a man of mystery. Member of the French nobility, trained in the King's Guard of noblemen's sons for a military life, suddenly and without explanation at the age of thirty-six, he had exchanged the luxuries of Louis the Magnificent's court for the meager amenities of Montreal.

There for four years he lived quietly. The annual fairs when the entire town went out of its mind over the furs brought in by western tribesmen left him cold. But little by little he became obsessed to know the Sioux, the one nation that sent no representatives to the St. Lawrence. To explain his odd ambition, he wrote:

No one believes it possible to explore the country of the Sioux or to have any trade with them, both because of their isolation, more than 1600 miles from our settlements, and because they are usually at war. This made me resolve to go among them.

No mystery englamored Robert Cavelier, Sieur de la Salle. Although also a member of the lesser nobility, he entered the Company of Jesus rather than the King's Guard. When he emigrated to New France, he exchanged the long, black robe of the Jesuit for the buckskins of the fur trader.

The better to intercept Indian canoe fleets from the west, he settled beside the rapids of the St. Lawrence. There he learned from passing tribesmen that the *Misi-Sipi* fell into the Vermilion Sea (Gulf of California), across which the flexible French geographers now felt sure lay the Orient. To win the coveted honor of being the first European to reach China from the New World, La Salle resolved to follow the Mississippi to its mouth.

Frontenac was delighted to take advantage of both men's ambitions. To Duluth he gave authority to explore and annex for France the Upper Mississippi Valley. And to La Salle, authority to do the same in the Lower Valley. To finance their expeditions, however, both had to go to Paris.

Duluth, a quiet, reserved man, was no promotor. Louis XIV refused him assistance of any kind. To enable him to finance himself, Frontenac awarded him monopoly over the fur trade west of Lake Superior.

La Salle was successful. Returning to Montreal, he encountered aboard ship a Belgian priest. Monuments in Belgium and in Minnesota now honor this man who did so little to honor himself. Vain and lazy braggart, cheat, coward, are only a few of the terms that describe Louis Hennepin. But La Salle, neither a judge nor a leader of men, invited the little priest to accompany him to China as chaplain of his expedition.

By coincidence both the Duluth and La Salle expeditions started west in 1678. Duluth's, as the culmination of long and ordered preparation. La Salle's, as the last of a series of disastrous starts. Now while La Salle again was forced to turn back, Duluth progressed steadily to the Mississippi, where the Forest Sioux eagerly welcomed him to Izatys.

The power of his personality is evident in the ceremony of annexation the chiefs permitted him to hold in their capital on July 2, 1679. Duluth thereby claimed all Sioux lands, again including Red River Valley, for France.

The Sioux also invited him to accompany a war party west, but to pacify various tribes now up in arms against the French and to organize his fur trade, he had to return to Lake Superior. In his stead, he sent three nameless French scouts with the warriors.

The scouts not only entered Red River Valley. They were the first Europeans, it is believed, to cross Red River to set foot in Dakota. At any rate, from Valley Sioux they obtained word of a lake of undrinkable waters "twenty days due west of Red River" and some handfuls of salt.

By another coincidence, the lake the Prairie Sioux described was Great Salt Lake. But the salt undoubtedly came from one of the two western tributaries of Red River, long known as Big Salt and Little Salt.[2] From these briny streams until a century ago, buffalo drank and Indians and fur traders recovered salt. But Duluth, convinced that Great Salt Lake must be the Western Sea, left Lake Superior early in 1680 to obtain guides and information about a route from his Prairie Sioux friends on Red River.

By a third and fatal coincidence, La Salle also had started west again. Before he reached the Mississippi, he was aware of flaws in his chaplain. To rid himself of the Belgian and at the same time hinder Duluth, he sent Hennepin, with two fur traders, to trade in the Upper Mississippi Valley. Almost at once the trio was captured by a Forest Sioux war party.

From Radisson and Groseilliers to Duluth, Forest Sioux had regarded white men as divinities. Now in the craven, helpless Hennepin, they found a very mortal man indeed. In him and his henchmen, however, the Izatys chiefs saw leverage to secure firearms from the French. But as week after week went by, even the chiefs grew skeptical.

When a hunting party started down the Mississippi, the Europeans were sent along, given a canoe of their own and every chance to escape. They clung to their captors.

With only two groups of white men west of Lake Superior, this had to be the moment when Duluth on his way to Red River reached

[2] Today's Forest and Park Rivers.

the Mississippi. There east-bank Indians told him of the three Divine Spirits held prisoner by the Sioux hunting party.

No matter that the captives, whether British or Spanish, had been poaching on the territory over which he held monopoly! If any Indian were permitted to interfere with the liberty of any white man, Duluth knew, no European would be safe in the interior. In a single canoe he rushed to the rescue, only to discover the three divinities to be members of the rival French expedition. Nevertheless, when the hunting party refused to release them, Duluth accompanied them all back to Izatys.

He won the trio freedom, but it cost him his friendship with the Sioux. Though he was to spend many years trading with Cree and Chippewa north of Lake Superior, he never again crossed the Mississippi.

His reports on the Sioux and their domain, however, roused feverish interest in Quebec. Colonial officialdom now recognized that of all western tribes, the Sioux were most powerful. That of all western lands, those of the Sioux were of greatest strategic importance. As the key to the richest fur preserve on the continent. As a base for western expansion. As the most direct route to the Western Sea.

Frontenac despatched Nicolas Perrot, clever young troubleshooter, to the Mississippi to set up Fort St. Antoine on Lake Pepin as an exclusive Sioux trading post. Such were the quantity and quality of pelts grateful Dacotahs brought in that on May 8, 1689, Perrot became the third Frenchman to take

possession for and in the name of the King, of all countries of the Sioux and of all rivers inhabited by said tribes.

To Chippewa, Cree, Fox, and other tribes around Lake Superior, the unmistakably powerful "medicine" Perrot had made over Dacotah lands was the last straw. Their lucrative trade as middlemen between Sioux and British traders on Hudson Bay, French traders to the east, Spanish to the south, would be ruined if the Dacotahs had their own trading posts and alliances. Promptly they barred passage across the Mississippi. Fort St. Antoine had to be abandoned.

This so enraged the Sioux that Perrot was hurried west to re-establish fort and relations. Instead he was almost burned alive by an unappeased Sioux war party.

That incident gave Frontenac and France the excuse they needed at the moment. The Sioux had tried to murder one of their best men! The Sioux had seized three of La Salle's men! In the past forty years the Sioux were known to have been at war, not once but two or three times, with fifteen different tribes east of the Mississippi, only God knew with how many to the west. The Sioux, in short, were

a race as unsteady as aspens and fierce as wildcats, full of mutual jealousies, without rules and without laws, for each was a law unto himself.

The truth was that largely through Sioux passion for iron and steel wares, more furs now filled French warehouses than European markets could absorb. Time was ripe, therefore, to engage British colonial forces in a fight to the finish for the western fur trade. For this, every able-bodied French colonist was needed. All licenses and permits to trade in the interior were revoked. By 1698 not a French post or trader operated outside the St. Lawrence Valley.

During the thirty years before this second chapter of the French March to the West and the seventeenth century ended simultaneously, Radisson and Groseilliers, Duluth, La Salle, Perrot and others had accomplished every French aim. They had extended French sovereignty in a great crescent from the mouth of the St. Lawrence to the mouth of the Mississippi. They had brought the French fur trade to the very door of the beaver El Dorado. They had discovered the most direct route to the Western Sea, due west from Red River of the North. Above all, they had held the friendship of the Sioux in the palm of their hand.

In tossing it away, France lost her grip on the New World.

3. THE VERENDRYES DISCOVER IT

No sooner had the French withdrawn from the west than British traders from New England and New York pushed into it. As they pushed, they undermined French prices and alliances. This pressure increased when the British won the war the French had started.

To save her colonial empire in America—and her fur trade—France had to accomplish two things quickly. Encircle British colonies on the Atlantic by joining New France with Louisiana. Reach the Western Sea first. Success or failure of both objectives depended on control of the Wilderness west of Lake Superior.

Cree dominated the northern section of that Great Beyond; Sioux, the southern. The Cree were not averse to resuming trade and alliance with the French. The Sioux were adamant. All hope of crossing Minnesota and Red River Valley to the Western Sea died. The only alternative was to discover a route to north or south beyond range of their deadly arrows and ambuscades.

During the past twenty years, daring independent French traders had penetrated the Wilderness. One or two had heard of a west-flowing river called Winnipeg. This mad artery, according to northern tribes, emptied into a vast inland sea, variously identified as Lake Winnipeg, Lake of the Assiniboines, Lake of the Cree. Into and out of it other rivers ran in all directions.

Lake Winnipeg might prove to be the long-sought Western Sea! If not, one of its rivers might lead to the great bay recently discovered on the Oregon coast which French geographers now believed to be an arm of that sea. To take formal possession of Lake Winnipeg became of supreme strategic importance to France.

As though in answer to this need, one October day in 1730, perhaps the least important fur trader in America arrived in Quebec. Before Governor Charles Beauharnois he placed his application to lead an expedition to the Western Sea, by way of Lake Winnipeg.

Up to this time, French explorers had been impoverished, adventurous youths of the lesser nobility who endured the New World only long enough to make a quick fortune. And western exploration demanded youth, audacious, tireless, free from responsibilities.

Though this weatherworn applicant bore the sonorous title of Pierre Gaultier de Varenne, Sieur de Verendrye, he was a local product. Born in Three Rivers, forty-five years before, he was ten to twenty years too old. As the father of a family, he had too many ties to take the necessary risks. And as the son of a petty colonial official, he could command neither financial nor political backing.

That last handicap had placed him when twelve years old in the colonial army. But from four campaigns in New England and France, he had gained only a lieutenant's commission and nine wounds. Since an officer without private resources could not survive in the French Army, he had had to return to Three Rivers as a recruiter.

THE GREAT MISTAKE. Two details from Chief Ochagach's map of the late 1720's which led Verendrye to
believe Red River the long-sought Northwest Passage to the Western Sea.

A. The two rivers Ochagach pictured as one: Red
   River, flowing into Lake Winnipeg from the
   south; the Saskatchewan, flowing out of Lake
   Winnipeg to the west.

B. Canoe route through the Wilderness from Lake
   Superior to Lake of the Woods.

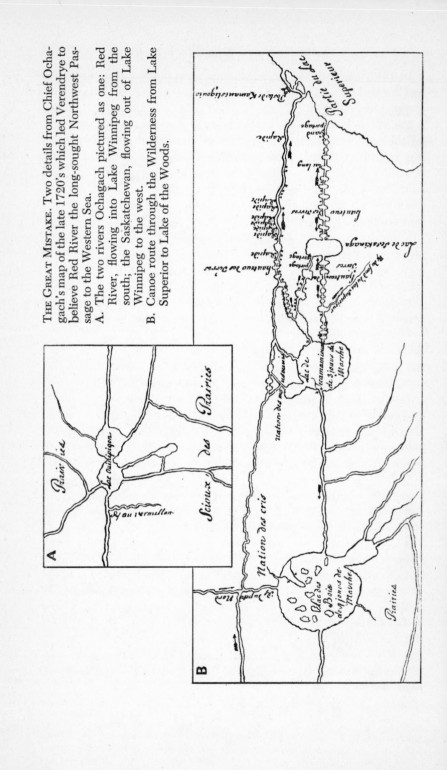

In 1717, married, the father of four sons, and again in need, he had applied for a fur trade appointment. Ten years later he received it. For Lake Nipigon.

Far north of Lake Superior, this most remote and isolated fort on the western frontier of New France perched on the very doorstep of the Great Beyond. Yet every sunset there reminded him that beyond that labyrinth of forests, lakes, swamps, rocky cliffs and haunting devils lay the Western Sea. The man who discovered it need never worry about the support of a growing family. About position or fame, either.

Verendrye's application did more than open the third and last chapter of French expansion in America. It initiated a new era in New World exploration. A masterly compilation of firsthand knowledge, it is unique in making no claim to the exact location of the Western Sea. "To be able to settle this point," it cautions, "we should establish a base at Lake Winnipeg."

Had Verendrye stopped there! Better still, had he remembered the ignominy and poverty in which his Three Rivers neighbors, Radisson and Groseilliers, died, or the humiliation heaped on Joliet, and torn that application to shreds!

But he went on to include a schedule by which an expedition leaving Montreal early in June could reach Lake Winnipeg in September. In conclusion, he promised that if permitted to head this expedition, he would give the governor *positive word* of the Western Sea during his second year in the west.

Considering the information he had gleaned from questioning every Indian who came to Fort Nipigon and a secret journey he himself had made, Verendrye may have felt he was practicing Spartan restraint. *For he knew where the Western Sea was to be found!*

From Ochagach, the Cree chief who made the map that accompanied his application, he had learned that Winnipeg River was not the only great artery in the Wilderness. First of four others was "one flowing north as far as Lake Winnipeg. . . turning west at the outlet."

The north-flowing river is Red River of the North; the west-flowing, the Saskatchewan. On Ochagach's mistaken conception that the two rivers were one, Red River cometed to glory.

Carefully Verendrye planted his words to permit the governor to cultivate for himself the idea that Red River flowed from the Western Sea (and incidentally to harvest for himself the credit when the great discovery was made):

On the left as you follow down the eastern shore [of Lake Winnipeg], you come to a river whose water looks red like vermilion and is held in great esteem by the savages. On the [west] side of this river but lower down is a small mountain whose stones sparkle night and day [Pembina Mountain]. The savages call it the Dwelling of the Great Spirit. No one ventures to go near it. This kind of mountain and Red River, where in places a very fine gold-colored sand is found, seem to all the nations of the region as something very precious.

He also summarized the Cree impression of Red River Valley:

They give a great account of that country, saying it is all very level, without mountains, all fine hard wood with here and there groves of oak. Everywhere are found quantities of fruit trees and all sorts of wild animals. The savage tribes are very numerous and always wandering . . . and always camping together to form a village. They call these nations Assiniboine and Sioux because they speak all the Sioux languages.

Still more carefully, in the words of an Assiniboine, Verendrye hinted at the location of the Western Sea and the reason it had not been discovered long since:

He says he has spent several nights within sight of the mountain whose stones shine day and night and that *from that point you begin to notice the rise and fall of the tide.* Also that from the land near [Lower] Red River to far below the mountain there are no settlements of savages. That he never heard whether it was far from the sea because he did not think any man brave enough to pass through the different [Prairie Sioux] tribes found in great numbers lower down.

Governor Beauharnois swallowed the bait. First he amplified Verendrye's statements with persuasive suggestions of his own that the country west of Lake Superior

is crossed by two great rivers which rise about the middle of it. One flows east—the St. Lawrence. The other south—the Mississippi. To the west, therefore, remains a territory 1400 to 1600 miles wide without any large river in it. This would be contrary to all knowledge we have of the known countries of the world. In so vast an area there is always some great river. . . . According to the course the savages give this River of the West, it flows into the bay recently discovered [on the Oregon coast].

Then the governor, in turn, passed on responsibility for decision and opportunity for glory to Maurepas, Minister of Marine and Colonies, in Paris.

To his aid, Maurepas called Charlevoix, Jesuit historian. By virtue of a visit to Eastern America twenty-five years before, the Jesuit was now French authority on all New World geography. Charlevoix was not at a loss:

> Discovery of the Western Sea is a matter which should be carried through . . . without a stop. The person undertaking it must have very exact maps of Mexico and California that he may not stumble on the Vermilion Sea into which there is every evidence that Red River discharges.

Had Charlevoix stopped there! But to him, discovery of the Western Sea, via Red River, now appeared routine. He also went on—to recommend that Verendrye take two or three New England Indians along to guide him through Red River country and several French children to sprinkle among Prairie Sioux camps to learn their languages.

Such nonsense Beauharnois could dispose of readily. Before one of the Jesuit's sentences he was powerless. That sentence damned Verendrye's explorations before they got under way:

> The whole expense needed for such an expedition would only amount to a stock of provisions easy to carry, arms and ammunition which could partly serve for hunting, and a few presents for the savages.

Convinced by Charlevoix's report that discovery of the Western Sea was merely a matter of following Red River to its source, Maurepas boiled with suspicion. Why should Verendrye, an insignificant, lowborn colonial fur trader, aspire to the highborn honor of discovering the route to the Orient? Fat profits must be his motive! And fat profits there would be from the trading "Posts of the Western Sea" he would be entitled to establish throughout Red River country. Curtly the colonial minister ordered the colonial fur trader to carry on, but at his own expense.

To equip an expedition of fifty men to spend two years in the interior, Verendrye had to enter into partnership with certain Montreal merchants. For the lion's share of any profits he might make from his posts of the Western Sea, they agreed to advance supplies.

Like a pouting lip, a tiny promontory thrusts out from Lake Superior's northwest shore into the vast and frigid waters. Within the curve of its northern shoulder excited Pigeon River tumbles into the lake. Its southern shore, however, shelters a quiet, crescent-shaped bay that parallels the river for several miles inland.

Theoretically, the mouth of Pigeon River was the entrance to the Great Beyond. Actually, because the final twenty miles of the river's course is a melee of cascades and rapids, Assiniboine and Cree long had made the bay serve instead. From its innermost point, by a nine-mile portage, the impossible twenty could be avoided and navigable water of Pigeon River reached.

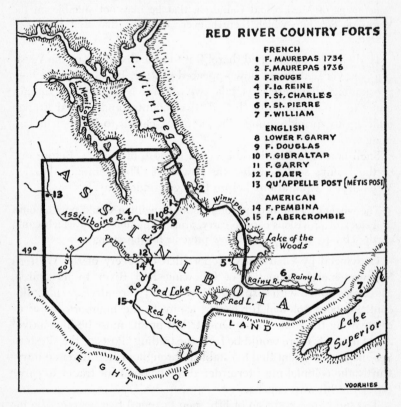

RED RIVER COUNTRY FORTS

FRENCH
1 F. MAUREPAS 1734
2 F. MAUREPAS 1736
3 F. ROUGE
4 F. la REINE
5 F. St. CHARLES
6 F. St. PIERRE
7 F. WILLIAM

ENGLISH
8 LOWER F. GARRY
9 F. DOUGLAS
10 F. GIBRALTAR
11 F. GARRY
12 F. DAER
13 QU'APPELLE POST (MÉTIS POST)

AMERICAN
14 F. PEMBINA
15 F. ABERCROMBIE

RED RIVER FORTS

As the only gap in the rugged hills, bluffs, and cliffs outlining Lake Superior's north shore, this nine-mile valley was to rise to fame as Grand Portage—historic and fabulous supply center and inland administration headquarters of the fur trade.

That fame was born on August 26, 1731, when fifty men, exhausted after eleven weeks of paddle and portage from Montreal, beached

worn and battered canoes on the bay's crescent shore. Out of the canoes stepped Verendrye; his three oldest sons—Jean-Baptiste, Pierre,
and François: his nephew, La Jemeraye; a priest, and assorted traders and boatmen.

Already the expedition was weeks behind schedule. Now, terrified
lest winter seal lakes and rivers before they could reach Lake Winnipeg, traders and boatmen mutinied. Verendrye sent La Jemeraye
with a few of the hardier spirits ahead to Rainy Lake. With the rest,
he wintered at what is now Fort William.

Before May, 1732, ended, however, he had reassembled his expedition on an island,[3] in Lake of the Woods. There, though haunted by
the specter of failure, he delayed still longer to build Fort St. Charles
as trading post and farm.

So soon had he made his first notable discovery! That expeditions
venturing west of Lake Superior must be self-sustaining.

While his men broke ground, sowed seed, he sent messengers to
invite every Cree chief to a great council. The chiefs came in state
and in state Verendrye presented them with two wampum collars.
By accepting the first, the Cree agreed to ally all their tribes with
France. By accepting the second, they agreed not to make war on
the Forest Sioux.

As Verendrye explained, the Forest Sioux, because of Fort Beauharnois on Lake Pepin (established to keep the Sioux busy while he
by-passed them to the north), also were French allies. Therefore,
they were allies of the Cree. Prairie Sioux in Red River Valley, however, were no man's ally or friend. On the Prairie Sioux they could
make war.

That second pact initiated the series of disasters that overwhelmed
the already doomed expedition. Within days, 650 barbarously
painted and feathered Cree warriors arrived to invite Verendrye's
oldest son to accompany them on an attack against the Prairie Sioux.

Twenty-one-year-old Jean Baptiste was eager to go. The priest and
most intelligent traders urged that he go. On condition that his son
have no military status, take no active part, the tormented father finally gave his consent.

Hardly had the war party set out than Jean Baptiste returned. The

[3] Until 1908, the Verendrye Expedition's first post was believed to have been
located on the Canadian mainland. Then a party of young priests from St.
Boniface, Manitoba, discovered the ruins of Fort St. Charles on Magnusson
Island in Lake of the Woods.

Cree had no intention of attacking Prairie Sioux. The Forest Sioux were their objective.

Forebodings haunted Verendrye. Not only the Forest Sioux but Legardeur Saint-Pierre, commandant at Fort Beauharnois, would hold him responsible for this Cree treachery. Though he now doubted that Red River issued from the Western Sea, he could do nothing. To renew his dangerously depleted supplies and quiet Maurepas' and Beauharnois' impatience with his slow progress, he must first return to Quebec.

Before leaving, he surrendered to his second son the honor of "discovering" Red River of the North. No historic account exists of Pierre Verendrye's expedition of 1734 and formal annexation of Red River Valley. Boyishly, the twenty-year-old youth reported to the governor:

I have established a fort at Lake Winnipeg, ten miles up Red River, on a point of land, commanding a distant view. There are many fish in this river. It's a fine spot, and a pleasant place to live; game abounds. . . .Fort and River now bear the name of Maurepas.[4]

Unfortunately, in Quebec, Governor Beauharnois was so pleased with the beaver skins Verendrye brought him that he wrote Maurepas:

When these posts [of the Western Sea] have been thoroughly established, they will increase substantially the total fur trade of New France.

His worst suspicions confirmed, Maurepas ordered Verendrye to give up all interest, direct or indirect, in the fur trade and to confine his efforts to discovery of the Western Sea. When his merchant backers heard of that edict, they refused him further credit.

To continue, Verendrye had to lease to independent traders any trading posts he erected and to borrow heavily to buy supplies. Then, expenses and debts doubled, he returned to Red River. With him came his fourth son, eighteen-year-old Louis Joseph.

Immediately, he and his sons explored Red River, other rivers that rose or fell in Lakes Winnipeg and Manitoba. Nowhere could they find a sign of the Western Sea.

But wherever Verendrye went, Indians told him of strange tribes who lived on the Upper Missouri. The Mandans were as pale-faced

[4] Later the name of Maurepas was transferred to the Winnipeg River and to a fort at its mouth.

as the French. They lived in towns and cultivated maize. Their Great
River of the West flowed southwest into the sea at a place where other
white men lived in towns, with forts, cannon, priests. The Mandans
could tell him how to reach the Western Sea.

While waiting for the supplies necessary to undertake that long
trek across the plains, Verendrye moved forty miles west to the
Portage la Prairie on the Assiniboine from which Cree and Assiniboine portaged to Lake Manitoba. There he erected Fort la Reine,
named to honor the Queen of France. And the moment the ice broke
in the spring, he sent Jean Baptiste with twenty-two men east to
hurry the Montreal canoes to the new headquarters.

Fell then the first blow of disastrous 1735. La Jemeraye mysteriously died, poisoned by vengeful Forest Sioux, Verendrye suspected.

Weeks, months passed with no word from his oldest son. When,
late in August, the Montreal canoes arrived, no man with them had
seen or heard anything of Jean Baptiste and his convoy.

But close on their heels came Cree and Assiniboine with news of
the convoy's horrible fate. On a little island near Fort St. Charles—
ever since known as Massacre Island—130 Sioux, both Prairie and
Forest, had fallen on Jean Baptiste and his men, left everyone dead.

And on *their* heels came hundreds more to implore the grief-
stricken Verendrye to lead them against the Sioux. He replied that the
French only made war on command of their king. But he wrote ur-
gently to Beauharnois and Maurepas to give him that command.

Beauharnois found it difficult to believe the explorer could consider a course "so opposed to the good of the service." To Maurepas,
the massacre was "most annoying." It again confirmed

the suspicion I have always entertained that the beaver trade had more
than anything else to do with Verendrye's Western Sea Expedition.

Under no condition, they ordered, was he to make war on the
Sioux or to permit war to be made. At great cost in effort and gifts,
Verendrye pacified Cree and Assiniboine. And thus, to the sorrow of
white men in Red River Valley for almost a century and a half to follow, confirmed the suspicion the Sioux always had entertained that
they were invulnerable.

To swell the disaster came word that Forest Sioux rage against
Jean Baptiste's brief presence among the attacking Cree had driven

Saint-Pierre from profitable Fort Beauharnois. And now, without the dependable aid of La Jemeraye and Jean Baptiste, French members of his expedition flatly refused to move farther west.

All this delayed Verendrye's departure for the Upper Misssouri until 1738. It, too, was a disaster. The Mandans were not white men but a branch of the Sioux. Terrified to remain in their vicinity, his Assiniboine guides and interpreter first stole both his personal effects and all the gifts with which he had hoped to enlist Mandan aid, then ran away. Rigors of winter on the open plains woke his old war wounds to add their tortures. Though now at the point from which Lewis and Clark some sixty years later took off successfully for the Western Sea, Verendrye had to make a painful return to Fort la Reine.

From that base, he explored in detail most of Lake Agassiz' bed, but griefs, hardships, disappointments and steadily failing health combined to forbid his attempting another western expedition. Finally, in 1742, he sent François and Louis Joseph to the Mandans to secure guides and follow the Missouri to its source.

Delays and disappointments harried them also. Mid-January of 1743 found them no farther west than within sight of the Black Hills of South Dakota. Abandoned there by their timorous Indian escort, the two young men buried a plaque[5] to signify they had taken possession for France of all Western America, then turned north. And in the north, Louis Joseph discovered Saskatchewan River.

Though it took twelve years, the Verendryes now could supply the promised *positive word* concerning not one, but two, direct routes to the Orient. As Louis Joseph reported:

By the northern [Saskatchewan] route is the most convenient way to pursue the discovery of the Western Sea, from the ease with which you can transport your effects thither by canoe, secure guides readily, and always have the same tribe, the Cree, to deal with. . . . This is not the case of the prairie [Missouri River] road. . . . On this southern route, you encounter different tribes, all enemies, and all with different languages, causes of hindrance and difficulty. . . .

Discovery of these two great Western waterways represents but a fraction of the Verendryes' total achievement. They explored, mapped, and claimed for France a larger, richer territory than that

---

[5] Found, in 1913, near Pierre, S. D.

covered by any other individual or group in the entire 200-year-chain of French explorers.

They not only discovered, but established the true relationship of,

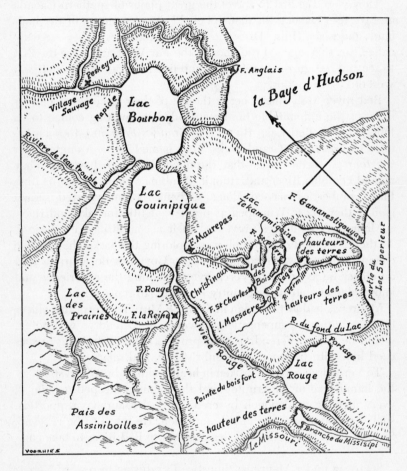

After Verendrye, 1750. Red River Country detail, from *New Discoveries in Western Canada,* the map made by M. de la Galissoniere from Verendrye's *Memoirs,* "but more inaccurate than (Verendrye) himself said."

North America's crossroads of waters. Rivers: Winnipeg, Red River of the North, Assiniboine, Upper Missouri, Saskatchewan, and many of lesser importance. Lakes: Winnipeg, Manitoba, Winnipegosis, and innumerable smaller ones. And they suggested the outlet of the Nelson to be Hudson Bay.

They were the first to travel the great plains of southern Canada and western Dakota, the first to behold the phenomena of the Badlands and Black Hills. "Discoverers of the Northwest," they are truly called, for they opened the door to the Far West and were the first to see and recognize the resources and potentialities of the continent west of Lake Superior.

Red River itself almost heads the list of their discoveries. One or more of the indomitable family ascended its twisting course to its junction with Red Lake River. *Les Grandes Fourches,* they christened that meeting—Grand Forks. They named Turtle Mountains for the *tourtes*—turtle doves—that thronged the tangled woods. They named Pembina River and, from it, Pembina Mountain, for the high bush cranberries massed along its banks. From assorted Indian names, they chose Winnipeg as permanent title for lake and river.

Maurepas' prejudices prevented their accomplishing even more. At the very time Louis Joseph was exploring the Saskatchewan, the colonial minister was recommending to Governor Beauharnois that an officer be assigned to Verendrye to acquire the experience and knowledge of Red River country necessary to replace him.

Maurepas had just the man in Sieur de Muy. To expect this officer to serve without compensation, however, as Verendrye was doing, would be unjust. Verendrye must provide the man training to succeed him with transportation, subsistence, and salary.

To Verendrye, already broken in health, almost broken in spirit, by the imminence of bankruptcy and the calumny heaped on him in every arriving mail pouch by creditors and Maurepas supporters, such a proposal was the final humiliation. He asked to be relieved. Sieur Nicolas Joseph de Noyelles was sent to Red River to take command.

Smarting under Maurepas' injustice in refusing to reward Verendrye with even a captaincy, Beauharnois sharpened his own pen:

I cannot refuse him the testimony which is his due, namely, that in this exploration he has but benefited the colony in the number of establishments he has founded in places to which no one previously has penetrated. . . . The idea that he has amassed wealth is flatly disproved by his actual condition of poverty. . . . I do not know of a single respect in which he has merited the mortification he has suffered.

Grudgingly Maurepas sent the captain's commission, though of junior grade, and the controversy over Verendrye waned until 1747. Then, Noyelles, having accomplished nothing, retired. Beauharnois promptly reappointed Verendrye. Though now sixty-five years of age, the old explorer rose gallantly to the challenge. In December, 1749, in the midst of preparations to return to his Red River base, he died.

At once, his three surviving sons applied to carry on in his name. This was denied them. The man chosen was none other than Legardeur Saint-Pierre whom Cree treachery had deprived of profitable Fort Beauharnois. Still bitter, Saint-Pierre refused to permit the Verendryes to accompany him even in subordinate posts.

And now a new colonial governor, more amenable to Maurepas' prejudices, conceived a final humiliation to erase the name of Verendrye from public memory. At this time the captaincies of three companies fell vacant, one of them created by Verendrye's own death. His three sons were in line for commissions. The governor nominated three men. All were accepted. Not one of them was a Verendrye.

The tragedy of the discoverer of Red River of the North epitomizes the tragedy of the French colonial empire in America. Like New France, Verendrye undertook two vast and unrelated projects—discovery of the Western Sea and promotion of the fur trade—on a shoe string. Like New France, his efforts were undermined at every turn by corruption and greed in the colony's political structure. Like New France, he extended himself physically too far, too fast. And finally, to him as to New France, opportunity for a second chance that might have meant victory came too late.

The analogy goes even further. New France outlived its foremost explorer by just one decade. In 1760, Montreal fell before the British. Three years later, by the Treaty of Paris, Great Britain acquired all French territory in North America between the Atlantic and Mississippi. In the America west of the Great River, including Red River Valley, France had claims that survived the Treaty. In the posts of the Western Sea, four of them in the Valley, the Verendrye sons had claims that survived their father's death. Both were to lose them all.

PART III

The Nelson Brings the English

1. PETER POND DISCOVERS RED RIVER VALLEY

For almost twenty years after Groseilliers opened the first trading post on Hudson Bay for Prince Rupert and his Honorable Company, English traders, distrusting Indian and Eskimo, refused to venture inland. Unlike the open-to-all posts of the French, their first establishments were dismal, stockaded strongholds, into which no tribesman was permitted to set foot.

Finally, in the summer of 1689, under repeated urgings from the London board of governors of what now was known as Hudson's Bay Company, the governor of York Factory at the mouth of Hayes River sent a small shallop to the Barren Lands, some sixty miles north of Churchill River. From it a ruddy-cheeked English lad of nineteen leaped ashore. But though Henry Kelsey walked north two hundred miles, he found only fog, mosquitoes, and the first muskox ever seen by European eyes.

That exploit moved London to order him to spend the next two years exploring the interior on his own, to find and reconcile warring tribes, and to persuade them all to hunt and trap for Hudson's Bay Company. This he did and much more, while traversing, mostly on foot, a good share of old Agassiz' bed.

When he returned, this first Britisher to see a buffalo and other phenomena of the interior was accompanied by a fleet of canoes buried beneath beaver pelts. On the information he brought back, the Company formulated its trade policy with the Indians, and for years its books testified to the success of his salesmanship. Unhappily for the young man himself, London now considered him too valuable to take further risks.

But happily for Red River of the North, on August 6, 1691, forty-three years before the Verendrye Expedition reached the River, he entered its name in British history as the River *Mith*[1]:

Now, ye water wch runneth down this River is of a Blood red Colour by description of those Indians wch hath seen it, wch makes me to think it may run thru some mine or other.

[1] *Mith*: contraction and corruption of *Miswagunmewesebee*, the Chippewa name for Red River.

From the beginning of his peacemaking, he found every Indian he encountered allergic to any form of truce with the Prairie Sioux. Too naïve to grasp that the northern tribes were determined to serve as middlemen between Sioux and English, he failed to press far enough south to discover the Mith to be the Assiniboine, long believed by both Indians and British to be one with Red River.

One of his discoveries won swift acceptance. With the Indian wife he brought back, Henry Kelsey, as mid-America's pioneer squawman, established a precedent enthusiastically followed by white men, whether British or French, in the interior.

Seventy-five years after he returned to York Factory, Hudson's Bay traders were just beginning to move south. But from Montreal, as soon as Great Britain's conquest of New France was complete, self-appointed British successors to the French traders rushed west to appropriate fur posts and customers of the defeated.

These were the Scotch, plus a few English, traders from New England and New York who, as the shadow of the imminent American Revolution deepened, had hastened to make the French fur capital their own. To avoid the Prairie Sioux, they by-passed Red River Valley to concentrate along the Assiniboine.

There they competed so bitterly for furs trapped by the Indians that the red men were debauched and corrupted. Infuriated, the northern tribes united to wipe out every European in the Northwest. Had not smallpox swept the interior, they might have succeeded. Before the plague ran its course, more than half the tribesmen were dead.

But for one obstacle, the whole Northwest now hung like a ripe plum within easy reach of Montreal's British traders. Still heady from that unreprisaled murder of the Verendrye convoy, the Prairie Sioux, using Red River Valley as warroad, carried on such relentless hostilities along the Assiniboine that by 1780 the British fur trade was in full flight to the region north of the Saskatchewan River.

Out of the deadly competition the Montrealers waged there, contenders began to rise to eminence as the "great Northmen." Alexander Henry. Simon Mactavish. The Frobishers, Joseph, Thomas, and Benjamin. The Ellices. Above them all rose Peter Pond. And behind him pressed always his cold and tenacious enemy, Alexander Mackenzie.

Neither rambunctious, illiterate Pond, nor respectable, ambitious

Mackenzie resembled the elegant, if dissolute, youths who dominated exploration and fur trade during the French regime. Mackenzie did fulfill the British contention that all important traders were Scotch, but Pond was a Connecticut Yankee.

In 1775 he arrived on the Saskatchewan, all set to battle Montreal's top-flight traders. Although thirty-five years old, the age when most traders retired, and with but two seasons' previous experience trading with Prairie Sioux in Minnesota River Valley, he shortly had pushed farther west than any other white man. And by thus tracking new customers to their very teepees, he built up such an enormous trade that the cream of the Montrealers fixed appraising eyes upon him.

Frobishers, Ellices, Simon Mactavish and others were fed to the teeth with the stark life of that remote wilderness. If they could find a man of sufficient enterprise, courage, and above all, integrity, to carry on for all of them, they would return to civilization. Peter Pond met every requirement.

His success outdistanced even his sponsors' most optimistic estimates. For he discovered Athabasca Valley, richest fur region in all America.

In surveying the valley with his outworn French instruments, however, he made the error that cost him his reputation in his own day and lasting fame as one of America's foremost explorers. Using three miles instead of two for the French league, he mapped Athabasca as practically on the Pacific Coast.

That mistake overshadowed his discovery of pemmican, a compact, nourishing, almost endlessly preservable food the Athabasca tribes concocted from powdered buffalo beef, berries and tallow. Overshadowed, also, the use he made of it to place himself shoulder to shoulder with the Verendryes as the discoverer of Red River Valley. For with pemmican he solved the problem of the white man's survival in the Northwest.

Remembering all he had learned from the Prairie Sioux of Red River Valley's buffalo, Pond returned to the forks of the Red and Assiniboine. With the pemmican he taught Chippewa and Cree there to make and with other Valley foods, he stocked a chain of supply posts that enabled his traders to travel freely to the remotest corners of the fur country.

To Peter Pond himself, neither Athabasca, pemmican, nor his success in organizing the Northwest into a formidably prosperous fur preserve for his sponsors equaled in importance his discovery of an enormous river. Flowing out of the west end of Great Slave Lake, it emptied, he felt sure, into the Arctic Ocean.

But when, in 1779, he returned to Montreal, he learned of the immense mouth of a new river on the North Pacific Coast that Captain James Cook had come upon the previous summer. Comparing his (erroneous) calculations with the Captain's, Pond estimated that only a narrow belt of land separated Athabasca from the Pacific.

He must be mistaken then in believing his river emptied into the Arctic. It must circle the northern end of the Rockies to spill into the Pacific at Cook's Inlet. It was, in short, the long-sought passage to the Western Sea!

Forthwith, he filed application with both the British Colonial Government in Quebec and the infant Continental Congress of the United States to lead an expedition to his river's mouth. But at that stage of the Revolution neither government had time or interest to study his maps, much less decipher the homemade phonetics he concocted to describe the British Northwest.

Thus absorbed, he gave little attention to what was going on among the fur moguls in Montreal. By this time competition between the big fur houses and their traders and the small had become so lawless that the trade itself was endangered. Now the giants wanted Peter Pond to return to Athabasca. The small fry wanted Waden, the trader then substituting there for Pond, to remain. As a compromise, both men were named.

Cooped up together through the long, sub-Arctic winter in Pond's bleak post on Athabasca River, the two men developed feverish rivalry and ill will. One bitter March night a bullet from the darkness killed Waden.

Pond and his clerk were exonerated from any responsibility for the killing. But Waden's death brought into the open the need long felt by the Montreal hierarchy for an organization with sufficient capital to conduct the fur trade on a scale to eliminate the small fry. Accordingly, during the winter of 1783-84, they formed a partnership known as North West Company.

Of the sixteen shares of stock issued, but one was reserved for the man on whose masterly organization of the trade their success rested.

Word of his small portion stunned Pond. He was not alone. To a man, the small traders were up in arms. One of them, Peter Pangman, joined Pond to form a rival organization. Hurrying to Montreal, the two Peters persuaded John Gregory, head of the fur house of Gregory, McLeod and Company, to back them.

To compete against North West's expert traders, Gregory had to find trader-partners of outstanding caliber for the new firm. Remembering a tireless, steel-willed and steel-tempered young Scotch book-keeper who had left his employ but a few months before to become an active trader at Detroit, Gregory offered Alexander Mackenzie a partnership. It was accepted with alacrity.

But when the trader-partners of "Little Company," as Simon Mactavish dubbed it, assembled at Grand Portage to inaugurate their first season, Peter Pond was missing. Dismayed to find the ablest trader in the Northwest in the ranks of this upstart rival, a Frobisher had humbled himself to induce Pond to remain with North West Company. From that moment Mackenzie was Peter Pond's enemy.

As a first expression of his feelings, the embittered young Scot stationed himself for the winter at Ile de la Crosse, a strategic site from which he could intercept Indian trappers en route to Pond's stronghold. John Ross, another Little Company partner, invaded Athabasca.

The following summer when the partners assembled for their first annual meeting at Grand Portage, John Ross did not appear. But soon a breathless messenger did. Their Athabascan partner was dead, he cried, "shot in a scuffle with Pond's men."

Horrified, the Little Company contingent burst in on the North West partners also in session at Grand Portage. Shocked by this second killing in Athabasca, the Nor'Westers didn't wait to investigate. To end the ruthless rivalry, they proposed that the two organizations merge.

If for Little Company the merger was a victory, for Mackenzie it was a double-headed triumph. To have become in one year a partner in the enlarged North West Company represented greater success than he could have achieved in twenty years on his own. More gratifying still was his appointment to succeed Pond as chief trader in Athabasca.

To stand trial for Ross's death, Pond had to return to Montreal. But already it was too late in the season to make that three-month journey. To Athabasca, Pond and Mackenzie went to spend the winter together.

Pond was neither aware of the Scot's enmity nor concerned that his days as a fur trader might be numbered. Now that the Revolution was over, he thought only of the expedition, financed by the British Colonial Government or by the American Congress, he would lead to the Pacific. So sure was he that he no longer could remain silent.

During the long winter nights he poured into Mackenzie's ears all he knew or surmised about his river and the lands, including Red River Valley, he had traveled. And to bolster his contentions, he produced his maps for the young Scot to study.

Mackenzie listened, studied, weighed every word—and secretly resolved to follow Pond's river to the sea himself. His first concern, however, as soon as the old trader left in the spring was to erase every sign of Pond's presence and work from Athabasca.

In Montreal, meanwhile, Pond had been acquitted of any connection with the death of John Ross. On the respect for his knowledge of fur trade and country and on the expectations excited by his constant talk about his Pacific-bound river, his prestige soared to new highs.

Only to have the further to fall. In 1790 came word that Mackenzie had traced Pond's river to its exit—in the Arctic Ocean!

Even Pond's North West associates and friends now looked on him as a charlatan and traitor. Bitterest of all was the man who believed so firmly in the river's Pacific exit that he had risked his life to prove it. "River of Disappointment," Mackenzie named Pond's river. But the man who had placed him on the road to fame and fortune he ever after minimized and maligned.

Completely discredited, Pond sold his share of North West Company stock and now an ancient of fifty, barred forever from the British Northwest, returned to his old home town in Milford, Connecticut. But, perhaps, after all, he had the last word.

As David Thompson, frequently called the "greatest practical geographer the world ever has produced," was to record, Pond's

was the hand that designated the boundary line between the Dominions of Great Britain and the Territories of the United States.

To define that boundary, the British Government appointed as commissioners two gentlemen completely innocent of any knowl-

edge of Northwest geography. And for their aid, it supplied them
with maps that pictured the entire country west of Lake Ontario as
a waste of uninhabitable rocks and swamps.

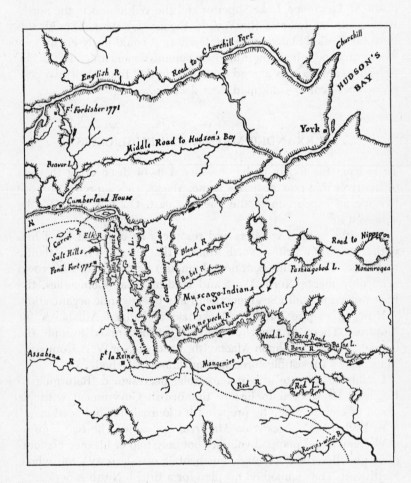

RED RIVER COUNTRY OF THE 1770's. From Peter Pond's Map of the
Northwest, presented about 1780 to the U. S. Continental Congress,
with his application to lead an expedition to the Western Sea.

Almost equally innocent, the American commissioners, though
prepared to accept a boundary running through the middle of Lake
Champlain, thence due west, first dug out Pond's maps and material

from Congressional files. Then Benjamin Franklin himself sought
out the old fur trader and explorer.

Pond recommended a boundary that passed through the middle
of the St. Lawrence, Lake Superior and the Wilderness to the northwest corner of Lake of the Woods, thence due west. Though this
gave the United States twice the territory it could justly claim, says
Thompson and others, the American commissioners asked for it. The
British commissioners agreed to it. And in due time, their two governments solemnly confirmed their decision.

2. ALEXANDER MACKENZIE PUBLICIZES IT

To redeem the fiasco—as he considered it—of discovering the exit
of the river that now bears his name, Mackenzie's supreme purpose
became an expedition to the Pacific Coast. On July 22, 1793, he
achieved it.

En route, natural wonders and resources he observed filled him
with a vision of a British North America that extended from Atlantic
to Pacific. To win this continental empire, he reasoned, the crown
need only merge North West and Hudson's Bay Companies, the
East India and South Sea monopolies into one gigantic organization.

Now an empire builder, Mackenzie exchanged Athabasca for
Montreal. There, as agent for North West, he worked to unite the
fur rivals. Alas, in Simon Mactavish, head of Nor'West Company,
Mackenzie's irresistible force met an immovable body.

Unable to tolerate a secondary role, he resigned. Returning to
England, he labored to inspire the British Government with his
vision of empire while he prepared his journals for publication.

In 1801, his *Voyages from Montreal* appeared. The two impressively bound and mapped volumes not only told of his own explorations and described (though much of it was hearsay) the whole
Northwest. They embodied his plan for a British North America.

As edition after edition rolled off the English presses and, in
Europe, country after country read *Voyages* in translation, all the
world acclaimed Alexander Mackenzie. And the king of England
dubbed him knight.

Few books have fostered such grandiose schemes. Oddly enough,
for good or ill, Red River Valley starred in most of them.

Napoleon read the French translation made for him and, studying its maps, conceived a plan to harass his perennial enemy, England, by an invasion of Rupert's Land, via the Mississippi and its tributaries. Had he acted promptly, French troops would have followed the Mississippi into Minnesota River, thence into Red River of the North, to challenge British sovereignty on Red River Valley soil. Napoleon decided to knock out Russia first.

Thomas Jefferson read Mackenzie's book and quietly took the step that culminated in the Louisiana Purchase, the Lewis and Clark Expedition, and that of young Lieutenant Zebulon M. Pike to the Upper Mississippi.

Louisiana Purchase included only those lands drained by the Mississippi. Red River Valley, with its northbound river, though the core of the great sprawling V formed by the junction of Mississippi and Missouri, Lewis and Clark mapped as "Red River of Lake Winnipeg" and passed by.

But Lieutenant Pike, on September 23, 1805, "for military purposes," made formal purchase from the Forest Sioux of nine square miles along the Mississippi between the mouth of the Minnesota River and St. Anthony Falls. Those nine square miles were to have more significance for Red River Valley than any equivalent area within its own boundaries.

Most important reader of Mackenzie's *Voyages*—from the Valley's standpoint—was Thomas Douglas, fifth Earl of Selkirk and Lord of Daerclough. In his Highland castle library in Scotland, coming on pages describing Red River country, he read one paragraph again and again:

There is not perhaps a finer country in the world for the residence of uncivilized man than that which occupies the space between Red River and Lake Superior. It abounds in everything necessary to the wants and comforts of such a people. Fish, venison, and fowl, with wild rice, are in great plenty; while at the same time their subsistence requires that bodily exercise so necessary to health and vigor.

Lord Selkirk knew a great many people who, to him, were uncivilized.

His inspiration was seventy-five years too late. During that time, uncivilized men, red, white, and red-white, had been playing hob with Red River Valley.

The carnage began when Chippewa scouts from the north shore of Lake Superior discovered Turtle Mountains. This 800-square-mile tangle of hills and dales, woods and streams, had everything. Beaver, moose, bear, mink and other prized fur-bearing animals. Partridges, prairie chicken, waterfowl. Wild plums, cherries, berries, and quantities of elder trees whose sap provided maple sugar to delight the red man's sweet tooth. Best of all, the mountains were enclosed by prairies where buffalo in untold numbers grazed.

To gain this paradise, the Chippewa waged a decade of unceasing war that, due to a misbegotten Forest Sioux strategy, ended in victory for the invaders. And to oust them, Prairie Sioux in turn waged such unceasing war that finally the Chippewa agreed to remain north of Pembina River if the Prairie Sioux remained south of the Sheyenne. That pact made the valley between the two rivers a warroad on which no life was safe.

But northern Red River Valley not only was populous with Cree, Assiniboine, and Chippewa. With French Canadians who, after the Conquest, refused to return to civilization. With all manner of British and American traders fleeing from North West's campaign to exterminate the small fry. As a result of the fervor with which French and British from Henry Kelsey on had allied themselves with Indian women, a new native, neither red man nor white, was peopling the prairies. The French called them *Métis* and took them in stride. The British called them half-breeds and looked with disfavor upon them.

Tall, straight, well proportioned, black haired and dark eyed, they were more powerfully built than the Indian, of greater muscular strength than the European. Because on little or no food they could paddle or trek and portage heavy loads long distances day after day, they were made to order for the fur trade. But even the first generations recognized themselves as a people set apart. They belonged to but one thing, but one thing belonged to them—the Valley where they were born.

Viewing this congestion as a menace to the chain of posts North West Company was erecting between Great Lakes and Rocky Mountains, Simon Mactavish ordered David Thompson to map the entire Valley, then assigned several of the great Northmen—Alexander Henry (the Younger), Peter Pangman, Archibald McLeod—to set up trading posts and monopolize its trade. (And to Alexander Henry's Pembina post, a blue-eyed Indian named Falcon quietly assigned himself.)

Nor'West's invasion promptly stirred the independent traders to amalgamate as X.Y. Company and brought Hudson's Bay traders south to "occupy" the Valley also. Before the eighteenth century ended, in the Turtle Mountain region alone, twenty-one rival posts functioned, each alert to destroy the others.

As though such competition were not enough, Mackenzie—now *Sir* Alexander Mackenzie—returned, in 1802, to Montreal. Shortly, as head of X.Y. Company, he was focusing his tremendous abilities on the downfall of Simon Mactavish and North West Company.

Mackenzie versus Mactavish made Turtle Mountains the scene of such violence as the violent Northwest had never known. Before the beaver were depleted and the warfare swept on to the Saskatchewan, a lurid chapter in diabolical villainy and vice had been inserted in Red River history.

In 1804, as both North West and X.Y. tottered on the brink of ruin, Simon Mactavish died. The two companies merged under the name of North West. And Mackenzie, again victoriously a partner, returned to England as its London representative.

Now only Hudson's Bay Company remained to challenge North West determination to monopolize the fur trade. But despite the Honorable Company's inferiority in organization, financing, personnel and methods, it still held one crowning advantage. Its route to the fur country, via Hudson Bay, was more than one thousand miles shorter than the Montreal company's, via St. Lawrence, Great Lakes, and the Wilderness.

In Red River Valley, Alexander Henry, like Peter Pond, found the winning weapon for North West. From his arrival in 1800, he began to record its riches in animal, vegetable, soil and water resources. Within a year, he was establishing farm after farm about the mouth of the Pembina River and amplifying Pond's manufacture of pemmican until his fortified post became known as the pemmican capital of the fur trade.

An inexhaustible base of supplies now assured, North West Company hastened to erect Fort Gibraltar at the forks of Red and Assiniboine Rivers. Possession of this strategic site did more than insure safe transport of Pembina's supplies to all corners of the fur country. It did more than guarantee protection to North West's lifeline of trade and communication between Lake Superior and the Rockies. With Red River Valley, now recognized as the most vital and valuable area in the entire Northwest, under its control, the Mon-

treal company became "perhaps the most terribly effective organization ever to be created in the New World."

Lords of the Lakes and Forests, Washington Irving called its
twenty-three partners. And in Montreal and Quebec they did live
with all the magnificence and prestige of feudal lords. But each summer when William Macgillivray, the new head, and his retinue of
partners, with titled guests, clerks, servants, exotic foods and wines,
returned to Fort William[2] to meet with the "wintering partners"
from the fur country, they traveled in the state and manner of ruling
monarchs.

As their Red River Valley base produced more and more, Mr.
Macgillivray's annual reports to the rank and file of partners proved
more and more satisfactory. While North West costs were decreas-
ing, its production of pelts increasing, Hudson's Bay Company stock
was falling—from £250 a share, down and down to £50. By 1809,
it paid no dividends at all.

In the light of such exhilarating news, his listeners were astonished
to be told of the arrival of letter after letter from Sir Alexander
Mackenzie in London. North West Company, their London agent
urged, must lose no time in purchasing control of Hudson's Bay.

To the Nor'Westers such a proposal was a sheer waste of money.
Their rival, they cheerfully agreed, was dying. Let it die.

3. LORD SELKIRK WINS IT

The reason Sir Alexander's was a voice crying in the Wilderness
dates back to a dark and stormy night in April, 1778, when the
American corvette, *Ranger,* dropped anchor off St. Mary's Isle on
the southwest coast of Scotland. This charming spot, for centuries
the ancestral seat of the Douglas clan, had been the childhood home
of the *Ranger's* captain.

To John Paul Jones's young eyes, Dunbar Douglas, Lord of Daerclough and fourth Earl of Selkirk, had appeared the mightiest and
richest man on earth. Now one of the daredevil privateers who
harried the British Isles during the American Revolution, the cap-

[2] After the Revolution, North West Company left Grand Portage to found
Fort William on the north shore of Lake Superior as its inland administration
headquarters.

tain had come to seize the mighty clan leader as a hostage against
release of Americans captured by the British.

The earl was not at home. So while seven-year-old Thomas
Douglas watched, Jones's disgruntled men looted the family plate.
Later, John Paul bought it back, returned it to Lady Selkirk. But
nothing ever erased from the mind of Thomas Douglas his memories
of that black night. As a man, he was to write:

> When I was but a youth I developed an antipathy for the United States,
> due almost solely to the buccaneering of John Paul.

Youngest of seven sons, Thomas Douglas had little prospect of
attaining to his father's titles. But with the blood of generations of
fighting Douglases in his veins, plus all the advantages of his historic and cultured background, a University of Edinburgh degree,
and the grand tour, he was too spirited and intelligent to live the
life of merely a personable, highborn, rich young man.

And at Edinburgh he had become so absorbed in the issues
raised by the French Revolution that he went to Paris to study
liberty, equality and fraternity at first hand. What he learned sent
him back to Scotland to study conditions among the tenants on the
huge Highland estates.

Victims of both the agrarian and industrial revolutions, they were
being evicted ruthlessly from the small plots of land they and their
ancestors had cultivated for centuries to make way for herds of
sheep and cattle. Only two precarious alternatives were offered
them. On the coast, the life of a fisherman. In one of the growing
industrial centers, slavery to a machine.

By the time twenty-one-year-old Thomas Douglas arrived, thousands of the dispossessed had discovered for themselves a third
alternative—the New World. Young Selkirk agreed that emigration
was their only salvation. But that the great majority had gone or were
going to the United States filled him with alarm.

Until 1799 he was powerless to act on his own idea—to settle
colonies of the desperate Scots in British North America. Then, his
father and six brothers dead, the titles and all the influence and
wealth that went with them came to him.

But now the precocious young man was convinced that in all
British North America no land fit for colonization remained unoccupied. In applying to the Colonial Office in London for a land

grant, he recommended that Great Britain immediately purchase the Mississippi Valley from Napoleon. In Louisiana he proposed to colonize not Scotch, but *Irish,* peasants.

Colonial Office indifference did not faze him. In the meantime, he had read Mackenzie's *Voyages.* Using Sir Alexander's own words, and others borrowed from collateral reading, he penned a second application—for a land grant in Red River Valley:

At the Western extremity of Canada, upon the waters [Red River] which fall into Lake Winnipeck. . .is a Country which the Indian traders represent as fertile & of a Climate far more temperate than the Shores of the Atlantic of the same parallel & not more severe than that of Germany and Poland. Here, therefore, the Colonists may, with a moderate expenditure of industry, be certain of a comfortable subsistence and they may also raise some valuable objects of exportation.

Rebuffed again, Selkirk made a third choice—the pass around Sault Ste Marie. This time the Colonial Office agreed, on condition that he choose colonists "more tractable than the Irish." By means of expensive promises, he persuaded one hundred Highland families to join his colony. Only then did he realize that to transport some eight hundred Scots, plus goods and chattels, across the Atlantic to mid-America would cost a small fortune.

The Colonial Office tried to hold him to his agreement. The same money invested in United States lands, he suggested, would prove a much more profitable "speculation." Hastily the Colonial Office granted him land and most liberal concessions on Prince Edward Island. It also offered him any unoccupied twelve hundred acres in Canada he might select.

His Prince Edward Island colony eventually was a success. His second, Baldoon Farm, on the lowlands between Lakes Erie and Huron, was a failure. While he decided on his next venture, Lord Selkirk visited Montreal.

There as a distinguished Scotch nobleman, he was feted. Most attentive hosts were North West partners, Highlanders largely, like himself. Frequently they entertained him at their exclusive Beaver Club where he was fascinated by their vivid, nostalgic ceremonies and reminiscences of their years as traders in the Great Beyond.

Flattered by his interest, the Nor'Westers freely answered his innumerable questions. In confidence, they even revealed their methods, profits, and details about the most potent element in their success—their supply base in Red River Valley.

Sure now that a colony on Red River was feasible *if it had the support of one of the two leading fur companies,* Lord Selkirk sailed for London. There, in 1807, the decision as to *which* company was made for him when he married Jean Wedderburn-Colville. She brought him both wealth and close association with her brother and other relatives who were major stockholders in Hudson's Bay Company.

From them, Lord Selkirk learned that ever since North West's supply base in Red River Valley had canceled the advantage of Hudson Bay's shorter route to the interior, the fortunes of the Honorable Company had been going from bad to worse. Many of its stockholders would sell out for whatever they could get.

Thus fortified with inside information from both rivals, His Lordship consulted five of the leading British lawyers. As one voice they assured him the validity of the Royal Charter of 1670 granting Prince Rupert's Land to Hudson's Bay Company was unassailable. He began to buy stock.

To his surprise, he found his idea was not original. The man whose *Voyages* had roused his interest in Red River Valley also was acquiring shares! Soon as friends and allies, Lord Selkirk and Sir Alexander Mackenzie were buying on joint account. They had several thousand pounds invested in common before North West's London representative discovered his noble ally's intention.

Sir Alexander was outraged. A British colony at the forks of Red and Assiniboine Rivers, the solar plexus of North West's entire system! Farmers exploiting the Valley that had placed in North West's hands the weapon that was forcing Hudson's Bay Company to the wall! This interloper's sly scheme spelled ruin for the Montreal company.

Aloud he called Lord Selkirk a cheap speculator. Selkirk called him a sordid fur trader. In no time, their fighting blood roused, the two Scots had passed beyond the bounds of reason.

Both continued to buy stock. Both labored to win supporters. Mackenzie's urgent pleas failed to waken North West partners in England and America to their danger. Lord Selkirk succeeded in persuading members of his wife's family to increase their holdings and also induced several influential friends to make large investments. By 1811, he owned or controlled about one-third of all Hudson's Bay Company stock.

Even before achieving this goal, he was so sure of victory that he asked the London board of governors for Red River Valley. On condition that his colonists would not interfere with its fur trade and other rights in Rupert's Land, the board assigned him 116,000 square miles "to underwrite the cost of establishing his colony."

Mackenzie protested furiously. No such grant could be made without the approval of the stockholders.

In May, 1811, the stockholders assembled. All they heard was the formal announcement that the board had granted Lord Selkirk Red River Valley for the purpose of establishing a farming colony at the junction of the Red and Assiniboine. Again Sir Alexander was on his feet to force a two-day adjournment.

Too late, his fellow partners in London grasped the enormity of the danger threatening their fur empire. To prevent Red River Valley, the very "root of North West Company," falling into the hands of this nefarious nobleman, they hastily organized formidable opposition.

They could have saved their breath. Never in Hudson's Bay Company's 141 years had any meeting approached the tumult and passion of that adjourned session. When it was over, Lord Selkirk had what he wanted—Red River Valley.

How skillfully he had questioned his Nor'West hosts in Montreal became apparent then. His 116,000 square miles not only included the Valley proper, from Lake Traverse to Lake Winnipeg. They embraced—from the fur trade's point of view—Red River's two richest tributaries. The Roseau Valley, a veritable larder of wild rice, berries, fish, wildfowl, running east to Lake of the Woods. The Assiniboine Valley, a treasury of beaver, extending northwest to that river's ultimate sources.

One thing he had not learned. Under the mistaken impression that the Assiniboine and Red Rivers were one, Lord Selkirk named his 74,000,000-acre land grant, Assiniboia.

Months before Assiniboia became his, he had privately distributed among the landed gentry an "Advertisement and Prospectus" for a joint stock company. Though this document failed to locate Assiniboia as 1,500 miles from Atlantic, Pacific, and Gulf of Mexico, on other points it was specific:

If a tract of the same extent and fertility were offered for sale in Lower Canada or Nova Scotia, purchasers would be eager to obtain it at one hundred or perhaps two hundred thousand guineas. [Conservatively speaking, for from $500,000 to $1,000,000.]

This stock company, His Lordship proposed, should buy Assiniboia from him at one or two pence an acre and sell it to the evicted Scotch and Irish peasants for ten shillings an acre. As each prospect would buy one hundred acres for fifty pounds and the expenses of transporting a family to Red River would not cost more than ten pounds, investors were assured of an initial "nett advantage" of forty pounds. Though in conclusion his "prospectus" warned that twelve years might elapse before the venture paid a dividend, after that

the amount to which profits may ultimately rise seems almost to baffle imagination. . .the result comes out so extraordinarily great that it might appear like exaggeration to state it.

That "prospectus" might have been written with liquid dynamite. North West partners held a field day refuting its every statement as false or misleading. Since, like Sir Alexander Mackenzie, many of them were widely known and respected, their opinions carried solid weight. Britishers in all manner of high places deduced that Lord Selkirk, in the belief that England must fall before Napoleon's imminent invasion, was preparing a refuge for wealthy cowards on remote Red River. To voice that view and another, the Rector of York (Toronto) personally wrote His Lordship:

Your projected settlement on Red River. . .appears to me. . .one of the most gross impositions that ever was attempted on the British public. [It] must be attended with the most baneful consequences to all those unfortunate men who, deluded by false promises, shall leave their homes for such a dreary wilderness.

As a result, only a few relatives of Lady Selkirk and personal friends subscribed. Forced to abandon the joint stock company, Lord Selkirk himself undertook to colonize Assiniboia on a greatly curtailed scale.

In this, too, the adverse publicity defeated him. Despite all promises of fertile land, long-term payments, high profits, freedom of religion, both Scotch and Irish peasants preferred their miserable known to any golden unknown.

Even Hudson's Bay Company was not enthusiastic, though it

had to be devious in expressing opposition. Usually each summer its ships sailed for Hudson Bay from Gravesend on the Thames. For this memorable 1811 sailing, the port selected was, of all places, Sir Alexander Mackenzie's home town—Stornoway, Scotland.

There, in early June, Red River emigrants began to assemble. Adventurous youths, on fire to hunt buffalo, fight wild Indians. Failures, eager to get away from it all. Old men, unfit for hardships and hard labor. Only a few in the prime of life. And most of these candidates for the agricultural life were fishermen.

Of the hundreds expected, 125 arrived. As 35 of these were to enter Hudson's Bay employ, only 95 were bona fide settlers. Connaught Irish. Orkneymen. Glaswegians. Each was suspicious of all the others. All of them resented the Glaswegians who had been promised high wages. And when they saw the difference between the two sturdy Company ships and the *Edward and Ann,* a decrepit old hulk awaiting them, some deserted, others wavered.

Rallying loyally, Mackenzie's relatives and friends warned the Selkirkers of the dangers ahead on sea and land. The port customs officer, uncle by marriage of Sir Alexander, urged them all to desert. His son-in-law, an army recruiter, forcibly induced several to accept the king's shilling, marched them ashore. Before he could return, the *Edward and Ann* stood out to sea. The ninety colonists had shrunk to seventy.

In charge of this first contingent, as superintendent of Red River Settlement and governor of Assiniboia, was Captain Miles Macdonell, a retired army officer Lord Selkirk had met in Canada. By virtue of a brother who had been for years a Nor'West trader on the Assiniboine and a cousin recently appointed chief trader at Fort Gibraltar, the captain was not ignorant of the situation at Red River. Now, acting under His Lordship's written instructions, he viewed the enterprise as a military expedition to occupy alien territory. Daily he turned out the unhappy seventy for military drill and duty.

Two dreary months later, the *Edward and Ann* dropped anchor in Hudson Bay. The Selkirkers' eagerness to feel firm ground beneath their feet chilled at sight of the barren shore, studded with rocks and blighted vegetation. And chilled again when the ungainly, leadroofed buildings of York Factory proved hardly less cold than the reception tendered them by William Auld, overseas governor of the Company, and other officials.

These officials were antagonistic on sight to Macdonell's energetic confidence in his own ability to overcome all obstacles. The captain hid his disapproval of their dogtrot methods, but he could not conceal his resentment for the winter camp site they had selected for his men on Nelson River. And his rage boiled over when, after they had selected the newcomers they wanted, his colonists were reduced to thirty-six. Two of these were so ill they had to return with the ships to England.

A really capable, conscientious man, Captain Macdonell did surmount both winter and obstacles. In spite of a riot among his cold, homesick flock that resulted in two being jailed for shipment to London. Of an armed insurrection, slyly abetted by York Factory, that lost nine more to Company employ. Of an epidemic of scurvy that took the life of one. When the ice left the rivers in mid-June, he and his twenty-two remaining colonists had built four crude copies of the York boat used by Bay brigades throughout the interior.

Early on the morning of July 6, a bull, cow and wheat seed were stowed aboard, though, strangely, for an agricultural colony at the junction of two fish-filled rivers, not an item of either farming or fishing equipment was included. All was ready for departure. At that moment three emigrants refused to go.

But now Macdonell's dander was up. Reach Red River he would if he had to go alone! Sheepishly, under the mocking eyes of Company personnel and ex-Selkirkers, eleven Scots and eight Irish climbed into the boats. Escorted by experienced Bay traders returning to their posts, the little flotilla set sail.

Fifty-five days crawled away before Red River Valley's first European settlers—footsore, weather-beaten, mosquito and black-fly bitten—arrived at the forks of the Red and Assiniboine. Their troubles were not over when they attained the promised land. A group of Company traders camped there greeted but did not welcome them. And the captain's cousin, Alexander Macdonell, as chief trader at Fort Gibraltar, made plain his loyalty to North West Company by sending mounted *Métis*, hideously painted as savages, to strike them cold with fear.

Nevertheless, on September 4, 1812, flags flew at the junction of Red and Assiniboine. Alexander Macdonell and his Nor'West traders, armed Hudson's Bay traders, colonists, *Métis*, and Indians stood more or less at attention. And Captain Miles Macdonell, as governor of Assiniboia, in the name of Lord Selkirk, took formal possession of Red River Valley.

PART IV

Red River Settlement [1]

[1] In the beginning, Red River Settlement was used as a synonym for the colony's changing names. Gradually, it became an inclusive title, synonymous with Assiniboia. When the settlement at the forks of the Red and Assiniboine Rivers reorganized and rebuilt after the Great Flood, the British Protestant community on the west bank took back the name for its own use; the east bank settlement retained its parish name of St. Boniface. To clarify confusion, the following series of the original colony's changing names may be helpful: 1812, Point Douglas; 1813, Colony Gardens; 1817, Kildonan; 1826, Red River; 1858, Fort Garry—or Garry, for short; 1873, Winnipeg.

1. "THOSE UNFORTUNATE MEN"

Prairie Sioux determined the location of Assiniboia's capital. Those savages, the captain was advised, had no curiosity about Red River north of its junction with the Assiniboine.

Accordingly, Macdonell chose as the site of Red River Valley's first white settlement, a triangle on the west bank of Red River, just three-quarters of a mile north of the junction. Bounded on two sides by the thickly wooded River, on the third by golden prairies, it was a really pleasing location. To honor Lord Selkirk, he named it Point Douglas.

Neither Fort Douglas nor homes could be built, however, because of the acute food shortage. Nothing could be secured from Indians or *Métis*, who also were near famine. What surpluses there were, Fort Gibraltar owned. But at Pembina, Macdonell was assured, food was plentiful.

Leaving five men at Point Douglas, he led the rest seventy miles south to make their first American homes near the Hudson's Bay post at the joining of the Red and Pembina Rivers. There he erected a fortified cluster of cabins and storehouses which, again to honor His Lordship, he christened Fort Daer.

Before the rude shelters were completed, a sorry procession straggled across the prairies to their gaping doors. Its sixty-odd members made up the second contingent of Selkirkers from Scotland and Ireland. Among them were the first women and children, including a baby born at sea. Their story was even sorrier.

Since sailing from England in June, 1812, they had endured such brutal treatment from the counting house clerk Lord Selkirk had placed in charge that several mutinous colonists had been sent back to London in irons. At York Factory, to keep them free of corrupting influences, he had confined them to tents. This so affronted Company officials that they had delayed for weeks to supply the boats to take them to Point Douglas.

And there they had been told they still had seventy miles to travel to Fort Daer. Fearful of the *Métis* in their escort, terrified of the Chippewa, they found the greatest hardship and humiliation of the entire journey the fact that they had to walk or creep along in crude carts while those "barbarians" rode horseback.

Food was plentiful at Pembina for traders, *Métis,* Indians, but not for so many additional mouths. Yet though always hungry, always cold, fearful alike of natives and the elements, the Selkirkers did enjoy two pleasures. Damning Lord Selkirk as the author of their woes. Repainting into rosy memories the privations they had known in the "Old Country."

To the third contingent of Selkirkers who arrived in Hudson Bay late in October, 1812, even the hardships at Pembina would have appeared rosy. These were the Sutherlanders, nearly one hundred strong. By far the best settlers yet sent to Red River, they were the only ones to come joyfully.

Of all the ruthless evictions of more than 450,000 tenants from Highland estates, those practiced by Lady Sutherland were the most shameless. And of all the 15,000 people she dispossessed, those in the parish of Kildonan suffered most. Memory of their homes a reeking mass of smoke and ashes, of the match applied while the sick and aged were in their beds, moved 700 of them to apply in one body to join Lord Selkirk's colony. Had York Factory been equipped to care for so many, the history of Red River Settlement might have rivaled Utopia's. But His Lordship had to limit this third sailing to 100, all Scots. No more Irish! Too intractable.

Hardly had the Sutherlanders sailed than typhus swept their ship. When it entered Hudson Bay, seven were dead, thirty dangerously ill. The captain, an obstinate man at any time, now in abject terror of the disease, anchored off a barren spot two hundred miles from York Factory, drove his passengers ashore. Before Governor Auld learned of their plight, hastened to them, several more had died.

After much bickering the captain took the survivors aboard, but at the first opportunity ran his ship aground. It soon was freed, but beyond that point he would not sail. Somehow the Sutherlanders wintered on Hudson Bay's north shore, somehow survived the treacherous trek over snow and ice in April to York Factory.

Late in May, 1813, the strongest set out for the settlement that Captain Macdonell, in a fever of wishful thinking, had named Colony Gardens. They found it neither a colony nor a garden. Though Macdonell had allotted each householder a one hundred-acre tract on Red River, helped them build homes as good or better than they had ever known, bought seed from Fort Gibraltar, nothing could please the Selkirkers already in residence.

As fishermen they had no interest in farming. Speaking Gaelic, they resented the English and French of the traders, French Canadians, and *Métis*, the outlandish gutterals of the Indians. Accustomed to brief vistas and changeable, misty weather, they felt strange and exposed on vividly green prairies rolling to unbroken horizons, disliked the succession of clear, warm days, of clear, cool nights. Suspicious and jealous of one another, they were unable to make friends or co-operate to their mutual advantage. In short, they were homesick.

Watching his charges grow thinner daily on the meager diet he could provide, Captain Macdonell grew bitter, too. For he was watching Indians and half-breeds stream into Fort Gibraltar with Red River pemmican, venison, bear meat, fish, waterfowl, cereals, fruits, even maple sugar and salt.

North West's distribution depot needed every mouthful of food it could lay hands on. Almost immediately after the United States declared war against Great Britain in June, 1812, American troops en route to attack Montreal had cut Nor'West's supply line. On Fort Gibraltar and Pembina, therefore, rested full responsibility for maintaining every North West post west of Lake Superior.

To Captain Macdonell, however, these Canadian trespassers on Lord Selkirk's private property were stealing foods that rightly belonged to the colonists. Now with the Sutherlanders added to his charges, he was forced to winter once more at Fort Daer.

There both the unaccountable immigrants and Red River Valley surprised him. The weather was mild, food abundant. French Canadians and *Métis* brought fiddles and drums to entertain the settlers. Sutherlanders enthusiastically adopted their fast-paced Red River Jig, made community festivals of the two marriages and four births among the Selkirkers, assumed ways and buckskins of the country. Little by little, following their lead, all the Scots and Irish began to put down roots in Red River soil.

Heartened by all this, the captain took the drastic step he had long been considering. On January 8, 1814, as governor of Assiniboia, he posted a Proclamation:

It is hereby ordered that no person trading in furs or provisions within Assiniboia, for the Honourable Hudson's Bay Company, the North West

Company, or any individual or unconnected trader or any persons whatever, shall take out any provision, either of flesh, grains, or vegetables,
procured or raised within said Territory, by water or land carriage, for
one year from the date thereof.

To insure food for his colonists was the least of Macdonell's three
reasons for issuing that embargo on provisions. More important was
his need during the coming summer to feed Lord Selkirk and a company of four to five hundred armed men. While recruiting colonists
in Scotland, His Lordship had discovered that North West propaganda had destroyed all hope of securing the tens of thousands necessary to people Assiniboia. Now he was coming himself to rid his
land grant of every Nor'West interloper.

But the embargo's most important function, as both Macdonell
and every York Factory official saw it, was as a weapon to rid Rupert's Land of their rival. On Red River pemmican, North West's survival, literally now, depended. Take it away and every post in the
Montreal company's empire must perish.

At Fort Gibraltar, however, Chief Trader Alexander Macdonell
and Duncan Cameron, another wintering partner, saw in the embargo a chance for a brilliant coup. Unable, because of the war, to
ship their mounting pelt packs to Montreal, they proposed a compromise. If Captain Macdonell would arrange for Hudson's Bay
ships to carry Nor'West furs to England, they would furnish him
with all the food he required. Since food was his object, the captain
agreed.

Food prospects now were so bright that for the first time the colonists need not winter at Fort Daer. During the summer of 1814, more
homes were built at Colony Gardens, more fields broken, more
seed sown. Small wonder the captain felt justified to believe himself
capable of handling any future challenge North West could offer.

He reckoned without Sir Alexander Mackenzie and other powerful Nor'West strategists. To these gentlemen, Red River Valley had
assumed an importance that far transcended its value as provision
basket for their trading posts. On absolute control of Pembina and
Fort Gibraltar, they now pinned their hopes to crush forever not only
Lord Selkirk and Hudson's Bay Company, but a new and potentially
more dangerous rival.

For long after his arrival in the American colonies of 1783, with
seven cheap flutes as his only capital, John Jacob Astor had been a

figure of fun to both Canadian and American fur traders. Unmoved, the tenacious German, barefoot in summer, wooden-shod in winter, had continued to plod the forests of Upper New York to exchange beads and swigs of rum for pelts with the Indians. In the same methodical way he had invested his profits in New York City real estate.

By 1809, he had the experience, organization and million dollars necessary to incorporate himself as The American Fur Company. When the War of 1812 forced him to suspend operations, he was not dismayed. In the meantime, like Lord Selkirk, he had read a book.

The published report of the Lewis and Clark Expedition inspired him with a continental vision of a United States that extended from Atlantic to Pacific. In this vision, he beheld Johan Jakob Astor in sole control of the American fur trade west of the Mississippi.

To achieve this goal quickly, he invited the venerable North West Company to merge with his brand new Pacific Fur Company. Umbrageous at such impudence, Sir Alexander Mackenzie and associates replied by preparing to make good their claims to all territory on the Pacific Coast between Spain's California and Russia's Alaska. To do this, Nor'Westers had to reach the Pacific overland before Astor's ships could arrive there by way of Cape Horn.

In general, their "preparations" included three major items. One: to expand Pembina's production of pemmican. Two: to enlarge Fort Gibraltar to double as distribution center for Nor'West trading posts *and* as a supply base for expeditions making the long overland haul to the Pacific. And three: by fair means or foul, to wipe Red River Settlement from the face of the earth.

But the partners had burned their fingers once in attempting to prevent Lord Selkirk from winning Assiniboia. Burned them again trying to prevent the Selkirkers from reaching Red River. Wary now, they awaited *the opportunity.*

When William Macgillivray and retinue left Montreal in that summer of 1814 for the annual meeting at Fort William, they still had no practicable program in mind. But at the fort, they learned about Captain Macdonell's Proclamation. In that embargo on provisions, they recognized *the opportunity.*

Picture then their rage and humiliation when they also learned of the compromise Fort Gibraltar had proposed and Captain Macdonell had accepted. To restore themselves to favor, the two wintering partners responsible for the compromise returned to Fort Gibraltar sworn to vengeance.

Alexander Macdonell left at once for Qu'Appelle River where the *Métis* had their headquarters. There he had little difficulty to convince the half-breeds that, as native sons of Red River Valley, they formed a New Nation whose lands the Selkirkers were stealing and would continue to steal. In the absence of Captain Miles Macdonell at Fort Daer, Duncan Cameron, resplendent in scarlet coat and sword, also had little difficulty in impressing the unsophisticated Scots and Irish with his authority.

Posing as a fellow Britisher, horrified at their sufferings, he offered them all free passage to Upper Canada where fertile lands were available in a long-established community. Alexander Macdonell added further inducement by sending mounted *Métis* to ride round Colony Gardens day and night shouting threats and firing muskets.

So successful was this joint campaign that on an early April morning, Cameron moved 120 men, women and children, their personal goods, and the field pieces of Fort Douglas to Fort Gibraltar. Despite all threats, the remaining thirteen families refused to budge.

When Captain Macdonell, warned, hurried back from Fort Daer, Cameron sent over a bailiff with a warrant for his arrest. Macdonell countered by ordering all Nor'Westers out of Assiniboia. Thereupon, his cousin trained Fort Douglas' own captured cannon on Colony Gardens, placed it under seige.

Irked by such moderate methods, Fort William ordered an immediate attack. It began on the night of June 10, ended a week later. By that time several Selkirkers were dead, others captured. To save further bloodshed and destruction, Captain Macdonell submitted to arrest.

He and the deserters—now 140 strong—were hurried by canoe to Fort William. The remaining Selkirkers fled in small boats for Norway House, a Hudson's Bay post at the northern end of Lake Winnipeg. Next day the Nor'Westers razed Colony Gardens, trampled the grain fields, killed or appropriated cattle and horses. Others hastened south to seize Fort Daer.

Fort William hailed with joy the arrival of the governor of Assiniboia, the deserters, and word that Red River Settlement was no more. Watching and listening to that joy, the Selkirkers knew, too late, they had been duped.

2. "GOOD NEWS!"

Where was Lord Selkirk and the company of armed men who could have saved his colony? All unaware of the storm centering over Red River, he was in England hard at work on what seemed a better plan.

Sometime before, a disgruntled ex -Nor'Wester, with six years, experience in and around Red River Valley, had arrived in London to place before Hudson's Bay's Board of Governors a scheme to ruin his former employers. In general, Colin Robertson's plan called for a wholesale adoption by the English company of the Montrealers' methods. In particular, it offered a sound and permanent measure for the security of Assiniboia.

North West's primary reason for placing so high a value on Red River Valley, Robertson insisted, was that its pemmican and other foods insured uninterrupted trading in prized Athabasca. The sooner the Honorable Company seized that Nor'West prize, the sooner Nor' West opposition to Colony Gardens would end.

To Montreal, in 1814, Lord Selkirk, accordingly, sent Robertson to hire every available French Canadian for an invasion of Athabasca. He himself remained in England to recruit a new contingent for Red River, to find a new governor of Assiniboia in response to Miles Macdonell's request to be relieved, and to inject Robertson's ideas into Hudson's Bay administration.

By the following spring, Robertson had assembled a hundred men. From them he heard of the all-out attack North West was planning against Colony Gardens. Pausing only long enough to send a warning to His Lordship, the ex-Nor'Wester, with twenty French Canadians, started posthaste for Red River.

At Lake of the Woods he learned he was too late. Colony Gardens had been destroyed a month before. Its survivors, more dead than alive, were at Norway House.

Speeding north, Robertson persuaded the refugees to return to Point Douglas. Under his competent direction and with the aid of his hundred French Canadians, new homes were built, fields sowed, hay cut. By fall, everything promised well for the winter.

Early in November, however, the new contingent of one hundred Scots arrived. With them came cattle, sheep, implements, seed, and —the new Governor.

Had Lord Selkirk scoured the British Empire for the most unsuitable successor to Miles Macdonell, he could not have made a better choice. A Boston Tory, Robert Semple had fled to London immediately after the American Revolution to become a traveling agent for a commercial house. As a result of his observations in Europe, Asia, Africa, and South America, he had written six books.

A pompous ass personally, he knew nothing of farming, military service, or government. He was not impressed by the buckskinned Nor'Westers at Fort Gibraltar. He understood at once that the destruction of Colony Gardens stemmed from Captain Macdonell's "grossest mismanagement."

To a man of action like Robertson, a man of words like Semple was a disaster. Fortunately, as the Settlement was not prepared to feed one hundred additional mouths, the governor and most of the newcomers had to winter at Fort Daer. Robertson remained in charge at Point Douglas.

Within a few months he had uncovered the reason for Alexander Macdonell's prolonged absence from Fort Gibraltar. A new Nor' West plot to destroy Colony Gardens was afoot. Promptly, he arrested Cameron, shut him up in Fort Douglas. And, searching the North West fort, he found more incriminating evidence in letters. One from Cuthbert Grant, the *Métis* leader at Portage la Prairie, left no room for doubt:

> The halfbreeds. . .are all to be at [Colony Gardens] in the spring. It is to be hoped we shall come with flying colors and never see any of them again in a colonizing way at Red River. In fact, [Hudson's Bay] traders shall pack themselves off also. . . . We are to remain [there] to pass the summer for fear they play us the same trick as last summer of coming back.

Alarmed, Robertson seized Nor'West's fast mail canoe from Fort William. In its pouches he found "most diabolical schemes" for the total elimination of Red River Settlement.

When Governor Semple returned, Robertson placed before him all his sinister proofs, urged that they destroy Fort Gibraltar at once. Semple refused. Unable to do more, Robertson, taking Cameron with him, departed for York Factory.

Too late, the governor realized he had neither forces nor leadership to defend the Settlement. But—with Alexander Macdonell and Cameron absent, only lesser men remained in charge of the Nor'

West fort. Impulsively acting on Robertson's ill-considered advice, he seized and razed Fort Gibraltar.

This blow to the solar plexus of their system removed the last curb on the Montrealers' lawless arrogance. Shortly an armed expedition left Fort William for a more or less mythical rendezvous with Alexander Macdonell and forty Canadians some miles south of Lake Winnipeg. Actually, confident of the inevitable explosion that must ensue if two such inflammable elements as Semple and the half-breeds were exposed to each other, Macdonell remained at Portage la Prairie. Cuthbert Grant at the head of seventy mounted *Métis* set out for the rendezvous.

On the afternoon of April 19, 1815, a guard in the watchtower of Fort Douglas sighted the mounted company cutting across the prairies from the Assiniboine to Red River. His shout of alarm brought men, women and children milling into the fort. Both hubbub and its cause annoyed the governor.

In all his travels to foreign lands, Semple had found the Anglo-Saxon to be above challenge, the natives docile and obsequious. These barbarous Red River half-breeds wouldn't dare to defy a British governor and man of letters! Ordering every male Selkirker within earshot to follow, he rushed out. Twenty-six men, muskets in hand, obeyed.

About a mile from the Fort, they beheld the *Métis*, garbed and armed for war. Their appearance was so formidable that even the governor paused to send back for more men and a field piece. But, too angry to wait, he again advanced toward the clump of seven oaks where the horsemen had halted.

One look at their painted faces and the colonists began to retreat. At that, a young *Métis* broke ranks to gallop toward the governor.

"What you want?" he demanded in broken English.

"What do you want?" Semple retorted.

"Why you destroy our fort, you damned rascal?"

Damned rascal! Furious at such effrontery, Semple grabbed the miscreant's bridle. Affronted also, the *Métis* leaped to the ground. In the tenseness of the moment someone pressed a trigger. As though that shot were a signal, both sides opened fire.

Twenty-three men, only one a half-breed, died in that so-called "Massacre of Seven Oaks.[2] Semple was among the first to fall. By

[2] Technically, a massacre is considered the slaughter by armed attackers of unarmed and unwarned victims.

surrendering or leaping into Red River, four Selkirkers, though wounded, lived to tell the tale. After stripping and mutilating the bodies of the dead colonists, the victors retired.

That evening Cuthbert Grant sent an ultimatum to stricken Colony Gardens. If one gun was fired from Fort Douglas, every man, woman and child would be shot. But if all properties were surrendered peaceably, he would give them safe conduct toward Norway House until they were clear of the route by which the Fort William expedition would arrive.

To Portage la Prairie another messenger sped with word of the victory. There Alexander Macdonell "and all the gentlemen with him" shouted, "Good news! Twenty-two English have been killed!" Immediately, the chief trader sent word to Grant to hold all prisoners until he came.

The order reached the Settlement just as the Selkirkers were entering their boats. All was despair until some sly soul suggested that Macdonell wanted them held that he might reap all the glory and rewards of victory. His own suspicion voiced, Grant sped them on their way, though without the promised safe conduct.

With admirable timing, Fort William's expedition had delayed its arrival at the rendezvous for four days, waited there two more. Now, as they paddled up Red River, the Nor'Westers met and halted the refugees. Failing to find the incriminating North West documents, hidden in the voluminous petticoats of one young woman, they permitted all but four men to continue.

At Colony Gardens the united North West forces plied the *Métis* with feasts and rewards for three days. Then, leaving the half-breeds to raze the Settlement, they returned to Fort William to report that this time Selkirk's "Rascally Republic" had fallen forever.

Meanwhile, Robertson's warning in hand, His Lordship was besieging the colonial minister in London to send troops to Red River. Assured by North West partners there that Selkirk's fears were both unfounded and malicious, and convinced himself that Red River Valley was a howling wilderness, the minister refused. Finally, in mid-September, Lord Selkirk sailed for America to see for himself how his colony fared.

In Montreal he found Captain Macdonell waiting, under bail, for his trial. From him, he learned of North West's first attack. But in that stronghold of the Nor'Westers, he could rouse no sympathy for his settlers. The governor also refused either to send troops to Red River or to permit him to take armed men there himself. And when, as a last resort, he tried to make peace with North West, the partners who finally consented to see him refused to withdraw their traders from Assiniboia or to permit the case to be brought to court. They did offer to divide Rupert's Land, *with the exception of Red River Valley,* with Hudson's Bay, but that, of course, was unacceptable.

By spring of 1816, however, Canada had a new Governor who was much more impressed with Lord Selkirk's social power and prestige than by the Nor'Westers' financial equivalents. To aid His Lordship to reach Red River, Governor Sherbrooke appointed him a justice of the peace to Indian territories, gave him a bodyguard of seven soldiers, and permission to recruit others.

In Montreal at that time remained many of the disbanded De Meuron Regiment of Swiss, Italian and other European mercenaries brought to Canada to fight for the British in the War of 1812. To any who would accompany him to Red River, His Lordship offered a small salary. And to every man who would remain there as a colonist, he promised land. Eighty enlisted men and four officers accepted. On the same terms, twenty recruits from two demobilized Canadian regiments signed.

Early in May, again as governor of Assiniboia, Captain Macdonell left Montreal with twenty men for Red River to prepare for Lord Selkirk's arrival. Daily his journey was beset with unaccountable delays, later proved to have been the work of a Nor'West agent among his boatmen. He was still some distance from Lake Winnipeg when he learned of the massacre and second destruction of Colony Gardens. Turning, he raced back to Sault Ste Marie to intercept Lord Selkirk and his party.

Too shocked and angry to listen to advice, His Lordship, with forces now totaling 120 men, headed straight across Lake Superior to take Fort William by surprise. He did.

William Macgillivray and other Montreal partners there agreed to release at once all Selkirkers and Hudson's Bay men held prisoner. And Macgillivray submitted without protest to arrest. When other Lords of the Lakes and Forests refused, they were arrested like common criminals.

Only for a few hours, unfortunately. Like Miles Macdonell and Robert Semple, Lord Selkirk underestimated his adversaries. Paroled and permitted to return to their own quarters, the Nor'Westers began that very night to secrete arms and ammunition, destroy or hide incriminating documents. Enough remained, however, to damn Nor'West practices in any British court.

Again overruling his advisers, Lord Selkirk insisted on wintering at Fort William to prepare his case himself. There he made an unwise if not meretricious agreement with a shifty old Nor'Wester left behind when the other partners departed. And when a few Montrealers returned, accompanied by a magistrate with a warrant for his arrest, he refused to accept it. Since he had more than a hundred armed men behind him, they did not insist. Next he had several nearby North West posts seized, their furs confiscated.

With the capture of Rainy Lake's important post, he cleared the way to regain his own forts, Douglas and Daer. Their recovery not only was imperative to control Assiniboia. Already he had seen enough pemmican in use to appreciate Colin Robertson's opinion of its superiority over the cumbersome, perishable foods imported from England for all Hudson's Bay posts.

Now that Fort Gibraltar was no more, he need only develop Colony Gardens as a pemmican manufacturing center to insure to the Honorable Company all the advantages this compact, enduring food had given North West. At this point the struggle between the English and Canadian companies for Red River Valley definitely became known as the Pemmican War.

To capture either fort but one strategy was feasible. Surprise. For this absolute secrecy was necessary. Yet days before Lord Selkirk's forces could reach Red River their presence on the open, snowy prairies must be spotted.

Into this impasse walked an unexpected ally—the blue-eyed Indian, Falcon. The time has come to tell—if sketchily—the story of Red River Valley's first American citizen and North West Company's unwitting Nemesis.

3. JOHN TANNER, FALCON

To the most remote American frontier of 1789—the forks of the Ohio and Miami Rivers—a few families from Virginia had emigrated. Among them was the Reverend John Tanner, whose second wife, with a baby of her own, had little time to watch over the brood the first wife had left. While she struggled to make a home of the crumbling log cabin whose previous owner had been tomahawked or captured by marauding redskins, she pressed rebellious, ten-year-old Johnny Tanner into service as baby-sitter for her own offspring.

"I wish the Indians'd get me," Johnny muttered one morning as he eased himself outside the cabin with his burden. There he employed a well-calculated pinch. His stepmother flew to the rescue of her screaming treasure. Johnny flew to the near-by woods.

Long before his family missed him, he had his wish. Bound and gagged at the bottom of a canoe, he was well on his way north to quiet the grief of a squaw whose own son recently had died. At the paddles were her husband, Manito, a hunter of an Ottawa tribe living near Detroit, and his eldest son.

The squaw accepted Johnny, tried to protect him from the white-man-hating Ottawas. But for two years his life was one long travail of starvation, brutal treatment, and intermittent attempts on his life. His capacity to endure and his incessant efforts to escape earned him the tribal name of Falcon, (*Shaw-shaw-wa-ne-ba-se*). Not until Manito convinced him—falsely—that he and his son had murdered the entire Tanner family was Falcon reconciled to his new home.

Escape of a sort came through a remarkable squaw, recognized by the Ottawas as their supreme chief and by the British at Detroit as rating a two-gun salute. For twenty gallons of diluted whisky and other considerations, Net-no-kwa bought Falcon. Until he was thirteen, he lived happily in her lodge on Lake Huron.

Then Net-no-kwa and her husband set out with their own two sons and Falcon to visit Chippewa relatives on Red River. In the wilderness west of Lake Superior, the husband and older son died. After a year of starvation and peril, Falcon and the remaining son managed to bring Net-no-kwa to the mouth of Red River. And there, miraculously, they found the unexpectant relatives encamped. Net-no-kwa's own son soon threw off all responsibility for her. At four-teen, Falcon became a trapper to care for her and himself.

Even before he reached Red River, he had forgotten both the English language and his strict religious training. During the next thirty years, as hunter and trapper in Red River Valley he became an Indian. The red man's code of right and wrong was his code. He even acquired a Guiding Spirit that appeared in his dreams to tell him where to find game or warn him of impending danger.

Nevertheless, in some ways he was no Indian. He neither drank hard liquor nor smoked a pipe. From the first he scoffed openly at the tribal medicine man. Rejecting the Chippewa custom of aban-doning old people to die, he cared for Net-no-kwa as long as she lived. By unremitting persistence, he trained himself to bring down every animal, bird or enemy he shot at.

Tall, black haired, sternly handsome, of unusual hardiness and strength, he was, at twenty, both feared and respected by Chippewa, Cree, and Assiniboine. To the white man he was a source of interest and concern. British and American traders in Red River Valley ad-vised him to go back to the States, even offered to send him. Alex-ander Henry urged him to turn white man, become a North West trader and share the Pembina post with him. Sure his family was dead and wedded now to the nomad life, Tanner always refused.

Each year had its cycle of activities, all delightful to him. In the spring, he set up his lodge in Turtle Mountains for the annual maple-sugar making. Followed for several weeks the thrilling spring buffalo hunt on the prairies. Then a leisurely canoe trip through Roseau River Valley, gathering wild rice, blueberries and other fruits. Just in time to fish for sturgeon, feast on wild duck, geese and deer, he reached Lake of the Woods. In the fall he returned to Red River for the bigger, longer, even more thrilling buffalo hunts. For his winter's trapping, he remained on Red River or traveled north to Lake Winnipeg or the Saskatchewan. This to Falcon was life indeed.

As he matured, he passed through the various Chippewa ordeals to become a warrior and accompany war parties on their annual summer forays against the Prairie Sioux. And as an eligible bach-elor, possessed of four horses, many traps and an infallible gun, he was the choice of numerous chiefs as the husband for their daugh-ters.

Falcon resisted all overtures until one fine spring evening Red Sky of Morning smiled at him. But as he grew ardent, she turned coy, and remained that way until he lost all interest. At that, Net-no-kwa, shocked, forced him to marry the grieving girl. When Red Sky of Morning had borne him a son and two daughters, she and her children returned to her parental lodge near Lake Winnipeg.

By this time, the blue-eyed Indian not only was the greatest hunter in Red River and Lake Winnipeg Valleys. As the only trapper to penetrate Upper Red River to hunt beaver with unprecedented success under the very noses of the Prairie Sioux, he was held to be the bravest and offered the title of chief. Though he refused that honor, his prestige was now so high he was obliged to take a second wife to perform the menial tasks of his tepee.

His choice was a sullen bride from a Chippewa lodge on Lake of the Woods. Although she bore him several children, she shared her family's hatred and fear of Falcon's disdain of medicine men in general, their own model in particular. Several times, only the warnings of his Guiding Spirit saved him from death at the hands of his irate in-laws.

With every other tribesman in Lower Red River Valley, Falcon remained aloof from the battles and intrigues between Hudson's Bay and North West traders. But he definitely was a partisan of the Montrealers. Each fall from Alexander Henry's Pembina post, he obtained a substantial advance credit to buy his winter supplies. Each spring he paid it off with pelts. So satisfactory an arrangement imbued him with a deep and mystic sense of "belonging" to North West.

When Alexander Henry left Pembina in 1808, Falcon transferred his allegiance and trade to Fort Gibraltar. But there the chief trader had established a new policy. No Indian could secure credit for so much as a needle.

His pride irreparably bruised, Falcon trapped that winter with such zeal that his catch was phenomenal. Caching his pelts near Fort Gibraltar, he trekked the seventy miles to Pembina. There Hudson's Bay's chief trader gave him all the credit he desired.

When he returned north to collect his furs, Fort Gibraltar's chief trader, an apparently changed man, invited him into the fort, plied him with food and wine. But even as Tanner ate and drank, clerks entered, Falcon's pelt packs in their arms. Tossing them into an inner room, they locked the door. When the key was in his pocket, the chief trader's courtesy abruptly ended.

Fury was no word for the white Indian's emotion. He never rested

till he gained access to that inner room. He had succeeded, was tossing his last packs out a window when the chief trader, gun in hand,
opened the door. Behind him stood several men, also armed.

Falcon waited. The Nor'Wester didn't shoot. Contemptuous of a
man who would draw a gun, then lack courage to use it, Tanner
struck it from his hand, stalked out.

Thereafter, until the offensive Nor'Wester died, he delivered all
his furs to Hudson's Bay posts. Then he returned to Fort Gibraltar,
but the damage had been done. His mystic sense of belonging to
North West had died, too.

And the life that had made every foot of Red River Valley dear to
him was palling. Persecutions of his wife's family increasingly har-
assed him. More and more he resented the endless strife between the
rival fur traders. Advent of the Selkirkers, with ensuing troubles, was
almost the last straw. The Massacre of Seven Oaks when "white men
killed white men like savages" was. After months of indecision, he
decided to return to the United States.

Unaware that Lord Selkirk's forces now occupied North West's
Rainy Lake post, he arrived there with corn to exchange for supplies
for his journey. Miles Macdonell welcomed him as heaven-sent. And
when the captain assured him that the white warriors were there to
restore peace to Red River Valley, Falcon agreed—for forty dollars—
to guide them to Fort Douglas. More: he planned the strategy for its
capture.

Early in December of 1817, with Captain Macdonell, twenty-
nine De Meurons, and twenty Chippewa braves he himself had selected, Falcon set out. By way of Roseau River Valley, established
Indian route between Lake of the Woods and Red River, but un-
traveled by white men because of its treacherous bogs, he brought
them, unseen and unsuspected, to the east bank, opposite Pembina.
Taken completely by surprise, Fort Daer's Nor'West captors surrendered without a shot.

Macdonell was jubilant. Fort Douglas never would expect danger
to approach from the south! Confident of victory, the little troop
moved north. Within ten miles of its objective, it camped to wait, as
Falcon had planned, to attack by night.

There Peguis, a most astute Chippewa chief and friend of North
West Company, came upon them. Learning the expedition's purpose, he persuaded the captain to wait till daylight, march openly on

the fort. Why Macdonell, a military man himself, cast aside Falcon's well-proved strategy never has been adequately explained. But agree he did.

His pride again lacerated, Falcon decided to vindicate his own tactics. When darkness fell, he and his Chippewa warriors slipped away. Making a ladder of a dismantled tree, they crept noiselessly to the foot of Fort Douglas' stockade, scaled it, dropped inside.

Next morning when Macdonell and his men, guns at the ready, marched up, Falcon threw open the gates.

Grateful for the bloodless campaign that had restored Assiniboia to him, Lord Selkirk offered to send Falcon back to his people or to take him to England. These months of association with white men, however, had convinced Tanner that he now was too much of an Indian to care for civilization. With eighty dollars instead of forty in his pocket and Lord Selkirk's promise to pay him twenty dollars a year for life (a promise kept for five years), Falcon returned to Lake of the Woods.

Still concerned, His Lordship prepared a pamphlet on the white Indian's life with the Chippewa. Published later in Ohio, it eventually united Falcon with his family in Kentucky.

A nine-day wonder to the entire country, Tanner decided not only to remain in the United States himself, but to bring out and educate his children as Americans. He recovered the three children of Red Sky of Morning. But when he tried to leave Lake of the Woods with those of his second wife, she and a young relative tried to kill him. Rescued and cared for by Nor'Westers, he again returned to the States.

An expert on Indian languages and customs, he served for two years as interpreter to Indian agent, Schoolcraft, at Sault Ste Marie. And now a white man, he felt he should have a white wife. In Detroit he found one.

But he still was all Indian in his attitude toward women. The young bride was horrified to find three of his Indian-mothered children, wild as foxes, in the crude home he took her to. And terrified to be treated herself as a squaw. When her own child was born, sympathetic Americans helped her and her baby to escape.

Some years later, suspecting the attentions of the Indian agent's brother to one of his daughters, Tanner shot the man and fled. Back, everyone assumed, to the life he loved in Red River Valley.

Long afterward in a swamp not far from the Sault, hunters stumbled on a skeleton, a gun at its side. The gun was the Falcon's.

4. LORD SELKIRK FOUNDS FORT SNELLING

Fort Douglas regained, Captain Macdonell ousted every Nor'Wester from Assiniboia, sent a messenger to Norway House to bring back the refugees. They had just returned and buried the bleached bones of the massacre's still exposed dead when Lord Selkirk arrived.

What were his emotions as he beheld his colony a pinpoint of ruin in that vast green sea of prairie? When he met the gaze of his tragedy-worn people? The answer lies in his strenuous efforts to place Red River Settlement on a firmer footing.

For this, too, an unexpected ally appeared. In Lord Selkirk, that astute Chippewa chief, Peguis, recognized the shaping hand of the future. Forthwith, he transformed his young hunters into a food battalion and in all things else made himself provider and protector of the great white chief's people.

His Lordship renamed the Settlement to honor the many emigrants from the Scottish parish of Kildonan. To insure protection for the new Kildonan, he awarded land about Fort Douglas to his soldier-settlers. To twenty-four families who had lost everything, he gave small farms, land for a school and church. To all remaining householders, he sold 100-acre farms along Red River. Finally, he had the whole Settlement surveyed, roads, bridges, mill sites and a huge experimental farm laid out.

While Kildonan hummed with activity, two very different Scots arrived on two very different missions.

By this time Governor Sherbrooke, shocked by the massacre and lawless rivalry between Hudson's Bay and North West, had appointed two commissioners to visit all scenes of violence and to arrest any member of either company found guilty of violence. To Red River came Commissioner W. B. Coltman to investigate the Massacre and to take Lord Selkirk into custody for resisting arrest at Fort William. His duties done, and His Lordship released on bail, the fat and genial commissioner settled back to wait to escort his noble charge to Montreal for trial.

More than a word must be said about the second Scot, tall, grim,

"Colonel" Robert Dickson. As a youth, this pioneer squawman of Upper Red River Valley landed in Canada to fight for Great Britain in the Revolution, remained to win fame as a North West trader and superintendent of the Western Indian Department of Canada.

While operating a chain of posts in Minnesota, Dickson discovered that the Great White Father in Washington had not paid a bead of the promised $2,000 in trade goods for the nine square miles of Upper Mississippi Valley Lieutenant Pike had purchased from the Sioux. This knowledge he used to such effect that during the War of 1812, all but one Sioux tribe sided with the British.

When the War ended, Dickson felt justified to add "and of the Conquered Countries" to his Indian Agent title. Choosing Upper Red River Valley as the conquered country to rule himself, he established his trading-post capital on Lake Traverse, married the daughter of a great Sioux chief, and lived in the grand manner of a viceroy.

Nor for long. In 1816, Congress passed a law forbidding foreign fur traders to operate on American soil. As North West Company vacated its American headquarters at Prairie du Chien (Wisconsin), Astor's revived American Fur Company moved in, to send swarms of aggressive traders into Dickson's Conquered Country. On their heels pressed Joseph Rolette, Joseph Renville, Alexis Bailly and other British traders who, to continue to trade in Red River Valley, turned American citizen. Numerous American traders, all belligerently aware of their new rights, came too.

His every move reported to U.S. authorities, his trade reduced to nothing, Dickson caught like a drowning man on a straw of news. Lord Selkirk had arrived at Red River Settlement! North he sped to lay before His Lordship a most ambitious plan.

Lord Selkirk need only secure Indian title to Red River Valley, said the colonel, then have that title confirmed by the U.S. Congress, to enjoy the same authority over the Valley south of the Boundary he now held over the north. Moreover, he promised, if His Lordship would supply him, via Kildonan, with trade goods, he would fortify his Lake Traverse post to hold and exploit the American Valley to the exclusive advantage of Hudson's Bay Company. His Lordship agreed.

Thus it was on a brilliant July afternoon that the most important event of Lord Selkirk's sojourn in America took place. Impressively

garbed to fulfill his Chippewa title of Silver Chief, he met with
Cree and Assiniboine chiefs who cheerfully agreed in return for
so many lengths of good black tobacco each year to give him the
entire valleys of both the Red and Assiniboine Rivers. Neither they
nor Dickson thought it necessary to mention that the Turtle Mountain region belonged to the Chippewa, most of the American Valley
to the Sioux.

This first pact ever made between a British subject and Rupert's
Land tribes, nevertheless, paved the way a half-century later for
Great Britain to acquire the British Northwest. And on it, Lord Sel-
kirk and his heirs for almost twenty years based claims against the
American Government for compensation or title to Red River Val-
ley south of the Boundary. Equally innocent of all knowledge of
Chippewa and Sioux property rights, their American lawyer was
confident of victory.

But Daniel Webster also was a politician. Fearful of losing votes
if the American public reacted against placing American terrain
in British hands, he endlessly postponed presenting to Congress the
bill that would affirm Lord Selkirk's title. When, in 1836, Webster
became a candidate for President of the United States, the Selkirk
estate, abandoning all hope, sold Assiniboia to Hudson's Bay Company.

In that summer of 1817, however, the only fly in the ointment was
Commissioner Coltman, still placidly waiting to escort Lord Selkirk
to Montreal. Dickson had a solution for that, too. Shortly after the
Indian Treaty was signed, he left Kildonan for Lake Traverse. Two
months later, in the darkness of a September night, Lord Selkirk,
attended only by his personal physician, slipped away—to Fort
Daer. There the colonel waited with a band of Prairie Sioux to conduct them to Prairie du Chien and thence down the Mississippi to
St. Louis.

More far-reaching events took root on that clandestine journey.
While riding up Red River Valley, down Minnesota River Valley,
His Lordship decided that by this route supplies could be sent more
quickly and cheaply to Kildonan than from Canada or England. In
Prairie du Chien, ignoring the American flag now flying over Fort
Crawford, he and Dickson distributed so many gifts among the
Sioux that two entire tribes and part of a third deserted Astor's
posts for Dickson's. In Ohio, they paused to have Lord Selkirk's

pamphlet on John Tanner published. In Missouri and Kentucky, they bought cattle and sheep to be sent overland to Kildonan. In St. Louis, they lingered to be feted as distinguished visiting foreigners.

All this took so much time that Lord Selkirk remained in Washington only long enough to arrange for presentation of his Red River claims to Congress. Then with a last stop in New York to authorize a young lawyer to colonize the American section of Red River Valley, he went on to Montreal to stand trial.

Fortunately he was not required to remain for the trials of all the accused Nor'Westers and Hudson's Bay personnel that cluttered Canadian courts for years. After paying a fine for resisting arrest, he sailed in the fall of 1818 for England.

He boarded his ship with a heavy heart. That four-month trip to Red River Settlement had broken his health. His dubious legal victory was going to cost him his fortune. And after seeing with his own eyes that scratch on the prairies he had renamed Kildonan, he knew now that all the years, money, and effort had been wasted. Red River Settlement was a failure.

Had he known the repercussions his American journey had set off, his heart would have been heavier still. The irate Indian agent at Prairie du Chien had reported to Washington that Lord Selkirk

is plotting with his friend Dickson for our destruction, sharpening the scalping knife, and colonizing a large tract of country at Red River for the purpose of monopolizing the fur and peltry trade.

John Jacob Astor and the Army officers at Fort Crawford charged that Red River Settlement not only menaced American possession of Red and Upper Mississippi River Valleys, but the very integrity of the United States. "The military force of this country," the Army report declared,

is too small to keep Dickson and his emissaries in check. . .a force should be posted here sufficiently strong to enable the commandant to send a company with suitable officers. . .to awe the establishment of Lord Selkirk into a proper respect for our laws.

Roused to action, Congress confirmed the long-delayed agreement with Great Britain on the International Boundary. In 1819 the War Department ordered Major Stephen H. Long to explore and map the country between Upper Mississippi and Rocky Mountains. A year later, the General Lewis Cass Expedition, sent in to follow the Mississippi to its source, came upon the first waters of another great system which it mapped officially as "Red River of Hudson Bay."

And in September, 1820, two companies of U.S. Infantry at last arrived at the mouth of the Minnesota River to pay the Sioux for those nine square miles and to begin construction of Fort St. Anthony. Completed two years later by Colonel Josiah Snelling, the fort was renamed in his honor.

Fort Snelling's jurisdiction embraced both Upper Mississippi and Red River Valleys. And its functions were clearly stated:

> To cause the power of the United States Government to be fully acknowledged by the Indians and settlers of the Northwest, to prevent Lord Selkirk and others from establishing trading posts in United States territory, to better conditions among the Indians, and to develop the resources of the country.

However well founded American suspicions of Lord Selkirk and Colonel Dickson may have been, those applied to Red River Settlement were wasted energy. Three months of providing for Lord Selkirk's large retinue had exhausted all supplies. Nor, during that winter of 1817, were any to be had at Fort Daer. French Canadians, half-breeds and Indians spent the long, cold months far out on the prairies south of Pembina trailing buffalo. To obtain food and shelter, the Scots, trailing, too, but of little value as hunters, had to act as servants to the Indians.

That experience sent them back to Kildonan early in the spring to plow and sow like demons. In vain! Late in July, a great cloud, lead-colored, whirling, droned out of the west to fall and flow in a living river over their ripening barley and corn.

Grasshoppers! The deadly Rocky Mountain locust!

Again the Selkirkers had to winter at Fort Daer. Again in the spring they hurried back to Kildonan to sow what seed had been saved from the crunching jaws.

But now from the ground where millions of eggs had been laid, larvae swarmed in an oily sea, three and four inches deep. The desolation was indescribable, the stench of decomposing bodies more offensive than the living creatures.

Even the long-suffering Scots could take no more. Turning their backs on Kildonan, they joined the hundreds of French Canadians and *Métis* already living permanently at Pembina. They were not good hunters. They had no skill with snowshoes. No flair for the dog teams, trimmed with ribbons, bells and feathers, Indians and *Métis* vied to own. But in all things else they were far on the way to adopting the vagabond life of the buffalo hunters.

The women, however, were uneasy. Watching the effect of that carefree, nomad life on their sons and daughters, they began to plead for one more attempt to establish decent homes at Kildonan. Without seed and supplies? said the men. Impossible! Why impossible? persisted the wives. If Lord Selkirk could go to Prairie du Chien, others could.

Late in December, a snowshoe delegation left Fort Daer. To cross Sioux-guarded Minnesota in dead of winter took three dreadful months. Three more passed while heavy boats were built at Prairie du Chien, loaded with wheat, oats, barley and a few precious chickens, rowed and poled up Minnesota River, down Red River to the doors of Kildonan.

Seed from that body-breaking Odyssey ripened before frost. There and then was founded the tradition of saving a certain per cent of each harvest for next year's sowing. But to inaugurate it required still one more winter at Fort Daer.

The Selkirkers traveled south with apprehension at their side. The August mail had brought word of their benefactor's death. Surely drastic changes were inevitable.

Drastic changes already were in the making. Lord Selkirk's death followed Sir Alexander Mackenzie's by just twenty-seven days. The passing of these irreconcilable enemies opened the way to unite the two fur rivals. On March 26, 1821, Hudson's Bay and North West Companies merged, for a period of twenty-one years, under the name of the English organization.

Although members of the enlarged Hudson's Bay Company still were at violent odds on many scores, on one they saw eye to eye. Farm colonies and the fur trade could not prosper side by side. Red River Settlement could continue to exist—in peace and obscurity. But no further attempts to people Rupert's Land would be tolerated.

5. EXODUS, RED RIVER STYLE

Peace and obscurity do not come by decree. Lord Selkirk's visit had so publicized Red River that as early as the summer of 1818, two unsolicited groups had added themselves to Kildonan. Orkneymen retiring from Company service, with their wives, white or brown, and assorted families, made up the first. Two Catholic priests from Lower Canada, with their respective French Canadian flocks, formed the second.

On the east bank of Red River, opposite the forks, Father Provencher founded the parish of St. Boniface. Father Dumoulin chose Pembina or "Upper Red River Settlement," as it now was more popularly known, for his.

Now, in this summer of 1821, the vanguard of the host of Company employees to be released by the merger, turned with their families to Kildonan. And all unannounced and unprepared for, 170 Swiss emigrants descended by way of Hudson Bay.

The newcomers were no more dismayed than the Selkirkers. With reason. On his return to England, Lord Selkirk, responding to his De Meuron soldier-settlers' pleas for wives and fellow countrymen, had commissioned a Captain de May to recruit colonists in Switzerland. Paid at so much per head, the captain had accepted watch and clock makers, weavers, merchants, pastry cooks, peddlers, old and young, ne'er-do-wells, well-to-do or penniless, lawless or law-abiding. If they had marriageable daughters, they were twice eligible.

They need take little with them, he had said; everything, including homes, would be provided at Red River. By embarking the credulous Swiss at an obscure port, he kept from them the news that Lord Selkirk was dead.

Autumn also brought another unexpected but highly welcome contingent to Kildonan. From Prairie du Chien, Alexis Bailly came down the Valley, driving a herd of cattle before him. The overjoyed colonists did not quibble over his inspired prices.

Bailly's venture proved Red River Valley a two-way street that, by way of the Mississippi, extended to the Gulf of Mexico. From States as far south as Louisiana herds of cattle and sheep began to make that long, overland trek. But its real inauguration was the decision of five Swiss families to return with Bailly to Prairie du Chien.

They got no further than Fort Snelling. Hazards and hardships of those first 700 miles were too much for the untried Swiss. Touched by their pitiful condition, Colonel Snelling permitted them to remain on the Reservation.

Word of this electrified Kildonan. Thirteen more families set out. Their ragged, half-starved arrival again moved the colonel. Other groups were making ready to follow when the horrible fate of the Tullys changed their minds. This Scotch family, starting out alone, had encountered Prairie Sioux.

For good or ill, Kildonians now were pinned to Point Douglas. They couldn't even go to Upper Settlement. In 1822, the administrator for the Selkirk estate, arriving to inspect the colony, had been shocked to find so large a percentage of its population living permanently on American soil. Ordering everyone back to Kildonan, he had Fort Daer and Hudson's Bay's post dismantled. The majority of French Canadians and *Métis* obeyed, but some 350 remained to continue "Pembina" as Red River Valley's first American settlement.

Lord Selkirk dead, Hudson's Bay Company now demoted York Factory to port of entry. Transferring its administration headquarters to Kildonan, it took over the government of Assiniboia. And to discourage further growth of the Settlement, it first induced the settlers to give up farming, then saw to it that every effort in other fields failed. First, and typical of a dozen similar enterprises, was the Buffalo Wool Company which manufactured cloth from the shaggy hair of the bison at ten dollars a yard, sold it briefly in England for a fraction of that cost.

Their hopes of quick and easy wealth dashed again and again, Kildonians conceived a practical idea of their own. After bartering food and clothing for pelts with the Indians, they slipped across the Boundary to sell them profitably to American traders. Hastily, the Company offered special privileges to all who promised not to engage in the fur trade. European colonists agreed. The half-breeds, as natives of the Valley, insisted on their right to trade when and where they pleased. Resulted a trade war so ruthless it approached the pitch of the old North West—X.Y. feud.

Victory was leaning toward the Company when two historic events stepped in to rip the situation wide open. Early in the summer of 1823, the S. S. *Virginia* steamed up the Mississippi from St. Louis to dock at Mendota, an American Fur Company post opposite Fort Snelling. Two months later, the Major Long Expedition rode into Pembina to erect a row of oak posts along the International Boundary.

Arrival of the first steamboat did more than open navigation on the Upper Mississippi. It provided American fur companies with a cheaper, faster route to the world's markets than the English Company enjoyed through Hudson Bay. It made competition against the Americans for pelts of Kildonan's bootleggers or "free traders" no longer possible to the British.

But pheasant feathers would have served as effectively as those oak posts to signal the United States's intention to control its share of Red River Valley. Both north and south of the Boundary, their significance only gradually became visible. It was the Prairie Sioux who regulated traffic on the Valley thoroughfare until that year to be remembered, 1825.

Rains fell all summer, to overflow every lake, river and hollow. With them came that curious biological phenomenon of the early Northwest, mice, almost as numerous and destructive as the grasshoppers. In December one of the worst blizzards the Valley ever recorded killed thirty-three people, froze hundreds of hands and feet. Followed a winter when snowdrifts piled to the eaves of Kildonan homes and Red River's ice thickened to five, almost six feet. Spring came late, to melt accumulated snows of Upper Red River, its lakes and tributaries, then push their combined waters north to hurl a solid wall of ice floes across still frozen Lake Winnipeg.

Week after week on a wooded ridge three days' travel east, the cold and hungry colonists huddled while waves and ice cakes of an horizonless sea bowled over every structure in Kildonan, ripped out every bridge. By mid-June when they returned to the sites of their vanished homes, they were of two minds.

One group had decided to remain, begin again on higher ground. The other had had enough. And why should they endure incessantly harried Assiniboia, they demanded, when Fort Snelling welcomed every Red River family with land, homes, protection?

To Group One, Group Two was composed solely of worthless, lawless characters whose departure would be an unmixed blessing. To speed them on their way, Group One dug into its own small stores to supply food and other necessities for the exodus.

On June 24, almost 450 people started south. . . .

While they suffer that slow and fearsome three-month journey, there is time to talk of the two new and this time permanent settlements Group One built on either side of Red River. Again on the west bank, a mile or two north of obliterated Kildonan, the British members of Group One laid out a two-parish settlement, definitely known as Red River. The southern parish, still called Kildonan, housed the stern-living Scotch Presbyterians. The northern or Anglican parish of St. Andrew's largely was made up of retired and active Company officials. And again on the east bank, opposite the Forks, the French-Canadian Catholics rebuilt their parish of St. Boniface as an independent community.

More oak and cedars came down in the already depleted woods along both banks to provide walls, floors, and furniture for the new homes whose living quarters below were not nearly so important as the lofts above. Here, wheat was stored in one corner, barley in another, oats in a third. And in the fourth were the shelves for the cheeses, dried fruits, candles, buffalo sinews, and innumerable other essentials the women prepared.

With everything from grindstones to durable pottery imported from England, nothing that could possibly be made or devised from wood or stone was ordered. Imports not only were expensive. Goods ordered one year arrived twelve or twenty-four months later.

Furniture, therefore, consisted of packing box beds, topped with straw mattresses, covered with Hudson's Bay blankets or buffalo robes, three-legged stools, open cupboards, tables, and, of course, a spinning wheel. Wooden utensils as cutlery, wooden trays as pots and pans, supplemented the iron pot eternally aboil in the open fireplace.

Simple, yes, but with their whitewashed walls and bright fires, they were snug shelters against winter's seven-to-nine-month seige. Shelter was the word for them. From the moment the ice broke in the spring until the first frosts of fall, men, women, and children were busy out of doors. In the fields. Gathering berries and fuel. Shearing sheep for the winter's spinning, weaving, clothing making, tanning hides for "beef shoes."

Spring and fall, many of the men were off to the lakes to hunt geese and ducks for the family larder. For weeks in August they camped on the prairies behind the settlement to cut wild hay for their horses and cattle.

Meanwhile the women, British and French, held the fort at home. Rearing children, grinding wheat into flour between the two roughly rounded stones of their querns, milking, making butter and cheese, drying fruit, picking and carding wool, defending life and property against fire, wild beasts, and other perils, theirs was the courage of desperation. When a bear started off with a lamb from one farmyard, the housewife, too horrified by the imminent loss of food and wool to be frightened, rushed out to berate the astonished bruin so severely that he slunk away, empty-pawed.

The British female of the species was adamant on another matter. Let the men adopt the long-tailed, high-collared, brass-buttoned and hooded blue wool coats, the buckskin trousers, hip-high buffalo leggings and moccasins the fur traders and *Métis* affected. Let the young men even add the bright red sash with tasseled ends which young French Canadians felt necessary to complete their costumes. Not the women, young or old.

Out of necessity they wore moccasins which they cut to their own pattern and sewed with buffalo sinews. Otherwise, they not only continued to wear tight basques, long, full skirts, and enveloping blue capes, reminiscent of Puritan styles, but topped them with mutches. Plain, high-crowned and starched white caps, tied beneath the chin, were good enough for week days. But for church-going and weddings, these had to be embellished with pleated frills and topped by a black silk kerchief. Whatever husbands or fathers might have forgotten or deemed unnecessary to life in the uncharted wilderness, no Red River woman left behind the heavy Italian iron cylinder required to make those pleats.

Out of necessity also, there was little intercourse between west bank and east. What the constant battle for food, shelter, clothing didn't do to discourage social life, the babel of languages—English, French, Gaelic, Orkney, Indian—did. Fur traders, of course, spoke English, French, and one or more Indian idioms. But the single-tongued British and French-Canadian colonists, *Métis* and tribesmen were forced to evolve a "prairie pidgin" to talk with one another. By 1860, this mixture of French, Orkney, and Cree, known as *Bungay*, was a full-fledged Red River dialect, but in these days following the Great Flood, it was still in its infancy.

Except for weddings, always saved for the cold months, New Year's, and brief pauses in spring to speed the brigades on their way to York Factory with the winter's accumulated pelts, mail and orders, and in the fall to welcome their safe return with the years's supplies and mail, life was real and very, very earnest. So was death. No matter whether a colonist died in his own bed or forty miles away, his casket was carried on the shoulders of slowly pacing men to its grave in Red River cemeteries.

Saturday night all work stopped that everyone might return home for a Sunday of prolonged devotions. Afoot or by sledge, Anglicans and Scotch Presbyterians set out for St. Andrew's Church, the Bonificians for their Cathedral.

The churchless, pastorless Calvinist Scots derived small comfort from their worship. In vain, to make them feel at home in St. Andrew's, the Anglican minister simplified the altar until it was little more than a platform, eliminated distasteful "worldly" hymns and other ritual. The obdurate Scots stood up to pray, sat down to sing and, in church and out, prayed and petitioned ceaselessly for a pastor and kirk of their own.

Alas, by the time their supplications were answered in 1851, the younger generation had acquired a taste for hymn singing and organ music. And though the Reverend Mr. Black who arrived to lead them was stern enough in all conscience, not a word of Gaelic could he speak!

PART V

The Nor'men March South

1. "PIG'S EYE, CONVERTED THOU SHALT BE"

Life at Fort Snelling, now in its fifth year, a well-established military post, couldn't have been more different. The Colonel and his officers had brought their families to the Reservation. Among the women were several of excellent social background who furnished their homes richly and with taste. Life in the Minnesota wilderness was gay with hunts, balls, entertainment of distinguished travelers arriving by steamboat from St. Louis. Especially gay when an occasional character like Giacomo Beltrami came along.

In Pittsburgh, Major Lawrence Taliaferro, Indian agent at Fort Snelling, had met this bizarre lawyer, linguist, army officer and, currently, political exile from Italy. Impressed with the Italian's commanding figure, culture and buoyant spirits, the Major brought him west by way of the Mississippi. While ascending the Great River, Beltrami became inspired to follow it to its source.

Arrived at Fort Snelling on the eve of the departure of the Major Long Expedition to Pembina, he obtained permission to go along. Although annoyed by the Major's way of doing things, he maintained a comparatively gentlemanly reticence until the expedition reached Pembina. There Major Long countermanded an order he had given. Insulted, he sold the horse and equipment Taliaferro had loaned him and, with a *Métis* guide and two Chippewa boatmen, paddled off in a small canoe to add his name to that glorious roster of Italian explorers headed by Marco Polo.

By streams and portages, he ascended eastern Red River Valley to Red Lake River. In the mistaken belief that this tributary was Red River of the North, Beltrami renamed it Bloody River. He had not gone far up its wriggling course when his escort abandoned him and canoe. Both at once capsized. Thereafter, his dashing uniform in dripping rags, a bit of bark for a hat, he waded slowly upstream, towing the canoe in which his soaked gun, sword, and provisions reposed under an open umbrella.

Ultimately he reached Red Lake. Though this really notable body of water had been occupied for half a century by fur traders, mapped by David Thompson and again by Lieutenant Pike (whose map he was using!), the hallucinated Italian declared himself its discoverer. Then, naming rivers and lakes as he went, he pushed on to a small rise which he declared to be the highest point of land in North America outside the inaccessible, snow-capped peaks of the Arctic.

From its pinnacle he beheld the waters of the entire continent dividing to flow to the four horizons. And the little pond (by Minnesota standards) at the base of the rise, he recognized as the northernmost source of the Mississippi and the southernmost source of Red River of the North. So he named it Lake Julia.[1]

In triumph he returned to Fort Snelling. Hailed as risen from the dead, he was forgiven all and sent on his way to New Orleans. There he wrote the book on his *Pilgrimages* that set a precedent for misinformation about Red River Valley faithfully followed to this day.

Ex-Red Riverites living on the Reservation saw little of such picturesque guests. They were too busy selling all they could produce to officers and men. Already a few were well on the road to prosperity. None of them took seriously the intimations made from time to time that they, too, were guests of Fort Snelling.

But now it is late fall of 1826 and the 443 survivors of the exodus from the Great Flood are staggering in. They were in truly desperate straits. Only faith that at the reservation they would receive food, care, land, and farming equipment had kept many of them going.

The snug, self-sufficient military post was shocked and surprised at their arrival. Even more so when it learned that these hundreds of gaunt Scotch, Irish, Swiss and French Canadians looked on the fort as their destination.

Since Colonel Snelling had neither authority nor desire to colonize the reservation, most of the refugees, when able to travel, went on down the Mississippi to established river ports from Galena to St. Louis. Some crossed the river to become earliest residents of the trading post of Mendota. Others, learning that plans were afoot to acquire and open to white settlement surrounding Sioux and Chippewa territory, remained at the Fort to be on hand when the treaties

---

[1] Believed to be today's Turtle Lake, Minnesota.

were ratified. Red Riverites thus became founders of St. Paul, Minneapolis, Stillwater, and other of the oldest towns in Minnesota.

Each summer from then until 1851, large or small groups of Red River emigrants swelled this peaceful Nor'man invasion of the United States. Altogether it is estimated that Red River Settlement contributed some thousand citizens to Minnesota, Wisconsin, Illinois, Indiana, Missouri, and Iowa.

Wherever they settled, they carried their quern stones to grind wheat into flour (later, to serve as doorsteps), introduced scones, fried pies, wild grapes to honey-making, Gaelic words to the forming American language. As they could, they first built churches, then schools, or sent their children to near-by or Eastern colleges. By crossing the International Boundary, these Sutherlanders, Massies, Gervais, Sinclairs, Perrys, Livingstones, Roses, Mathiesons, Campbells, Rondons, MacIntyres, and all the rest became law-abiding, industrious pioneers of the American Midwest.

In so remote a wilderness, where the Commander of Fort Snelling ruled as king, his officers as heirs apparent, their whims as wells as their wishes were expected to be accepted as law. Inevitably, as the emigrés remaining on the reservation enlarged their families, homes, fields, herds, they progressed in the eyes of the nobility from refugees to squatters to intruders.

By 1837, when the Sioux and Chippewa Treaties were signed, tension between hosts and guests had reached such a pitch that the Red Riverites ignored Fort Snelling to appeal directly to President Van Buren. The officers countered with a report that the 157 interlopers, with more than 200 cattle, had neither legal right nor claim to overrun Government property.

While they argued, Mendota's bootleggers planted themselves along the newly released east bank of the Mississippi to ply their trade openly. Among them was a most unsavory old rascal with one eye always alert to the main chance. The other, marble-hued, crooked, with a sinister white ring round the pupil, was blind.

A former French-Canadian *"voyageur,"* kicked out of Sault Ste Marie for vicious practices, Charles Parrant had been forbidden to enter U. S. Indian Territory on any pretext whatever. Nevertheless, he had slipped into Mendota, disguised as a fur trader, to select a choice location in advance of the treaty signing.

He found it in a lovely little gorge north of Fort Snelling. The site offered easy access to Indians, traders, and soldiers, yet was out of range of Indian agent and fort authority. Its Fountain Cave was the perfect hiding place for his liquor stores. The creek that ran out of it into the Mississippi could dilute them endlessly. Just east of the cave he staked his claim and threw up a hovel as home and saloon.

Shortly a new commander arrived at Fort Snelling. Predetermined to tolerate no civilian nonsense, Major Joseph Plympton ordered the onetime Kildonians to move. A few families did cross the Mississippi to take up claims on the east bank. Abraham Perry, Benjamin and Pierre Gervais and Joseph Rondo moved into Parrant's gorge. And to help them build their new homes, Edmund Brisset, a young carpenter, took up his abode under the old bootlegger's roof.

One day while writing a letter, young Brisset was at a loss for a return address. Looking about, he spied his host's widely known blind and porcine eye. In due time he received a reply addressed to him at Pig's Eye, Minnesota. Parrant was furious, but the little settlement in the gorge had a name.

Before long it had no bootlegger. Losing his claim for debt, Parrant moved two miles north to a palisaded bluff where two ex-soldiers held adjoining claims, put down stakes again. With him went the name, Pig's Eye.

Meanwhile, Major Plympton had extended the reservation's boundaries to twenty square miles and ordered the Red Riverites to move beyond them. Again Abraham Perry, accompanied by his faithful friends, followed Parrant. The rest sat tight on claims that now stretched for five miles along the Mississippi's east bank.

Fort Snelling waited till spring. Then on that east bank were repeated the scenes that had brought the Sutherlanders from Kildonan parish, Scotland, to Red River. Forced at gun point from their homes, the ex-Red Riverites watched their cabins unroofed and burned. In a body then, they moved to Pig's Eye on the bluff to found a new colony about the nucleus of cabins built by Abraham Perry and his friends.

For the next few years, Pig's Eye might better have been called Arcadia. Its romantic setting one hundred feet above the Mississippi was enclosed by low hills dotted with groves of scrub oak that looked like aging orchards. With all but three or four of its thirty families from Red River, its language was French, its religion Catholic. And as founders of the settlement, they set its tone of quiet, almost dreamy industry and simplicity.

In winter the men trapped for the American Fur Company, which hastened to transfer its headquarters from Mendota to Pig's Eye. In summer, they cultivated small farms. Gradually, about the trading post, five little stores found place. And along wriggling paths, the increasing itinerant population of American trappers, boatmen, mechanics, and laborers erected huts and tents.

During that same summer of 1840, however, Father Lucien Galtier, sent to Mendota to establish a Catholic Church, found few parishioners to serve. But at Pig's Eye, devout French Canadians were so eager to have his ministry that they donated land for a church, garden, and cemetery.

While dedicating to St. Paul the little log church, so crude it reminded him of the stable in Bethlehem, Father Galtier asked that the new settlement also take that name.

Even more briefly an apocryphal couplet tells of the rechristening of this first city in Minnesota, founded by Nor'men from Red River Valley:

> Pig's Eye, converted thou shalt be, like Saul;
> Arise and be, henceforth, St. Paul.

2. RED RIVER'S MILLION-DOLLAR TRADE

One chill October dawn, just thirty-seven years before St. Paul received its permanent name, a tremendous "walla walla" opened every eye in North West's trading post at Pembina. Tumbling out with all the rest, Chief Trader Alexander Henry mounted to a watchtower to record for posterity the frenzied preparations of Monsieur Langlois, prominent half-breed, to visit Pembina Mountain to barter trinkets for pelts with the Indians.

Mr. Henry needn't have hurried. Ten o'clock passed before the procession finally straggled off across the prairies. At its head marched Anthony Payet, guide and second-in-command, leading two Indian ponies harnessed to a small, open box mounted on two wooden wheels distended by four straight spokes. Behind this primitive conveyance, filled with his personal possessions, walked his

Chippewa wife, very merry. On her back a year-old child slept placidly.

Next came Charles Bottineau. He also led two ponies and a cart piled with trade goods, his own baggage, and two button-eyed children. Behind walked his squaw, scolding furiously as she tossed her shoulders up and down to quiet the squalling infant on her back. Followed Anthony LePoint with a third cart drawn by two ponies. This not only held trade goods and his baggage but that of three French Canadians who walked more or less behind. Having imbibed various farewell drams and lighted their pipes, they filled the air with clouds of smoke as they cavorted along.

There was more, a half-mile more. But only those three little carts at the head of the procession count. Their successful completion of that sixty-mile round trip revolutionized buffalo hunt, fur trade, and life in both the American and British Northwest. In so doing, they laid the foundation on which St. Paul rose to eminence as fur trade and political capital, distribution center, metropolis.

Never before or since has their like been seen. Perhaps Red River Cart came into use during the last days of the French regime in Red River Valley. But it was Alexander Henry's *Journal* of 1801 that tossed it history's first bow:

· Men now go for buffalo meat with small, low carts, the wheels of which are of one solid piece sawed from the ends of trees whose diameter is three feet. These carriages are more convenient and advantagous than horses and the country being so smooth and level, we can use them to go in all directions.

From the original light box set on solid wheels, Red River Cart evolved into a freighter, capable of carrying eight hundred pounds, mounted on spoked wheels six or seven feet in diameter. The higher the wheels, the better for crossing marshes and muddy streams.

Made entirely of wood, the only tools necessary to construct one were an ax and an auger. With a strip of green buffalo hide, repairs could be made on any part at any time. The crude harness, first for Indian ponies, then for oxen, also was shaped from this enduring material.

Whatever the model, Red River Cart's outstanding features were endurance and the shrill, incessant squeal of each wheel. The first impelled a bemused observer to write:

It would make a white man wild to see these two-wheeled things go through the woods, smashing brush, tumbling over logs and fallen trees, plunging down banks, sometimes with ox or halfbreed under the cart, the next moment coming straight up on the other side.

The second ended church services, assemblies, even conversations, hours before a train of several hundred Carts came into view.

Now with these simple wooden vehicles, a thousand buffalo could be slaughtered in one afternoon. Now there no longer was need to wait for open water to transport trade goods, supplies, pelt-packs. Now each summer from Red River Settlement and Pembina hundreds of Carts left for all parts of the Northwest. Before returning, some would cover more than three thousand miles.

After 1844, when the first little Cart Train blazed the first Red River Trail to St. Paul, the Valley's soil was cut and rutted from east to west. For Cart Train routes were not trails but ways. In general, from Pembina to St. Paul, there were three—the West Plains Trail, East Plains Trail, and Woods Trail. (See Map.) From Pembina to Red River Settlement, the Trains, depending on the wetness of the season, followed the River or spread all over the prairies.

Creeping along at fifteen to twenty miles a day, a Cart Train required six weeks to two months to reach St. Paul. As the Carts increased in capacity, the Trains lengthened. By 1854, Red River Settlement alone had fifteen hundred Carts traveling to St. Paul. Four years later, Settlement and Pembina were sending six thousand Carts south annually.

Because the outdoor, adventurous, not to say dangerous life appealed to them, French-Canadians and *Métis* took to carting like ducks to water. So did their families. An eight hundred Cart Train might include thirteen hundred men, women, and children.

Constant threat of Prairie Sioux called for strict discipline and organization. Each Train had its governor. Carts were divided into parishes, each under its captain. Every three carts had a driver.

Starting at dawn, Trains traveled until midafternoon, when the governor hoisted a flag to signal time and place to camp. In a rough circle, the Carts lined up, wheel to wheel, to form a barrier impassable to man or beast. Inside the enclosure, a hundred or more teepees for family men whisked up. Other drivers draped buffalo hides over their carts to lodge comfortably beneath. Until dark, animals grazed

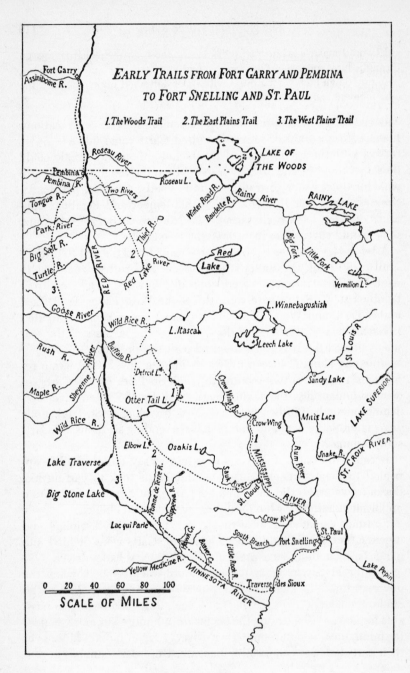

RED RIVER TRAILS

freely, then were herded inside, the entrance sealed. Throughout the night, thirty to forty men stood guard.

With plenty of pemmican and dried beef supplied, with game everywhere, these Cart *"voyageurs"* were the happiest people on earth. On the Trail, round campfires at night, they sang incessantly. For hours they danced or engaged in trials of strength. And for their further peace of mind, priests always accompanied the Trains to conduct brief services morning and night, mass on sundays.

At any time French-Canadian and *Métis* dress was gay, but to impress the Paulistas, they outdid themselves. Over their long, bright blue wool coats, with their hoods and rows of dazzling brass buttons, they wore sashes of brilliant red or varied colors and, crisscrossed on breast and back, a band embroidered with beads and porcupine quills. On their thick, shining black hair perched vivid beaded caps. And in addition to the gun and knife each man carried, fancy pouches to hold powder and shot, tobacco and kinnikinnick, firesteel and flints, dangled from sash and band.

Even the carters' efforts paled before the elegance of the merchant princes who owned or traveled with the Trains. Usually these nabobs rode finely trained buffalo runners. And they lived high. One entire Cart was necessary to transport the padlocked chest whose double deck of pigeonholes held tea, sugar, spices, cheeses, jams, assorted brandies, wines, and other delicacies essential to their comfort.

Well might they revel in style and luxury. Cart, ox, and harness cost but $80; a carter received about $20 a month. Red River Settlement Trains charged up to $105 for 800 pounds of freight; Pembina Trains, with a shorter haul, up to $90.

The first six-Cart Train in 1844 carried only $1,400 in pelts to St. Paul, but left some $12,000 for merchandise in its tills. Within twenty years, Trains annually hauled more than $250,000 in raw pelts, to say nothing of pemmican, buffalo robes, foodstuffs and other goods. Profits on these combined with the Red Riverites' lavish buying each year represented more than $1,000,000 to St. Paul's traders and merchants.

This was not all. Among the low buildings crowding onetime Pig's Eye's narrow, twisting paths, every other shop was a furrier's. Their windows displayed Red River beaver, otter, marten and mink. But, taking a leaf from London's book, where beaver and muskrat were transformed into "sable, mink, and other valuable furs and sold at fabulous prices," St. Paul's furriers concocted fine mink out of the mangiest skins, sable and ermine out of anything. Not one muff in a hundred was from the animal purported.

Still more. Fame of the picturesque Cart Trains' camp in West St. Paul drew tourists up the Mississippi to overflow hastily erected hotels and boarding houses and crowd the fur shops with purchasers. No wonder that arrival of the Cart Trains each summer became the high point of the hustling port's year.

For thirty years, Red River Carts pumped life and wealth into St. Paul. And for a decade longer, they continued to serve buffalo hunters and fur traders, particularly in the British Northwest. Then, one by one, as fuel for camp and home fires, they disappeared.

What brought this unique vehicle out of obscurity, returned it to oblivion? The buffalo, whose physical, social, political and economic impact on Red River Valley tops that of any other animal, including man.

Buffalo bones and flesh, deposited by millions of tons over centuries of time, had enriched the very soil. The myriad needs the great beasts satisfied not only transformed tribes of Forest Sioux into Prairie Sioux whose unparalleled ferocity was whetted in defense of the prairies the thundering herds made peculiarly their own. On Valley-born descendants of white fathers and Indian mothers, they repeated this mystic mating of man and land. *Métis* blood, too, ran hot and high at any threat to their right to the prairies the buffalo grazed.

Yet French and early English regimes ignored the brown herds. Not until the 1820's when supplies of beaver and other small fur-bearing animals began to decline and, in Europe, fur fashions to change, did attention swing to the buffalo.

Within ten years, more than 184,000 buffalo robes in one season sailed down the Mississippi to St. Louis. American dinner tables clamored for buffalo tongues and steaks. Many uses developed for buffalo tallow. But the primary demand was for pemmican.

Orders came in from all over the British and American fur country, from the East Coast, from Germany which found it the perfect food for its armies, from other countries in Northern Europe. As exporters joined the fur traders in all-out competition, pemmican manufacture at Pembina entered the realm of big business.

Opening of this world market galvanized Red River Indians and half-breeds on both sides of the Boundary. Tribesmen always had considered trapping small animals a nuisance and degradation. But long, exhilarating trips on horseback with large bands of fellow hunters, thrills and dangers of the hunt, glory and feasting afterward, were the breath of life to them.

And now they could indulge themselves the year round. Spring hunts began about June 1, ended in August, just in time for the fall hunts which continued until November. If buffalo lingered through the Valley winter, Indians and *Métis* did, too.

A change in the buffalo's own habits created only a momentary problem. Their annual migrations to the Saskatchewan now bypassed the forks of the Red and Assiniboine Rivers. Hunts, therefore, had to be staged south of the Boundary or on the high plains to the west. Red River Settlement hunters solved the difficulty by ignoring the Boundary.

And for a time there was plenty for all. Buffalo covered the prairies to every point of the compass as far as the eye could see. They came in such numbers that Indians, ear to the ground, could hear their trampling more than twenty miles away. Between 1821 and 1840, Red River Settlement hunters alone killed over 650,000.

But even ten buffalo robes, packed in a press, made so large and heavy a bundle that two men were required to handle it. No existing means of transportation was adequate. Red River Cart was the answer.

By 1820, the Settlement was sending 540 Carts to Pembina for the spring hunt; within a few years, 1,200. Hudson's Bay traders operated south of the Boundary as a matter of course. By 1856, as one British pen phrased it, "Pembina had become well established as the Canadian base."

Demand for buffalo robes and products so outmoded the fur trade that John Jacob Astor disposed of his American Fur Company. No matter. Red River prairies now became the equivalent of interior Africa today, a big game hunters' mecca which drew sportsmen from all the world.

And a buffalo hunt was something to experience. Although held from Lake Traverse to the Boundary, those of Pembina ranked first. From Red River Settlement and Pembina itself several hundred to a thousand or more men, women and children, with more than a thousand Carts, streamed out across the prairies.

Each hunter rode an ordinary Indian pony but led two or three blooded and highly trained buffalo runners, whose saddles of elaborately beaded scarlet or blue cloth were hung with fancy lariats and whips. The air rang with songs and squeals of Cart wheels. In a great circular enclosure, they made camp.

At the first assembly point, hunters elected a chief or president of the hunt and ten captains. The captains, each with ten responsible henchmen, policed the expedition. For each day a guide was named to supervise the Cart Train. His badge of authority was the flag with which he signaled orders.

At this time, too, laws of the hunt were proclaimed. The moment any article, no matter how trivial, was declared missing, no one could move till it was found. Stealing was not tolerated, nor hunting on Sunday. After final camp was made, no gun could be fired, no one leave without permission.

For a first violation, an offender's saddle and bridle were torn to shreds; for a second, the coat from his back. Few risked the penalty for the third—public flogging.

Before the Train reached its final camp, scouts already were far ahead spotting the herds. Excitement now burned at such a pitch that long before the following dawn, every hunter, mounted on his best runner, was ready.

That all might have an equal chance, officials rode ahead on the slowest horses. Until word was given, no one could pass them. As soon as the herd was sighted, a halt was called for final instructions.

Again the officials rode ahead. Behind them now, hundreds of hunters moved abreast in a great crescent that the "surround" might be as complete as possible. As suspense mounted, all insensibly increased their pace to a full gallop. Excited as their riders, the horses raced along, heads erect, eyes on the upraised arm of the president. Not until he was within four or five hundred yards of the quarry would that arm drop.

"*Now!*"

Already alarmed, the buffalo were pawing the ground, curving their brief tails, and gathering in a milling mass. Suddenly—they were off! Cows first, bulls in a compact, protecting phalanx at their heels.

Within moments, the fastest runners had borne their riders into the heart of the fleeing herd. Dust and smoke blackened air aroar with the thunder of pounding hoofs, clashing horns, bellowing, gunfire.

Soon cows began to fall out, blood pouring from mouths and wounds. Occasionally, a wounded bull pivoted to charge. The rider's expert mount merely swerved and turned to give him another chance for a shot. By the time pursued and pursuers vanished over the horizon and pandemonium dimmed to silence, hundreds to thousands of brown bodies lay still beneath settling dust clouds.

Even the best buffalo runners sometimes stumbled into badger holes. Hunters riding at full speed spit bullets into clumsy muzzle loaders, fired without lifting gun to shoulder. Bullets crisscrossed in all directions. Yet though the sport was alive with perils, fatalities were few.

The hour or two pursuit was but a prelude to the day's real hunt. As soon as the president signaled its end, each hunter had to work backward to identify, strip the robes, and hack off the meat of his own kill before darkness, wolves and crows rendered his labor futile. Eye, judgment and memory combined to tell him where each beast had fallen. Every man knows his own handwriting, they said.

As they worked, Carts crawled back and forth between field and camp. There women slashed the meat into long strips, pressed it by hand to quarter-inch thickness, hung it to dry on improvised wooden frames. Meat from the tenderloin, hump and undershoulders was tied into sixty-pound bundles for winter use. The rest was flayed to powder to be used in pemmican. Skins unfit for robes were scraped to be made into clothing. Bones were broken and boiled for their marrow. Tongues were sold on the spot to traders who first salted, then painted them with molasses to a dark, smoky color.

Even so, the waste was enormous. And each hunt included not only ten or twelve pursuits when every hunter took part, but any number of small forays.

Premium for the hunt that surpassed all others in importance, size, and waste goes to Red River Settlement's spring drive of 1840. For nineteen days more than 4,000 people, with 1,200 Carts and 500 dogs, ascended West Plains Trail to make final camp on the Sheyenne River. Three weeks later they returned home with 1,089,000 pounds of beef alone. Though this represented over 200 pounds for every man, woman, and child in the Train, it was but a fraction of the food left on the field.

The result of such prolonged profligacy was inevitable. While each year Red River Cart Trains bearing buffalo robes and products to St. Paul lengthened, the herds grew smaller. After 1870, they came no more to Red River Valley.

Together, however, buffalo and Carts had made Red River Trade a phrase that set fingers all over Canada and the United States to itching and minds to working.

3. RED RIVER BUILDS AND REBUILDS ST. PAUL

St. Paul storekeepers did not stop to question the miracle that brought the first six-Cart Train over 700 miles of swollen rivers and unprotected prairies from Pembina in 1844. To extract the last coin from the Red Riverites, they stripped their shelves, even their homes.

And when the Train departed, with promises to return in 1845 with more pelts and bigger orders for merchandise, they compiled such lists to restock that the Mississippi port towns receiving them were incredulous.

They had thought this most northern outpost in the wilderness of the Upper Mississippi fit only for savages and fur traders. But these orders called for every kind of home furnishing, including wallpaper, carpets, window glass, door knobs and locks, watches and jewelry, stoves and andirons, books and falderals.

To exploit this heaven-sent market, Galena, Illinois, immediately established regular steamboat service with St. Paul. As the news spread, businessmen with sharp eyes, settlers, and tourists boarded the boats to see for themselves. And the U.S. Land Office in St. Louis sent surveyors to plot the town site of St. Paul and the adjoining region around St. Anthony Falls.

These last arrivals woke the Red Riverites to the fact that they again were squatters. But this time they would not be caught napping! In Henry Hastings Sibley, former American Fur Company partner, now turned banker, they found their friend in need.

When St. Paul's town site was auctioned off, Mr. Sibley bought, one by one, every plot in the ninety acres that today form the commerical heart of Minnesota's capital. No one opened his mouth to outbid him. Though the Red Riverites said not a word, they were there. In his hands each grim-visaged founder of St. Paul held a formidable club.

This crisis ended, another loomed. In 1848, Wisconsin became a State. When it announced its boundaries, the entire region between Upper Mississippi and Missouri Rivers overnight was deprived of Government protection.

By this time, Red Riverites and American traders had founded two bustling lumber camps. In St. Anthony, beside the Falls; in Stillwater, a little to the north; and in St. Paul, white men in the abandoned area largely were concentrated. At once they held a joint meeting to petition Congress to grant the region Territorial status. By agreeing that when Minnesota Territory became a State, St. Anthony should have the university, Stillwater the penitentiary, St. Paul bagged the capital.

Such details were merely of academic interest to the Red Riverites. At peace at last on lands they had made forever safe, they laid out the future capital after the fashion of an old, provincial French village. Not a tree was left standing for shade. No thought was given to preserving the beautiful waterfront. Their wriggling paths became wriggling streets, broken by public squares that were merely "skewdangular lots as large as a stingy piece of gingerbread." On these lanes their eighteen chimneys haphazardly faced.

Six months later, on this crazy pattern, an American town of 142 buildings, complete with State House, hotels, boarding houses, two printing presses (one, a newspaper, the *Minnesota Pioneer*), saloons, gambling houses, and many more new homes were superimposed. And the air continued to ring as saws and hammers labored to transform the bluff into the "St. Louis of the North."

The metamorphosis had been wrought one early April night when in a lull of the furiously crashing, flashing spring thunderstorm, the village was startled to hear the first steamboat of the season whistle imperatively. Heedless of wind and rain, every man raced for the levee. There from the bridge of the S. S. *Argo*, Captain Russell Blakeley roared and reroared the great news. Congress had created Minnesota Territory! St. Paul was to be its *temporary* capital.

From then until late fall, steamboat after steamboat chuffed up the Mississippi, all laden with new settlers. Before 1849 ended, St. Paul had 1,000 citizens. And all about new towns were rising.

Most important arrival was the Territorial govenor, Alexander Ramsey, with his wife, in May. Though they stepped ashore on a quiet Sunday morning, they found their capital seething. With preparations for the arrival of the Red River Cart Trains. With high talk against Red River Settlement and Hudson's Bay hunters and traders who, continuing to ignore the Boundary, annually were robbing St. Paul of more than a quarter-million dollars in buffalo robes and prod-

MINNESOTA TERRITORY, 1849-51

ucts. "It's high time," everyone assured the governor, "that we had a fort at Pembina."

On June 1, 1849, Minnesota Territory officially was proclaimed. Six days later, Captain John Pope, a topographical engineer, left Fort Snelling for Pembina. With him went Major Samuel Woods and forty soldiers.

At Pembina, Pope selected two possible sites for a fort. One site he specifically did NOT recommend was the junction of the Red and

Bois des Sioux Rivers, 200 miles south of the Boundary. This, however, was the point the Army chose, then did nothing more for ten years.

The choice was eminently unsatisfactory to St. Paul. Red River Trade already had made the Territorial capital a booming commercial center. Now with Captain Pope reporting that Red River Valley,

from its vast extent, perfect uniformity of surface, richness of soil, and unlimited supply of wood and water is among the finest wheat countries in the world,

Paulistas saw no limit to their economic future—*if the Valley could be protected against British exploitation.*

When the Army remained adamant, Governor Ramsey, in the fall of 1851, set out for Pembina. To his amazement he found a community of 1,134 people, largely *Métis,* cultivating over 2,000 acres, with more grain stored in their barns than all Minnesota raised, and with hundreds of horses and cattle grazing the prairies.

This region need only be peopled by American farmers for St. Paul to have an inexhaustible market! Promptly, he negotiated a treaty with the Chippewa for thirty miles of land on both sides of Red River south of the Boundary.

Next he visited Red River Settlement, now a clean, well-organized community of more than 5,000 residents, not counting Indians. On his return to St. Paul, he described it in almost lyric terms:

Imagine a river flowing through flat, alluvial plain, and the west side of it continuously lined for over thirty miles with cultivated farms, each presenting a great appearance of thrift. Each has only a narrow frontage on Red River but extends inland for one or two miles. Each. . .has dwellings and farm buildings spread along the waterfront, with lawns sloping to the water's edge and shrubbery and vines literally trained around them and trees intermingled.

Fashionably dressed men and women driving about in carriages, quiet, deferential farmers and their families, turning windmills, almost twenty of them, to which Red River Carts were rolling from all directions with wheat to be ground into flour, whitewashed schools and parsonages, churches and, in St. Boniface, the cathedral, to say nothing of two huge and handsome stone forts, all caused the governor to be "lost in wonder at the phenomenon this settlement exhibits."

His own capital's stark, treeless streets, lined with low, unkempt buildings, swarmed with Indians and, due to lack of soap, unshaven white men. Even to State House affairs these men came in heavy boots and moccasins. And their wives shoved and grabbed about buffet tables to make up bundles of food for home consumption.

Governor Ramsey was not too overwhelmed by Red River Settlement's refinement to fail to observe that for lack of a market, it was "smothering in its own fat." For that, too, of course, he had an infallible remedy. St. Paul!

Congress' fourteen-year delay in ratifying his Chippewa Treaty defeated his plan to people Pembina, but his journey was by no means fruitless. As a result of his recommendations, Congress authorized the famous Sioux Treaty of 1851 which released to American settlement all lands between the Upper Mississippi and Red Rivers.

Shortly, steamers jammed with settlers and land speculators were ascending the Mississippi. Within a few years, 30,000 newcomers were arriving each season.

As one and all succumbed to speculation fever, the capital boomed. Mechanics, bankers, traders, ministers, farm boys made fortunes. Money lenders, advancing funds at thirty-six to sixty per cent annual interest, did too. What of it? was the cry. Millions in it!

Soon food and every other necessity had to be imported. Prices went insane. Crime and disorder were rampant. Gambling houses, race courses, taverns and every other vice and device, added to new hotels, business structures, and homes made St. Paul the fastest-growing, fastest-living town in the Northwest. What of it? Millions in it!

In the course of American migration westward, "town jobbing" had become the new big business. Crews of town jobbers, scouring the region between Mississippi and Red Rivers for desirable town sites, discovered eastern Red River Valley. One day its fertile soil must make it the Breadbasket of the World. Its tortuous River would be the outlet for the annual golden harvest of wheat. More: Red River would become the main street of trade and travel between the United States and Canada.

Rumors that Congress was to authorize a railroad from St. Paul to the junction of Red and Bois des Sioux, with a branch line down the eastern Valley to Pembina, furnished the crowning proof. "Millions in it!" now meant Red River Valley.

Even before the Sioux Treaty was signed, settlers and town jobbers were planting the eastern Valley to town sites, each destined to be the seat of a great metropolis. Lapham. Cold Springs. Holmes City. Winthrop. Mansfield. Reno. Bellevue. And many more. Some were real enough. But others, merely paper towns, extravagantly described in circulars distributed in the East, made—and lost—paper fortunes overnight.

After the signing, landseekers, refusing to accept Red River as the boundary, crossed to the west bank. Unable to cope with them, Indian Agent McLean warned Washington that "all the Valley, treaty or no treaty, will be occupied unless opposed by a stronger force than is here now."

Others believed the junction of Red and Sheyenne Rivers would be the future head of steamboat navigation and the point where the much talked of Northern Pacific Railroad would cross on its way west. Within eight miles, five town sites were laid out on the east bank.

But a few of the most optimistic Paulistas saw millions in the junction of Red and Bois des Sioux. Lest others think so, too, they secretly left St. Paul on New Year's Eve, 1857. An almost unbroken series of blizzards beset them and their slow-paced oxen during the month required to make the journey. Before howling winds lessened to permit use of surveying chains, they had endured months more of storms, forty-below-zero temperatures, snowdrift beds, and soup made from corncobs stolen from their own oxen. What of it? Millions in it!

After platting Breckenridge on the east bank of the junction and Graham's Point a few miles to the north, they moved downriver to buy up the five town sites laid out opposite the mouth of the Sheyenne. Then, well satisfied, they returned to St. Paul to wait for the millions to roll in.

They found their fellow citizens reeling with shock. In far-off New York City, on August 24, the Ohio Life Insurance Company had closed its doors. Depression gripped the entire country.

Its body blow was reserved for St. Paul. Hardly one out of five commercial houses survived. Real estate could not be sold at any price. Every town site in Red River Valley was wiped out. Loans had to be paid and there was no money. Fifty per cent of Minnesota's population departed. And when navigation opened in the spring, not one new settler came.

On May 14, 1858, Minnesota became a State. Its capital did not celebrate. With script down to forty cents on the dollar, crops a failure, trade and immigration paralyzed, Paulistas lay prostrate, under a blanket of gloom.

They need not have despaired. Their deliverer even then was en route.

4. THE EMPEROR OF THE NORTH

Born in 1787 on the wild and isolated west coast of Scotland, George Simpson was at twenty-three so tenacious, adventurous, realistic and superlatively canny that an uncle gave him a clerkship in the London firm of which he was a member—Graham, Simpson and Wedderburn.

The third member was *the* Andrew Wedderburn-Colville who, as Lady Selkirk's brother, so strongly had supported His Lordship in the fight for control of Hudson's Bay Company. As a reward, he was made a member of its new board of governors and, in due time, its chairman.

During the next ten years, Colville and his fellow governors were equally impressed with young Simpson. When the Hudson's Bay-North West controversy reached Canadian courts, they sent him over to take command, if necessary, as acting overseas governor.

The need did not arise, but in Montreal Simpson saw that British America offered quicker chances for advancement than the home office. Never shy, he asked for and received the appointment as chief trader in Athabasca.

The complete novice, he placed himself in the hands of a fellow trader to obtain boatmen, trade goods, and supplies. His sly benefactor took to himself the lion's share of everything, including territory. In the richest preserve on the continent, Simpson practically was stranded. That experience gave him an immediate and enlightened view of the fur trade.

When the rival fur companies merged the following spring, he was named governor of all Company territory west of James Bay. Four years later, largely thanks to his diplomacy and acumen, the Company was paying a ten per cent dividend, plus bonus. His authority, thereupon, gradually was extended until, in 1839, he was named overseas governor of Hudson's Bay Company.

But George Simpson was mortal, and mortals err. His first and greatest blunder was Red River Settlement.

Arriving there in 1822, on his initial round of his territory, he was shocked to find the colony at the end of its first decade a hodgepodge of bloods, nationalities, and religions, strung along Red River from Pembina seventy miles to the south to Netley Creek forty miles north. He was further annoyed to find the colonists haggardly emerging from a winter of semistarvation in a land of plenty.

Nevertheless, he undertook to turn this liability into a lucrative investment for the Company. No European resident, he ruled, could trade with any Indian or *Métis*. Anything they couldn't produce themselves, they must buy from the Company store—at one-hundred to four-hundred per cent profit to Hudson's Bay. Then, after communicating his irritation with the Settlement to all his chief traders, he wrote London their joint opinion that it should be discontinued.

But by this time the London governors saw in the Settlement their strongest claim to Rupert's Land. Displeased with Simpson's proposal, they ruled, "There never was such a mistake." And Colville personally wrote his protege a stinging rebuke.

Obedient if not docile, the young governor then set about reorganizing the colony on a sound basis as a source of food supplies and labor for the Company, and as a retreat to which employees leaving the service could retire. Despite his diplomatic abilities, however, he managed in so doing to unite the diverse elements against him.

Protestant and Catholic missionaries, struggling to legalize unions of white men with Indian or *Métis* women, were the first. In Athabasca, Simpson had taken a sister of his half-breed interpreter as wife without benefit of clergy. By Margaret Taylor he had had four children. But when he returned to England on furlough in 1825, he married the daughter of the uncle who had given him that springboard clerkship.

Though he also married his *Métis* wife to a *Métis* and provided generously for his children, the clergy could not condone such conduct in the overseas governor of the Honorable Company. With his second marriage, they said, he had destroyed all their good work.

On behalf of his British wife, Simpson, for the first time in the history of Red River Valley, drew an arbitrary color line. This further incensed the missionaries and automatically alienated the aristocracy—active and retired Company officials living there with their native wives and families—and the French *Métis*. And when he dismissed a young Scotch breed for daring to aspire to marriage with the daughter of a prominent white resident, the British mixed bloods joined the opposition.

One by one, the remaining groups did, too. The Scots held the governor responsible for their lack of a kirk and pastor of their own. The French Canadians resented his ordering all public meetings and notices to be voiced in English. The Indians made the antagonism unanimous when he threatened to stop their supplies unless they delivered all their pelts to Company posts.

Yet just four years after the Great Flood, when Governor and Mrs. Simpson came to live in Red River Settlement, it had done much more than recover from disaster. Thanks to the governor's own vision, Fort Garry, just south of the forks, and Lower Fort Garry or Stone Fort, twenty miles north, were imposing and reassuring structures. Stone Fort covered as much ground as St. Paul's Cathedral in London. Its high stone wall enclosed the Governor's own residence, an impressive building even today. Fort Garry, because of its central location, was headquarters for the colony's political, commercial and social life. Its thick sixteen-foot high wall sheltered Assiniboia's Government House, Company offices, courthouse and jail, officers' homes, barracks, storehouse and granaries.

Between the forts on the west bank of Red River, homes of the European aristocracy were far on the way to becoming the charming, even pretentious dwellings Governor Ramsey admired so much. And about them spread the orderly farms of the British half-breeds.

Protestant, industrious, law-abiding, these British *Métis* imitated as closely as they could the virtues of the English and Scotch whose blood ran in their veins. Some of their sons and daughters attended the academies Governor Simpson had established for children of the aristocracy. Others went to Montreal or the British Isles to study law, medicine, theology. Several rose to high places in the Company.

On the east bank, the French-Canadian community of St. Boniface rayed out from its massive twin-towered Cathedral in ever-lengthening streets of small, neat houses. And along the Assiniboine, French *Métis* were setting up more or less permanent homes.

Despite every misfortune and obstacle, Red River Settlement was becoming an oasis on the prairies where man, particularly the poor

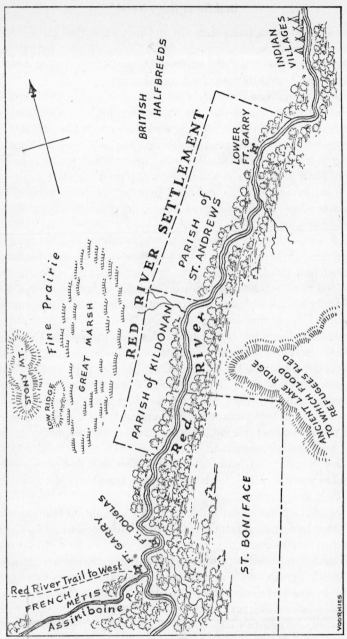

RED RIVER SETTLEMENT, AS REORGANIZED AFTER THE
GREAT FLOOD OF 1826

man, enjoyed more independence and privileges than in any other part of the nineteenth-century world. The catch was that its residents didn't know it. Ridden with a growing anxiety that couldn't be spoken aloud, they turned their resentments and fears first on the governor, then on one another.

The aristocrats, many of them men of wealth, and the frugal, devout Scots directed their spleen against the French Canadians. They deplored the buffalo hunts that flooded the Settlement with meat, rendered every *Métis* and Indian idle while it lasted, and stopped the sale of farm produce. Even more they deplored the Cart Trains. St. Paul's stoves, chairs, sugar and other luxuries, they complained, were giving residents of the east bank illusions of equality with their betters on the west.

They scorned St. Boniface men as windy talkers and boasters, the winter weddings and other festivities that after days of boisterous feasting and drinking, usually ended in four-alarm brawls. They ridiculed the French-Canadian passion for fine horses, decked with bells and ribbons, and for gaily painted carioles. With these, said the Britishers, the Bonificians dashed about frenziedly to give the impression that the entire burden of the Settlement's political and commercial life rested on their shoulders.

To Calvinist Scots, the French Canadians turned Sunday into a day of carnival with their noisy arrivals and departures about the Cathedral and with their races on the river ice. And they damned young French Canadians for giving young Scots a taste for bright blue coats, dancing, racing, and for crossing the Boundary to find work among the Americans.

The easygoing east-bankers went their way, but they were neither unaware nor insensitive to these British assumptions of superiority. And they, too, were uneasy.

Root of the general alarm derived from a condition Hudson's Bay Company had exacted from Lord Selkirk before granting him Assiniboia. By this condition, ten per cent of the colony's land always must be available to Company employees of three or more years' standing.

Though British and French-Canadian families were moving in, each year saw more leaving for Canada or the United States, or joining the groups Governor Simpson sent west to hold Oregon against the influx of American immigrants. And Company employees, particularly the *Métis*, now viewing the Settlement as "home," arrived in such numbers that within a few years the population had doubled. The colony fast was becoming a community of half-breeds.

Nor were the half-breeds a united, homogeneous people. As a rule, French *Métis* were athletic, good-looking, lively, fond of a fast pony and merrymaking, freehearted, openhanded, so emotional they could be roused to extraordinary acts of friendship or revenge, bravery or daring. British breeds were industrious, provident, stable. Or so the Europeans saw them and compared the first to wild mustangs that roamed the prairies, the second to the patient, dependable dobbin.

Actually, as one English observer wrote, life at the Settlement so influenced all of them that

I doubt if a halfbreed dressed and educated like an Englishman would seem at all remarkable in London society. . . . They recognize no chiefs except when they elect a Chief for their great hunting expeditions. In all respects they are like civilized men, not more uneducated, immoral or disorderly than many communities in the Old World.

On the denial of what they considered two basic rights, however, all factions sank their differences to stand together. For these denials, Governor Simpson also was held accountable.

Ambitious to rule themselves, they resented the council and court, sheriff and police he had set up to govern them. Appointed and paid for by the Company, these authorities were regarded as Company tools.

Eager to prosper, the colonists longed to take advantage of the lucrative market for their produce offered by American trading posts along Red River and its tributaries. Governor Simpson contended that the Company's monopoly included a monopoly of the Settlement's market.

Red River Settlement, consequently, had neither trades, occupations nor stores. Every man had to be his own carpenter, mason, wheelwright. Every wife and daughter had to spin and weave the family's clothing. With limitless reaches of fertile land theirs for the taking, they were restrained, for lack of a market, to cultivating little more than enough for their own needs. French Canadians and *Métis* were further incensed because Company personnel now preferred farm produce to pemmican. The Company, therefore, bought less and less buffalo meat.

"Take our products," Europeans, French Canadians and *Métis* joined to cry, "or give us an export (American) market."

Ignored, the Britishers farmed doggedly on. But French Canadians and *Métis*, using Pembina as their base, retaliated by free trading in furs with the Americans. Again and again Governor Simpson warned them, but the Selkirk estate supported the colonists. It was to cut this Gordian knot that, in 1836, Hudson's Bay Company bought Assiniboia.

Though its purchase was kept secret for years, the governor now was free to act. Homes of suspect bootleggers were invaded, sometimes destroyed, in systematic searches for pelts. All furs found were confiscated. Finally, he had a persistent *Métis* offender publicly flogged.

That brought the French half-breeds out en masse to demand, "Either deliver George Simpson to us to be punished as we see fit or we will seize and deal with him personally." In return for abandoning that idea, they asked better prices and the right to an American market. Nothing came of those demands either. But the Company, fearful that word of the unrest at Red River might spread abroad, in 1837—five years before its twenty-one-year license was due to expire—applied for its renewal for another twenty years.

The triumphant return of the great buffalo hunt of 1840 evoked another threat to Company security. Of the more than one million pounds of beef brought back, Governor Simpson would buy but a few hundredweight. The surplus smothered all demand for farm produce. Yet south of the Boundary, American buyers were eager to purchase any or all of both harvests.

Again the Settlement united to implore the council of Assiniboia to grant it this American market. The council did nothing. Again the British colonists farmed doggedly on. But the *Métis* broke out in a rash of petitions.

They asked the governor of Assiniboia to make official their status as "native sons" of Red River Valley. They asked the British crown to define the powers of Hudson's Bay Company. They asked the U.S. Congress to annex Assiniboia.

The governor ruled that they held the same status as British subjects. The crown delayed its decision for years. Congress refused to consider their petition.

Governor Simpson's reaction to all this was still sterner measures. He raised duties on American imports to twenty per cent, punished the *Métis* leader of the petitioners, asked the Catholic Church to recall the priest who had assisted in preparing the documents. On the ground that feeling over the Oregon Question was running so high in Red River Valley that Americans might attack Assiniboia, he obtained 500 soldiers of the Sixth Regiment of Royal Foot to man Fort Garry. To cut down American competition for free trade pelts, he offered traders south of the Boundary $1,500 a year to go somewhere else.

That offer brought young Canadian-born Norman W. Kittson, one of the most successful of Astor's traders on the Upper Mississippi, to Pembina on the gallop. With him came able, if untrammeled Jo Rolette, Jr. While Kittson established a line of competitive American posts along the Boundary, Junior joyfully seized a Hudson's Bay post south of it, sent its traders north. The following spring, Kittson led that first six-Cart Train, largely filled with "free trade pelts," to St. Paul.

Dismayed to discover the criticism Hudson's Bay Company was reaping both in Canada and the British Isles, the London board of governors took stern measures of its own. It secured the recall of the Sixth Regiment from Fort Garry and its replacement by a company of ex-soldier pensioners. It appointed the company's commander governor of Assiniboia. It notified Governor Simpson and other Company officials to keep hands off the colony.

Almost at the same time, unfortunately, arrived the crown's belated answer to the *Métis* petition. The Company, it declared, was acting completely within its rights. Thus fortified, Governor Simpson ordered the arrest of four *Métis* free traders.

The day their trial opened, both British and French half-breeds gathered outside the courthouse. As an earnest of their intentions, they fired several rounds from their muskets. This so intimidated one of the judges that he paid a bystander to take his place while he slipped out to his horse and sped to safety.

Nevertheless, the jury found the first defendant guilty. The Company's counsel then moved that, the legal point established, no sentence need be imposed.

Although growing competition south of the Boundary motivated Hudson's Bay compliance, to the half-breeds this was a personal victory. "Trade is free!" they shouted. *"Le commerce est livre!"*

Like prairie fire the cry swept through the fur country. Then from the valleys of Lakes Manitoba, Winnipegosis, and Winnipeg, Cart Trains rolled openly for the Boundary. Joining those of Red River Settlement and Pembina, they swelled Red River Trade to greater and greater volume.

PART VI

The Old Order Changes —— Fast

1. YORK FACTORY YIELDS TO ST. PAUL

Throughout the 1840's and '50's, American influence more deeply infiltrated Assiniboia. Pembina's prosperity under Minnesota's administration accounted for some of it; Americans, pushing into Assiniboine and Saskatchewan Valleys to take up land, for more. But the chief culprit was eastern Red River Valley, now abloom with new settlers, towns and filling pockets.

French Canadians and *Métis* who accompanied Settlement Cart Trains up and down the Woods Trail first asked why Assiniboia, with practically the same soil and climate, did not prosper likewise, then devised their own answer. While Assiniboians were crushed under the dictatorship of a fur trading monopoly, they said, Americans under a representative government lived as free people. Carried away with their own logic, they went on to criticize everything British, praise everything American. Even the Scots, watching the mushrooming population of half-breeds, began to wonder if they wouldn't be safer if Assiniboia were under the American flag.

From the four British colonies on the Atlantic, eyes also were turning more and more critically on this miniature colony on Red River. In 1846, the British crown had lost Oregon because Hudson's Bay Company's few trading posts and the handfuls of Red Riverites Governor Simpson sent out had not been enough to hold it against inrushing Americans. Three years later, American goldseekers had overrun California. The worst—or best—of it was that wherever Americans went, their steamboats and railroads were sure to follow. Yet like Assiniboia, the maritime colonies remained static within less than one-third of the northern half of North America.

Why? Because, reasoned the Easterners, the other two-thirds were controlled by an English fur company for the exclusive benefit of 250 stockholders.

As facts and rumors about the fortunes Red River Trade was pouring into American tills spread over Canada, this conviction ripened. Toronto merchants sent a representative to Red River to investigate.

143

He returned to corroborate the reports and to add that since by far the greater share of that Trade came from Rupert's Land, it should be directed east into Canadian markets.

He also brought back a petition to the Canadian Parliament, signed by 574 residents of Rupert's Land, to ask that renewal of the Company's license in 1857 be denied. When Toronto's Board of Trade learned that the Rupert's Land document concluded with the ominous warning:

> Just as surely as the Company obtains a power as despotic as that it has exercised for so long, every halfbreed will cross the Boundary and, finding themselves stronger, they will then show who was wrong to have scorned their complaints,

it promptly submitted a similar petition.

Letters from Red River, smuggled out through Pembina, also told of the *Métis* petition to the U.S. Congress, of the delegation of half-breeds that had traveled to St. Paul to ask Governor Ramsey and Fort Snelling for military aid against Company oppression. Of another delegation that had appeared before the doors of a political convention in St. Paul. Refused admittance, its members had insisted that since all Red River Valley soon must become American territory, they were entitled to enjoy the benefits of democratic institutions *now*. They were admitted.

Suddenly, Canada and the British Isles saw all the troubles at Red River in a bright new light. Wasn't the doctrine of Manifest Destiny rampant in American politics? Wasn't peaceful penetration of Oregon and Texas the first step toward American annexation? Hadn't Americans for years been quietly spreading over Assiniboine and Saskatchewan Valleys? Ergo: it was the Americans, intent on acquiring not only Rupert's Land but all the British Northwest, who were stirring up the *Métis!* Obviously, a fur trading monopoly was not powerful enough to resist such pressure.

At this point, Chicago merchants, long jealous of St. Paul's monopoly over Red River Trade, organized to get their share. In 1856, they founded Superior, Wisconsin, as western terminal for a line of steamboats on Lake Superior and eastern terminal of an overland route to Pembina and so to Red River Settlement.

Loyal Britishers there hastened to warn both Canadian and British Governments of the immediate danger which threatens the integrity of the present imperial rule in British America from the subtle ingression of a foreign power to its very center.

Even Canada's Chief Justice Draper took up his judicial pen:

The effect of the commercial intercourse of Assiniboia being necessarily with the United States will be to make all the interests of the inhabitants American, all their dealings American. . . .

By 1857, Canadian fears were soaring like St. Paul's fantastic land boom. Minnesota soon must attain statehood. When that happened, Red River Valley south of the Boundary would become part of a new Territory. Americans always rushed into a new Territory. They would pay no heed to an invisible Boundary. In no time, all the Valley would be solidly American "with great factories taking the place of windmills and railroads replacing Red River Carts."

Canadian aspirations soared with their fears. Only one obstacle stood between them and acquisition of Red River Trade. Only one obstacle stood between them and acquisition of a continental territory bounded by Atlantic and Pacific.

At this most inauspicious moment the obstacle again applied to renew its license. Hudson's Bay Company's application served as a flare to signal all hostile forces to unite against it. Unable to ignore such a demonstration of public sentiment, British and Canadian Parliaments each appointed a Select Committee to investigate the Company's administration of a fur empire that now extending from Labrador to the Pacific, International Boundary to the Arctic, embraced some 4,500,000 square miles.

Before the Crown's Select Committee in London, friendless Hudson's Bay could marshal but two witnesses—Governor Simpson, now Sir George Simpson, and Edward Ellice, a member of the board of governors. Against it, not only witnesses from Red River, but representatives of Canadian trade associations, of the Grand Trunk Railway and other vested interests with eyes on Red River Trade, ranged themselves.

Thus it was that while St. Paul rocketed toward catastrophe, in London the Crown's Select Committee was asking 1,424 pertinent questions. Of these, the three most crucial were put to the man who had ruled that vast empire for almost forty years. With the wordage august bodies always employ, it requested:

*Will you have the goodness to give an account of your impressions
of the territory of Hudson's Bay Company with reference to its adapta-
tion for the purpose of cultivation and colonization?*

I do not think any part of Hudson's Bay territory is well adapted for
settlement.

Would you apply that observation to the district of Red River?

Yes.

Why so?

On account of the poverty of the soil.

Whether or not Governor Simpson was an honest convert to his
own opinions or a reluctant subscriber to the will of his Company,
his testimony fell on stony ground. His nineteen inquisitors simply
did not believe him.

Canada, they ruled, should be free to annex any portions of the
British Northwest it wished to colonize. Two districts should be
acquired at once—Red River and the Saskatchewan. Furthermore,
within those two districts, Hudson's Bay authority "would, of course,
entirely cease."

Canada's own Select Committee also came to two crisp conclusions. Hudson's Bay Charter of 1670 was null and void. If Canada
were not to lose Red River Trade to the Americans, it must take
immediate steps.

Realistic Governor Simpson long had seen the handwriting on
the wall. Not only was the great empire he had governed so long
crumbling. Steamboats and railroads were transforming the entire
economic organization of North America. For almost a decade steamboats had been ascending the Mississippi to St. Paul. Soon the long-
bruited Northern Pacific Railroad must become a reality. The time
had come for York Factory to step down as the Company's port of
entry to America. Even before the Select Committees rendered their
decisions, he had begun negotiations with the U.S. Secretary of the
Interior.

Early in the summer of 1858, the result of his efforts burst like an
exploding sun over the prostrate Paulistas. All Hudson's Bay goods
and those of Red River Settlement would be carried in bond, to and
from Fort Garry, via St. Paul!

In streets, offices, and homes, at all hours, they fell on one another's
necks with joy and relief. Newspaper headlines ran a fever. Public
meetings everywhere discussed how best to exploit this miracle that
literally had raised Minnesota's capital from the dead.

Next came word that gold had been discovered in British Columbia. St. Paul was to be the supply center also for the goldseekers!

And when Governor Simpson and Mr. Ellice arrived to set up headquarters and arrange for the first shipments of furs and goods, plans and excitement spread to Red River Valley.

A few miles north of the junction of Red and Bois des Sioux Rivers, the U.S. Army at last erected Fort Abercrombie. Some miles below it, Hudson's Bay Company founded Georgetown as trading post and shipping center. At Pembina, a U.S. Customs House was established. Burbank and Company of St. Paul started a stagecoach and freight wagon line to Fort Abercrombie. From there, Hudson's Bay personnel and goods would travel north by Red River Cart.

Optimistic as they were, Paulistas were unprepared for the volume of freight the Company's 152 posts, 3,000 traders, and 100,000 Indian trappers required. The first three shipments wrought two immediate changes.

With all goods addressed to Fort Garry, the Company's headquarters, Red River Settlement's name, so far as Americans were concerned, was Fort Garry. And so it became in fact. Though 6,000 Carts labored mightily to transport the new assignment as well as the now really tremendous Red River Trade, they were totally inadequate. Steamboats were indicated.

Russell Blakeley made a quick trip to Red River. Returning, he reported that for five months of the year, the 417 miles of its course between Forts Abercrombie and Garry were navigable.

Within weeks, St. Paul's Chamber of Commerce was accepting the offer of "Captain" Anson Northup to transfer—for $2,000—his good ship, *North Star,* from the Upper Mississippi to Red River and to have it operating by April 15, 1859.

Announcement of this forward step moved James W. Taylor, U.S. Treasury Agent in Minnesota, to cry:

When the whistle shall sound the advent of this boat in Garry, Archbishop Taché. . .will spring instantly to his feet and, raising his hands reverently above his head, will exclaim, "In the name of God, let the bells of St. Boniface ring, for civilization has arrived."

By late February Captain Anson had dismantled his boat on the Crow Wing River, lashed it to ox- and horse-drawn sleighs, and was on his way, attended by thirty doughty Mississippi boatmen, to Red River, 150 miles away. Even today to transfer such cumbersome freight across Minnesota in midwinter would be an undertaking. In 1859, with bitter temperatures, blizzards, deep and drifting snow harassing every foot of the way through trackless forests, it was epic.

Yet no thought of employing guides entered the captain's head. A compass had served him on the Mississippi; a compass he used now. Weeks later, a searching party found his expedition hopelessly lost near Detroit Lakes.

But by April 1, everything was at Georgetown. Seven weeks more, and to the crash of a bottle of dubious whisky on its duck-bottomed stern, the S.S. *Anson Northup* floundered into Red River.

An up-ended shoebox structure rose midway of an oval, ninety-foot deck that barely skimmed the water. From the engine room below, the funnel, running straight up, overheated the salon above, blinded the sky with smoke and sparks. A crude paddle wheel threshed furiously behind. From the bow, a long, log sweep, powerfully manipulated, assisted the helm to negotiate Red River's eternal bends.

Its machinery, well aged on Maine's rivers, had not been rejuvenated by the long voyage, via New Orleans, to St. Anthony Falls. Now after eight years of service, its boiler, originally built for a locomotive, was so cracked that despite a thick coat of river gumbo, disconcerting jets of steam popped out thick as freckles on a farm boy's face.

That maiden voyage of Red River's first steamboat definitely falls under acts of God. Among its cargo and clouds of sparks were one hundred kegs of gunpowder! Yet eight days after it struck the water, a hoarse bellow interrupted two little girls braiding each other's hair on Fort Garry's wall. Said Mary Ramsey to Maggie Murphy, "Somebody's blowing in a bottle."

They were the only ones to take calmly the S.S. *Anson Northup's* arrival. Every Indian on the River had been terrified. The colonists were dumbfounded. Pouring out of their homes, they shouted, wept, prayed, fired muskets.

Within less than seventy-two hours, the captain was on his way back to Fort Abercrombie. Eighteen days later, he was in Toronto making headlines in the *Globe* with descriptions of his namesake's luxurious cabins and other marvels.

Although his was the fastest trip made up to that time between

Red River and Canada, he had paused long enough in St. Paul to collect his $2,000 from the Chamber of Commerce and to force Burbank and Company to buy his ramshackle boat for $8,000.

The Burbanks rushed Captain Edwin Bell and a crew of Mississippi boatmen to Fort Abercrombie to take over. But it was now late summer, the River low. Three weeks crawled away while they dug pits into which to roll, one by one, the twenty-two miles of boulders that created what was known as Goose Rapids. Days more were lost while they released the paddlewheeler from a sandbank. Meanwhile every passenger hung over the rail angling anxiously. It was fish or starve.

The boat reached Fort Garry just in time to be tied up for the winter. In the spring, patched up and renamed the *S.S. Pioneer,* the crazy craft curdled Red River nerves for two more seasons.

Then Red River's second steamboat was ready. In the spring of 1859, Captain John B. Pond, trying to hustle the *S.S. Freighter* up the Minnesota River before flood waters fell, grounded. Leaving a little Welshman in charge, the captain walked away. Three years later, at a sheriff's sale, Burbank and Company bought the hulk, sight unseen. The crew that arrived to dismantle it found the faithful Welshman, clad in long hair, beard, ragged coffee sacks, and cabin curtains, still on guard.

Rebuilt at Georgetown as the *S.S. International,* Red River's second nautical wonder celebrated her maiden voyage in the spring of 1862 by ramming a bar, losing her smokestacks, and rousing the wrath of the Prairie Sioux. And at Fort Garry, to crown misfortune, two immigrant families aboard brought Burbank and Company into head-on collision with Governor Simpson.

The naïve Burbanks had regarded the steamboat as a magic force that would people and develop the Valley from end to end. To the governor, an immigrant was anathema; the steamboat, merely an auxiliary of the fur trade.

Bowing to the inevitable, the Burbanks sold the *International* to Hudson's Bay. And at its convenience, the Company operated it. Except for a weekly mail service between Fort Garry and Pembina, Red River Settlement again was cut off from the outside world.

So, within less than five years, the first chapter of steamboating on Red River began and ended.

The sternwheelers, however, had had an offspring—the flatboat or barge. During the interim while the S.S. *Anson Northup* was an abandoned waif, Russell Blakeley had built a barge at Fort Abercrombie to carry a mixed party of British notables and British Columbian goldseekers to Fort Garry, there sold it at a handsome profit as lumber. That transaction gave St. Paul merchants an idea. Fitting out flatboats as itinerant shops, they floated them downriver until all their wares were sold, then disposed of them on the spot.

The flatboats underscored what the S.S. *Anson Northup's* and *International's* stuttering engines had proclaimed. The long, long day of man, beast, and wind power in Red River Valley was done. Having come, steam must remain.

But the Old Order, as represented by Prairie Sioux and Hudson's Bay Company, still was all-powerful. Before steamboats could return, men and events as powerful had to rise to conquer it.

2. DAKOTA TERRITORY AGAIN PARTITIONS THE VALLEY

Early in the spring of 1857, a dozen self-styled "intelligent gentlemen imbued with the spirit of enterprise" left St. Paul. Garbed in jeans and buckskins, traveling by ox-drawn wagons, they resembled any band of town-site seekers roaming Minnesota. Captain Kidd and his pirate crew, however, would have envied them their bold and careful plan to seize a treasure.

Within a year Minnesota Territory was to become a State. As a State, she would be forced to reduce by half territorial boundaries that approximately enclosed today's Minnesota, North and South Dakota. White men in the area cast adrift, thereupon, according to standard procedure, would petition Congress for Territorial status.

It was to anticipate this that Alpheus G. Fuller and fellow members of the newly incorporated Dakota Land Company set their compass west-south-west. Its needle guided them overland to *Can-can-san Ha-ha Oton-wi,* or Whitewood Rapids, on the Big Sioux River. To the Paulistas' consternation, they found members of Iowa's Western Town Company already in possession.

The two groups merged to make this beautiful site, whose terraced cataracts were the backdrop for a favorite Prairie Sioux camping ground, the capital and industrial center of Dakota-Territory-to-be. From it, they could pre-empt town sites suitable for university, penitentiary, and other institutions, as well as all surrounding farm lands.

One group went north to found Flandrau and Medary. The rest remained to fell trees and quarry rock for the first structure of the metropolitan capital of Sioux Falls. Shortly, enclosed in a high, adobe wall, this tiny story-and-a-half building became Fort Sod. Here sixteen men spent a hazardous winter fighting off Prairie Sioux while in St. Paul and Sioux City, Iowa, Mr. Fuller and partners labored futilely to recruit citizens for their various town sites.

Before spring, Sioux Falls had two lusty competitors. On the Missouri River, Norwegian and Swedish immigrants from Nebraska, also with territorial plums in mind, had founded Yankton. And far to the north, Pembina was astir with political ambitions.

On one point, the three rivals could agree. Until their soon-to-be-orphaned land was guaranteed Territorial protection, neither settlers, industry, nor capital could be induced to enter. The indefatigable Mr. Fuller went to Washington. For two reasons, he got nowhere.

In 1858, the House of Representatives was Republican, the Senate Democratic. The House would consider no bill to create Dakota Territory that did not contain a clause forbidding slavery. The Senate would consider no bill that didn't authorize slavery. Impasse.

And now citizens of the newborn State of Minnesota were split asunder over location of their boundaries. One faction insisted that northern Minnesota and northern Dakota formed a wilderness that should be relegated permanently to savages and fur traders. Minnesota's future demanded the trade and traffic the Missouri and Mississippi Rivers would insure. Therefore, the Territory should be divided east to west along the forty-sixth parallel to embrace the area between the two great rivers.

The opposition argued for a north-south division with Red River of the North as Minnesota's western boundary. This would give the new State the incomparable advantages of a harbor on Lake Superior, control of the Mississippi to the Iowa border, and, above all, control of the whole navigable course of Red River of the North and of Red River Trade. Impasse.

If they could not obtain law-abiding and industrious settlers, until Territorial status was assured, Mr. Fuller and company knew they could count on an inrush of lawless elements. Unable to wait for one or both stalemates to be broken, they called a political convention for that very summer in Sioux Falls.

Though the white population between the Red and Missouri Rivers numbered less than one per hundred square miles and transportation difficulties were almost insuperable, the few delegates who managed to attend were in determined earnest. Taking Territorial Minnesota's constitution as their model, they set up a temporary government to function until Dakota Territory could be created. In their innocence, they thus inaugurated the first and only genuine "Squatter Sovereign Government" in American history.

Sioux Falls delegates then nominated S. G. Albright for Governor, their own town site as capital. Yankton delegates promptly reacted by nominating J. B. S. Todd for Governor, Yankton as capital. Red River Valley now held the balance of power. Norman Kittson of Pembina was a friend of Albright's. Sioux Falls won both governor and capital. And the Valley acquired a permanent political strategy.

The Squatter Government served less than three years. In that time so many Southern Congressmen left Washington that the Republicans gained a majority in both Houses. The Bill creating Dakota Territory (minus slavery) was signed on March 2, 1861, just two days before Abraham Lincoln took the oath as President.

True to form, American landseekers rushed into the new Territory. When this annoyed the Prairie Sioux into burning Yankton, twice attempting to wipe out Sioux Falls, the U.S. Government took title to Big Sioux, Vermilion and James River Valleys. The tribes holding them moved to the Missouri. Now more log shanties and settlements began to dot the released valleys and, on the Missouri, to cluster about Forts Pierre and Randall.

Meanwhile, Red River Trade had decided Minnesota's boundaries. Afraid of losing this invaluable commerce to a now aroused Canada, Congress gave the shortsighted new State a choice. Take the north-south division *and* a large railroad grant, it ordered, or the east-west and no grant. Privately resolved to leave the northern region to traders and savages anyway, Minnesota announced its western boundary to be Red River of the North.

Dakota Territory now became the largest organized unit in the United States. Extending from the Iowa-Nebraska line to International Boundary, from Red River to the Rockies, it included 350,000 square miles. Millions upon millions of settlers were needed.

Sioux Falls and Yankton began to advertise Dakota's attractions in Eastern papers. Like Mr. Fuller, they got nowhere.

Lest settlement spell death to its numerous military posts in the new area, the U.S. Army campaigned to restore the land to the

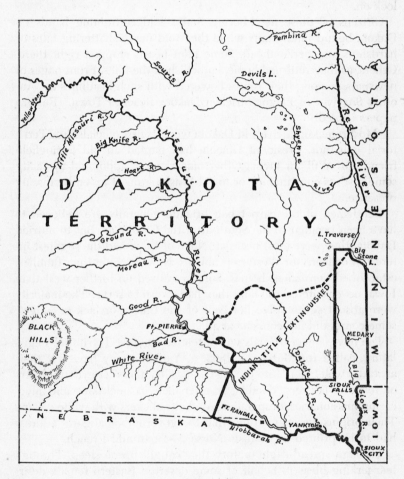

DAKOTA TERRITORY, 1866

Indians. The Union Pacific Railroad and other Southern interests, desperately recruiting population for their own huge land grants, spread grisly rumors about Dakota. Minnesota, Iowa, and other States with large areas still unoccupied took newspaper space to describe the new Territory as a land of incessant drought, death-dealing blizzards, grasshoppers so voracious they dug potatoes from the ground, tomahawk-brandishing Prairie Sioux. Favorite implication of one and all was that no man in Dakota died with his scalplock on.

Citizens of these neighboring States laid restraining hands on Dakota-bound immigrants while they told nerve-shattering tales of hardships and perils ahead. Some faint hearts stopped right there. Others, as they returned home, embellished the tales. Front pages of newspapers along their routes flowered with such headlines as "Another Survivor of Plague-Stricken Dakota Reaches Town." Eastern papers copied.

Most reluctant arrivals in Dakota were its first officials. For Territorial governor, President Lincoln had named an old Springfield friend, Dr. William Jayne. Other officers were appointed to pacify some restless constituency or to rid Washington of an embarrassing presence.

Gentlemen of the carpet bag brigade generally are believed to have been peculiar to the South after the Civil War. But to untried Dakota, they were most peculiar. None of them had the slightest interest or concern for Western problems. None brought their families, established permanent homes. Some ventured no further west than Iowa, never entered the land they had sworn to serve. The majority were absent seventy-five per cent of the time. For lack of judges, some courts did not convene at all.

The few pioneer officials who attended the first Territorial Legislature, called for March 17, 1862, in Yankton, may have felt their attitudes well taken. Into the log cabin "Chambers" crowded soldiers of fortune, lawyers, doctors, frontiersmen in buckskins and moccasins, missionaries, desperadoes, and city slickers with white collars. Their origins were so various that the governor's inaugural address had to be printed in English, Norse, German and French.

Through spread-eagle oratory they caught up on sleep. Through tear-jerking pleas in behalf of some deserted Eastern female desiring to be divorced from her husband, they howled with glee, roared, "Treason! Treason!" At their pleasure, they ate hard-boiled eggs, picked their teeth with jackknives, circulated bottles of whisky.

As there were no defined political parties, no clear-cut issues, any member, to further his own or public fortune, could—and did—propose weird, controversial measures. Big Bill Somers, for one, dressed in full Sioux regalia, a loaded six-shooter in each hand, first moved to solve the lack of population with a bill to legalize marriage between white men and squaws, then threatened to blow out the brains of anyone opposed.

Drawn guns, bloodshed, black eyes, trickery, tides of whisky, and general pandemonium accompanied Yankton's victorious fight to get the capital. While the Legislature was in session, Governor Jayne, though he cared not a whit what laws were made or not made, laid about vigorously with his veto. Outside the chambers or on the open streets, he used his fists.

Gambling, dancing, wine dinners, wine speeches, and quarrels also enlivened the legislators' leisure hours. As the session drew to a close, campfires aisled the streets of Yankton. Wigwam-fashion, the lawmakers sat about them, eating, drinking, smoking, while they planned torchlight parades, fife and drum corps, and other red-hot, ripsnortin' attractions to get out the vote in the fall elections. By one dawn's early light, six of them tried to extract milk for an eggnog from an inadvertently passing cow.

It didn't matter what they did. Nothing mattered. The time was now—April, 1862.

3. THE SIOUX "EAT GRASS"

Little Crow, the great Sioux chief, was a welcome figure each Sunday morning in the Episcopal Mission of the Lower Sioux Agency on Minnesota River. In his good black broadcloth suit, white collar and dark tie, he was outwardly distinguishable from the American and German farmers, Indian agents and traders about him only by his gleaming black braids and beaded moccasins.

As steadfast friend of the white man, Little Crow, in fact, was their guarantor of peace with the thousands of Sioux assembled since the Treaty of 1851 on two reservations on the Minnesota River and on a third about Lakes Big Stone and Traverse. Not only had he himself adopted the white man's ways and religion. He had secured a missionary to teach them to his people and to aid him to fight the rascally traders and agents who, to enrich themselves, plied warriors and squaws with bad liquor.

But inwardly Little Crow was still a Sioux. And steadily, since the signing of the treaty, resentment for the white man's justice had mounted in him. Even the signing had been accompanied by trickery. With the tacit consent, if not the connivance, of Governor Ramsey, the traders had duped the Sioux of the $275,000 down payment on their lands between the Mississippi and Red Rivers.

Every month since, the treaty provided, $45,000 was to be given the tribes for food, clothing, equipment and education. But, due to venal agents and traders, Government red tape and bungling, they seldom received it. When they did, Agency storekeepers palmed off on them spoiled and wormy food, wretched cloth and utensils. In every possible way, the proud, onetime owners of Minnesota and Red River Valleys had been humiliated, despoiled and exploited.

Or so Little Crow had thought. But in mid-August of 1862, Andrew J. Myrick, clerk at the Lower Agency store, conceived a new taunt. After weeks of waiting for the long-delayed funds to arrive from Washington, the Sioux—more than 3,000 of them—on the Lower Reservation were starving. With several brother chiefs, Little Crow went to the store to ask that food be advanced them. Myrick listened, then laughed in their faces.

"If your people are so hungry," he advised, "let 'em eat grass."

The following Sunday, Little Crow attended church as usual. Perhaps he went for a last meeting with his white friends. Perhaps in the crucible of that hour, his fatal decision was made. The service over, he mounted his horse and rode away—to call a council of his Soldiers' Lodges.

This was the Golden Hour, he told his warriors, for the Sioux to regain Minnesota and Red River Valleys. The Civil War had drained every possible white man from the lands west of the Mississippi. Only sixty soldiers manned Ripley and Ridgeley, the two nearest forts. Fort Abercrombie's garrison had been replaced by a company of Minnesota Volunteers, and half of them were at Georgetown.

Sioux warriors, on the other hand, on the Lower Reservation alone numbered 1,000. On all three reservations, they totaled 4,000. And, if need be, they could call on the Tetons, their Sioux brothers west of the Missouri, to swell those numbers beyond 6,000.

Early Monday morning, August 18, 1862, Andrew J. Myrick lay dead before the Lower Agency store, his mouth stuffed with grass. Forty-eight hours later, some 2,000 white settlers were dead. More than 300 women and children were captives. Some 30,000 people were in panicked flight toward the Mississippi. And in a territory 200 miles long by 50 wide, more than $3,000,000 in property had been destroyed.

During those same hours, the belated Government funds arrived.

To the white man, the uprising was a massacre. To Little Crow and his people, it was honorable war against a pitiless enemy.

Minnesota's policy of developing only the southern half of the State stood Red River Valley in good stead now. The area around Fort Abercrombie alone suffered death and destruction. On August 23, the fort was alerted by word that 5,000 Sioux were on their way to attack. Before sundown, the majority of settlers were safely inside its stockade.

Unable to obtain aid from Fort Snelling, Volunteers and settlers withstood seige for four weeks. Twenty-one white men were killed. Breckenridge, Dayton and Old Crossing, burned. And, after a Cart Train or two had been plundered, a stagecoach looted, its driver shot, all activity in Red River Valley ended.

At this, Minnesota newspapers began to clamor:

The importance of keeping open the great thoroughfare. . .to Fort Garry can hardly be overestimated. Some 500 Trains now in Transit are waiting at St. Paul and St. Cloud until protection can be given.

Protection was supplied promptly then. Cart Trains, mails, stagecoaches, and the *S.S. International,* tied up under Fort Abercrombie's guns, all began to move.

But life in the Valley south of the Boundary did not resume. Every settlement and farm was abandoned. Every settler gone. Even Georgetown was deserted.

By mid-September, Colonel H. H. Sibley had broken the uprising in Minnesota River Valley, freed most of the white captives, taken 1,500 Sioux prisoners. And the warring bands, their munitions and supplies low, had fled to the high plains west of Red River to concentrate about Devil's Lake.

On March 3, 1863, Congress authorized removal of all Sioux in

Minnesota beyond the bounds of any State. The next day 2,000 non-belligerents were crowded aboard a steamer for transfer to the new Reservation west of the Missouri.

The Sioux outbreak had shocked the entire United States, electrified the American Northwest. But with every Sioux now beyond its boundaries, and with more than one million of their fertile acres freed for white man's settlement, victory, so far as Minnesota was concerned, had been won. For six more years, however, punitive expeditions spent millions of dollars in marches and countermarches across Dakota Territory.

All the years and money were wasted. The fate of the Sioux was decided in Red River Valley within nine months after the uprising.

From mid-August until late September, 1862, Red River Settlement lived in a state of growing uneasiness. With every trail closed, only confused rumors seeped in of some terrible catastrophe to the south. Then, the Woods Trail partially opened, mail and Cart Trains brought details of the massacre.

Shortly, the horrified colonists were more horrified still to learn that a band of Sioux was on its way to visit them. If the band were not friendly, the Settlement was in no position to hold off a horde of inflamed warriors. If it were, the Settlement had no desire to see Assiniboia tribesmen fraternizing with murderers of white men in Minnesota. Least of all did it want Americans to get the idea that, as a British colony, it was giving aid and comfort to their enemies.

Just after Christmas eighty-six Sioux arrived. Members of the Lake Traverse Reservation, they had had no part in the outbreak. They came, they said, to learn the feeling of Assiniboian tribes toward them.

For three days, the Council of Assiniboia reluctantly fed and sheltered them in the courthouse. But when they left, as reluctantly, it was plain that they had not stated the real purpose of their visit.

That purpose came to light five months later when Little Crow himself arrived with eighty warriors. In the courthouse he received Alexander G. Dallas, Governor of Assiniboia, with all the state due one ruler from another.

For the occasion, he seated himself, cross-legged, on the judge's bench. Again he wore the good black broadcloth coat. But now his costume included a breech clout of fine blue cloth, a sash devised from some white woman's costly shawl, a turban from another, deerskin leggings, beaded moccasins, and a six-shooter. About him stood his warriors, resplendent with feathered headdresses and with medals and flags Colonel Dickson had given the Sioux during the War of 1812.

Throughout that war as well as during the American Revolution, Little Crow reminded the governor, the Sioux had aided and supported Great Britain. In return, they had been promised that the "red flag of the north" would protect them from their enemies. Now they were fighting with a rope around their necks. But if they had ammunition and food, victory would be theirs.

Food, Governor Dallas could give. Also a promise to intercede on their behalf with General Sibley. Arms to kill Americans, no.

In that refusal, Little Crow heard his people doomed.

Returning to Turtle Mountains, he dismissed his warriors. With his sixteen-year-old son, Wowpinapa, and a small group of non-combatants, he started south afoot. No longer had he heart to war on the whites, he told the boy. He would steal a few horses to provide for his children, then go far away.

An evening or two later, an unknown white man saw an old Indian picking red berries along a trail. Acting on the now insistent watch-word that "The only good Indian is a dead Indian," he shot twice. In a thicket, with only his son beside him, Little Crow died, unaware that chance had given his people a reprieve.

For the campaign of 1863, General Sibley with 3,000 men left Fort Snelling for Devil's lake, by way of Big Stone Lake. General Sully, with 3,000 troops, went to the east bank of the Missouri. Between their pincers, they planned to trap the Sioux before they could join the Teton tribes or cross the Boundary into the British Northwest. Sully's forces failed to meet the schedule. Seizing the advantage, hundreds of Sioux warriors streamed west. But other hundreds, weaponless, starving, turned east, to Pembina.

To Pembina, late in the fall, Fort Snelling dispatched the Hatch Battalion—a company of cavalry—to rout them out. Arriving without supplies, with most of its horses dead of exposure, forced to erect barracks in bitter weather, the Battalion offered little menace to the refugee Sioux. Nevertheless, its presence did disperse them. Some went west again, but 600 crossed the Boundary to camp within six miles of Red River Settlement. They had come, they announced, to live and die with their British friends.

Their British friends were nonplused. Among the newcomers were two leaders of the massacre now under sentence to hang—Little Six, brother of Little Crow, and Medicine Bottle. Feather headdresses sweeping the ground, each feather a symbol of a "deed of blood," identified most of the others as warriors of long and dangerous prowess.

They were not dangerous now. The death of Little Crow and want of food and arms were painfully evident in their spirit and bodies. They lacked "even sufficient wire to trap a rabbit."

On condition that they move to White Horse Plain, twenty-five miles west, Governor Dallas gave them a little pemmican. When that was gone, some Sioux, to get more, sold their children to sympathetic colonists. Others, in small bands, spread over the British Northwest. A large number went to Lake Manitoba to fish through the ice.

Little Six and Medicine Bottle, to the Settlement's acute alarm, remained near by. Finally, a few of the most unnerved colonists yielded to the persuasions of Hatch Battalion officers. Plying the two unsuspecting chiefs with whisky drugged with laudanum and chloroform until they fell unconscious, the conspirators bound them securely, carted them to Pembina for shipment to Fort Snelling.

This incident roused great indignation in the United States and in Assiniboia, great fear of Sioux reprisals. In the midst of this crisis, Governor Dallas received a message from 5,000 Sioux on the Missouri. It left no doubt whatever that the entire Sioux nation now looked on Assiniboia as its refuge.

Under the same impression, Minnesota beamed its wrath on the thoroughly dismayed colonists. St. Paul papers pictured them as laughing at the impotent indignation of the Americans and boasting that the murderers were now under the protection of the British flag.

To the rescue came one of Assiniboia's own tribes, jealous of even the little aid given the starving Sioux. In May, it attacked the refugees on Lake Manitoba, killed twenty, wounded many more. Taking the hint, some Sioux pushed farther into the British Northwest, but the majority began to drift back across the Boundary. Hatch's Battalion was withdrawn to Fort Abercrombie. Governor Dallas advised the Sioux on the Missouri to make peace with General Sibley.

Red River Settlement was just beginning to draw a long breath when it learned that 3,000 of the Missouri Sioux had crossed the

Boundary, were on their way east. To make it clear that the British colony offered no haven to them and their people, the governor met them far out on the prairies.

Their last hope dead, the despondent Sioux departed. But before leaving, they visited every family to whom a Sioux child had been sold, took it with them to share the four long years of attrition, battle, despair and death before peace was signed in 1868.

With the savages gone and fur traders going, eastern Red River Valley now served chiefly as the Woods Trail for reviving Cart and Wagon Trains. In the western Valley, grass grew over the Plains Trail. Only Fort Abercrombie showed signs of life. From Fort to Pembina, not a human being, cabin, or other mark of white or red man's presence remained.

Solemnly, George Catlin, whose paintings of frontier life had made him an oracle on the Northwest, penned an epitaph:

> *Dakota is that part of the Great Plains which is and ever must be useless.*

4. ANNEXATION; NEW BONE OF CONTENTION

Since that free trade victory of 1849, discouragement and slow decay had vanished from Red River Settlement. Now, via St. Paul, it had an ever more profitable export market with the United States. Now its population, not including Indians, was approaching 12,000. Now its farms and homes not only stretched for fifty miles along the banks of Red River of the North, but—with some sparse intervals—for seventy along the Assiniboine. It even had a neighbor.

In the summer of 1862, McKenney and Company had erected a long, log store in the hitherto avoided angle between Red and Assiniboine Rivers. When neither winter winds nor spring floods carried it away, other shops and homes rose about it. The result was called Winnipeg.

Yet, characteristically, as one of the original Selkirkers put it,

> Old Red River is going to the devil faster than ever. God only knows what is to become of us if the British Government or some friendly soul does not take us in hand.

The Great Fear had come to pass. Red River Settlement was, indeed, a community of mixed bloods. Almost 6,000 of its people were

French *Métis*, more than 4,000 British half-breeds. Only some 1,600 residents were white. And those included a number of "foreigners." Eager-beaver Americans who had hastened to Winnipeg to fill the need for shops and services. Canadians from Ontario, drawn west with blood in their eye by the publicity about the *Métis'* victorious battle for free trade.

All British and all Protestant, the Ontarians immediately focused their racial and religious prejudices on the Catholic half-breeds, their equally hot political prejudices on the annexation of Assiniboia by Canada. Treating the half-breeds as inferiors, they boasted that when the superior race they represented arrived on Red River in numbers, all this nonsense about the rights of the New Nation would end.

Most arbitrary and violent of them all was their young leader, Dr. John Christian Schulz, a titan in stature and energy. When he was refused a seat on the Council of Assiniboia, he and his followers threatened to seize the reins of government themselves.

They did found the *Nor'Wester*, Red River Valley's first newspaper, to ask pointed questions. Why was Assiniboia the only British colony in America without its own representative government? Why the only one anywhere forced to live in isolation from the world? Again and again its vociferous columns ridiculed Assiniboia's laggard growth when Minnesota, right next door, in a single decade had increased its population from 5,000 to 172,000. •

Astonishment was the word for the British colonists. Since its founding, Assiniboia had had no more contact with the four British colonies on the Atlantic than with Africa or the Argentine. Why, they retorted, should it join Canada now? If it joined anyone, the United States was the logical choice. But why join anyone? Great Britain soon must make it a crown colony. Then their own representative government automatically would replace Hudson's Bay's.

The *Métis* wanted no change of any kind. Hadn't they won free trade? With several of their leaders on the Council, weren't they steadily gaining voice in Assiniboian affairs? But, specifically, in the light of the Ontarians' aggressions, they wanted no truck whatever with Canada.

Among the Americans in Winnipeg—and Pembina—were sundry flag wavers. Irked by Hudson's Bay's dictatorial ways, they declared the time had come for freedom-loving Americans to give the little colony a great big helping hand. And in St. Paul, that ebullient agent of the U. S. Treasury, James W. Taylor, to swell Minnesota's financial contribution to the nation's welfare, assumed leadership of a movement to make Assiniboia safe for American trade.

Unless Great Britain acted soon, he reported to Washington, Red River Settlement either would declare its independence or ask for annexation to the United States. In the latter event, there were enough red-blooded patriots in Minnesota alone to "hold, occupy and possess all Red River Valley" against British interference.

From the Settlement's founding, one group constantly and loyally had supported the British crown. Suddenly, in 1863, to the amazement of colonists and Americans alike, its members said never a word. Active and retired officials of the Honorable Company were, in fact, too stunned and angry to speak. For to them, like a bolt from the blue, had come an announcement from London.

Hudson's Bay Company had been sold, lock, stock, and barrel!

Until the last detail of its transfer to a syndicate known as the International Finance Association was signed and sealed, not a hint had been permitted to leak out. Not a penny of the sale price had been allotted to any of the wintering partners in America, though tens of thousands of pounds were due them. Not a word of explanation, appreciation or farewell had been sent them by the outgoing board of governors with whom they'd worked so long.

As word of the sale flew from post to post throughout the British Northwest, rage boiled in its wake. The wintering partners considered resigning in a body. Some did resign. Many turned openly against the Company. Others supported Assiniboia's annexation to the United States. The majority, though covertly, backed the half-breeds in their determination that no part of Rupert's Land ever should be linked with Canada.

And when Red River Settlement grasped that sale of the Company to the International Finance Association included the sale of Rupert's Land, the lid on the caldron of its wrath disappeared into the stratosphere. Through its official organ, the *New Nation*, even the Government of Assiniboia began to voice its leanings toward American annexation in editorials that saw visions of

a great consolidation of peoples and interests such as can be parallelled nowhere else among the kingdoms of the earth.

That pretty bubble of wishful thinking was all Minnesota and its neighboring States needed to urge American annexation of the entire British Northwest. Eastern States, inflamed against both Britain and Canada for their aid to the Confederacy, joined the chorus to urge that annexation be extended to include Upper and Lower Canada, Nova Scotia and New Brunswick. Their newspapers, too, beheld visions, like that of the *New York Sun*:

The tendency of events on this North American continent is plainly toward consolidation of all the peoples dwelling upon it into one great nation around the United States as nucleus. From the Polar Sea to the Isthmus of Darien, there will be in time but one government. Canada, Rupert's Land, British Columbia, Mexico, all will have but one flag, and eventually Cuba and her sister islands will join us.

Feeling the direction of the wind, Great Britain called the Quebec Conference of 1864 to induce the four Eastern colonies to federate and accept responsibility for themselves and the British Northwest. The four colonies took such a jaundiced view of that maneuver that foreign observers foresaw the day when Mother Country and American dependencies would part forever.

And now the U. S. Congress, fighting mad over the Alabama Case, abruptly canceled its Reciprocity Treaty with the neighbors north of the Boundary. A year later it authorized purchase of Alaska. In both acts, the quartet of British colonies read American intention to force them to join the United States.

But it was Mr. Taylor in faraway Minnesota who exerted the final pressure that brought Alexander Mackenzie's dream of a continental British America to pass. Since 1857, in an effort to augment his U. S. Treasury income, he had been promoting the interests of one or another of the proposed north Pacific railroads. Recently he had become associated with *the* Northern Pacific Railroad.

Ambition to make good in an opportunity that clearly had a future warmed the pen with which he prepared a bill for Alexander Ramsey, now U. S. Senator from Minnesota, to present to Congress. This bill authorized the United States to admit, on request, the four British maritime colonies to the American union. In return, the United States was to buy Rupert's Land from the new Hudson's Bay Company for $5,000,000, organize new States and Territories throughout the British Northwest, *and construct on British soil a combination rail and waterway from Atlantic to Pacific.*

The bill died a sudden death in the House of Representatives. In a fury of demonstrations and protests against it, the four British colonies united. On July 1, 1867, they jointly proclaimed themselves the Dominion of Canada.

More! In the white-hot light of that achievement, *they* beheld a vision. Of Assiniboia as rampart against American imperialism. As the new Dominion's essential arch. As the keystone of a continental Canada.

In Assiniboia, alas, no eyes were free to enjoy that vision. Every gaze was fixed on another leaden cloud whirling out of the west to the accompaniment of a sinister drone.

By fall, locusts had devastated the country. That winter starvation came so close that some colonists, it is recorded, ate horses, even cats.

Hardly had they emerged to a lean summer than a crew of Canadian road builders (trailed by bands of Ontarians alight with get-rich-quick illusions) arrived. Sent out by Ottawa, they were to construct a road from Red River to Lake of the Woods. Their appearance was Assiniboia's first intimation that Canada was negotiating with Hudson's Bay Company for the purchase of Rupert's Land.

That neither Government nor Company had seen fit to consult Assiniboian wishes was shocking enough. That Ottawa had ordered the road built before it obtained legal title to Rupert's Land more shocking still. Such tactics smacked all too loudly of one British colony's intention to invade another.

Next, though throughout the summer of 1869 negotiations for Rupert's Land hung fire, Ottawa despatched John Stoughton Dennis to Red River to make a general survey of Assiniboia. His use of the American system of mile-square sections instead of the long, narrow strips, each with its frontage on Red River, which the colonists preferred underlined the Dominion's aggressive intentions.

British settlers were bitter. But the *Métis* were further incensed by the jubilant Ontarians who fell on the surveyed lands like a plague of human locusts. Around the now thriving village of Winnipeg, they were voracious. Dr. Schulz staked out so large an estate that had he been able to retain it, he would have died the richest landowner in Canada.

Of the *Métis* three chief sources of income, the buffalo and Cart Train were on the rim of extinction. Hudson's Bay's fur trade, facing bankruptcy under the new regime, required fewer and fewer woodsmen and boatmen. Loss of their small plots of land, therefore, meant death to their security.

Yet though only a night watchman now guarded the Settlement, they attempted no violence. The silent groups that gathered to watch his crews at work so unnerved Dennis, however, that he warned Ottawa to postpone the survey until it gained title to Rupert's Land. Back came instructions to proceed as ordered. He proceeded.

Small wonder if to Canada's first untried federal officials the anxiety of a few thousand half-breeds for a few thousand acres in remote Red River Valley appeared picayune. They were up to the eyes in graver problems.

How to weld four antagonistic British colonies into one smooth-functioning Dominion. How to ward off Washington's bellicose suggestions that Britain cede Canada to the United States to pay for damages American property had suffered through her aid to the Confederacy. How to ward off an even more immediate danger as Americans from coast to coast, citing the aid Assiniboians had given the Sioux, bombarded Congress to buy Rupert's Land to insure Alaska's safety. How to cope with Hudson's Bay's shrewd new directors who exploited the current American hysteria to jockey interminably for better terms for Rupert's Land.

Still bent on doing his best for the Northern Pacific Railroad, Mr. Taylor stirred the boiling pot to a second explosion. In the unrest at Red River and in Ottawa's attitude toward it, he—and Senator Ramsey—found reason to prepare a series of resolutions and a treaty for the Senate Committee on Foreign Affairs to present to Congress. One resolution read:

We regret to be informed of a purpose to transfer the territories between Minnesota and Alaska to the Dominion of Canada. . .without a vote of the people at Red River Settlement and of the settlers on the Saskatchewan River who largely consist of emigrants from the United States, and we would respectfully urge that the President and Congress represent to the Government of Great Britain that such action will be unwarrantable interference with the principle of self government and cannot be regarded with indifference by the people of the United States.

Another declared:

The Legislature of Minnesota would rejoice to be assured that the cession of northwest British America to the United States, accompanied by the construction of a northern Pacific railroad, are regarded by Great Britain and Canada as satisfactory provisions of a treaty which shall remove all grounds of controversy between the respective countries.

The treaty they proposed provided that Canada cede to the United States all British America west of Longitude 90 (the line on which lies Lake of the Woods).

The Senate Foreign Affairs Committee did more than approve both resolutions and treaty. In the belief that if the United States did not offer to build that railroad, "all British America would become irrevocably British provinces," it set up a committee on the Pacific Railroad.

In due course, word of two documents reached the sensitive attention of Ottawa. One was the Pacific Railroad Committee's first report which concluded:

The opening by us of a north Pacific Railroad seals the destiny of the British possessions west of Longitude 90. They will become so Americanized in interest and feeling that they will be in effect severed from the new Dominion and the question of their annexation will be but a matter of time.

The second document was a letter written by Mr. Taylor to the Hudson's Bay agent in St. Paul. In addition to repeating that the United States would pay $5,000,000 for Rupert's Land, it stated flatly:

I know that President Grant is anxious for a Treaty with England which will transfer the country between Minnesota and Alaska to the United States in settlement of the Alabama controversy and as a consideration for the establishment of reciprocal trade with Canada.

Convinced that the United States intended to perpetrate "this awful swallow for territory," the Canadian Government issued an ultimatum to Hudson's Bay Company. Then, without waiting for a reply, it created North West Territory out of Rupert's Land and provided that, as a Territory, it should be administered by an appointed lieutenant governor and council.

Within five days, Hudson's Bay Company capitulated. For $1,500,000, the right to continue its fur trade, and other considerations, it agreed to sell Rupert's Land to the Dominion of Canada.

Red River Settlement was chosen as the Place, December 1, 1869, as the Date, of Transfer. And as the Lieutenant Governor who would take formal possession of vast, if unwanted, Rupert's Land, Ottawa named the Honorable Mr. William McDougall.

Announcement of all this shattered forever Red River Settlement's dreams of becoming a crown colony. To be *given*, not offered, Territorial status, was the final blow. But when the colonists learned the caliber of the officials—all Canadians—appointed to govern them, their wrath and humiliation reached new highs.

5. RED RIVER REBELS

Like Dakota Territory's Governor Jayne and staff, North West Territory's officials were named to gratify or pacify certain political interests or, as in the case of the lieutenant governor, to remove from Ottawa a most unpopular presence. Cold, intractable, tactless, completely ignorant of the *Métis* and their problems, William McDougall was a most unhappy choice.

As usual, the Scots at Red River said little. But the English were vocal against this evidence that all the butter Rupert's Land afforded was to be spread on Canadian bread. The Catholic clergy feared that under the imminent influx of British-Protestant settlers, their thousands of half-breed parishioners would be lost to the Church. Loudest and bitterest of all were the Company's wintering partners. Once more, while they, the working bees, got nothing, the syndicate and stockholder drones would divide that $1,500,000 of honey!

With the exception of Ontario's boisterously rejoicing Orangemen, white Assiniboians resolved to give no support to the Government that had shown so little consideration for them. Two groups, in fact, were stimulated to even greater zeal on behalf of American annexation.

One was the Red River Republican Party, made up of recalcitrant elements who appeared merely to be "agin the Government." No one recognized in its leader, W. B. O'Donohue, an unfrocked Fenian priest. The other, though small and by no means composed of all the Americans in Assiniboia, was known as the American or Annexation Party.

And now the half-breeds began to suffer the fears native peoples in all parts of the world had known before the approaching impact of a competitive civilization. They were unequipped to compete with the white man and they knew it. Specifically, the French *Métis* knew they were unequipped to compete with a British-Protestant civilization.

In these frightened, volatile people, all the other factions recognized a tool to fashion their own ends. All began to use it.

At this point the picture blurs behind clouds of accusation and denial as to the roles played by clergy, Company personnel, and white colonists in the events that followed. It should be said, however, that the three men who exercised greatest influence over the mixed bloods—Hudson's Bay's William Mactavish, Governor of Assiniboia; Archbishop Taché, and Anglican Bishop Cochrane—offered Ottawa their services as mediators. All were ignored.

By October, American newspapers clearly and derisively were picturing the regal progress of Governor McDougall and his retinue of major and minor officials, clerks, household servants, across the United States. And all manner of fantastic rumors were winging about Red River. News and rumors added to fears convinced the *Métis* that this interim between the lapse of Hudson's Bay's government and inauguration of the Territorial regime was their last opportunity to act.

Even so, the Governor was descending Red River Valley before the French half-breeds assembled, as they did before a buffalo hunt, to elect officers and to proclaim Rupert's Land, *ipso facto,* a republic. As politically naïve as Dakota Territory's Squatter Government, they gave no thought to the fact that both Britain and Canada might view such action as treason. Their one idea was to prevent the Governor from crossing the Boundary until they could make terms with Ottawa concerning their status and land claims.

On October 21, Governor McDougall reached Pembina. Although informed of the unrest at Red River, he was not prepared for the hostility the half-breeds at the American frontier post demonstrated to make plain their sympathy for the *Métis* north of the Boundary. Nor could he credit his eyes when he found the road to the Settlement barricaded and guarded.

But two messages handed him there stopped him short. The first, from the Council of Assiniboia, warned him to remain on American soil. The second, in French, said briefly;

The National Committee of *Métis* of Red River Republic present to Monsieur McDougall the order not to enter the Territory of the Northwest without special permission of this Committee.

> *By order of the President,* JOHN BRUCE
> LOUIS RIEL, *Secretary*

Louis Riel came naturally by the courage, initiative, pride of race, and youthful foolhardiness necessary to sign that order. He was a member of the first family of Red River Valley.

During the winter of 1807-8, two white women—the first known to have reached Red River—upset the routine of North West Company's Pembina post. On December 29, an intrepid young creature from the Orkney Islands who, disguised as a man, had arrived, via Hudson's Bay, eighteen months before to seek a faithless lover, became the mother of a fine boy. Eight days later, an equally fine girl was born to Madame Marie Anne Lagominère, a French woman who with her husband had paddled the 2,000 miles from Quebec to Red River the previous summer to join the buffalo hunters.

The first white child born in Red River Valley returned with his mother to her native islands in 1808. The second remained at Red River to marry Louis Riel, one of the *Métis* leaders in the fight for free trade. Louis Riel, Secretary, was their son.

By the time he was born in 1844, St. Boniface was an established community with a Cathedral School. There Archbishop Taché, coming one day on thirteen-year-old Louis absorbed in a Latin grammar, was so impressed that he secured the necessary financing to educate him for the priesthood in the College of Montreal.

But when graduated, Louis Riel did not become a priest. Perhaps a certain instability that made him cool and dignified one moment, restless and irritable the next, told against such a career. Yet though neither tall nor large, with a remarkable head, capped by thick black curls, a good brow, and piercing, intelligent dark eyes, he was a striking figure. And when moved to oratory, he was a fiery and persuasive speaker.

Returning to Red River in 1868, he found no opportunity open to a *Métis* with his training. The job he was forced to take with a Cart Train gave him firsthand insight into what would happen to his people if Assiniboia were overrun by white immigrants.

Louis Riel did not instigate Red River Rebellion nor take any active part until the *Métis* had organized Red River Republic. Then he supported the decision to prevent Governor McDougall from crossing the Boundary. Soon, as a natural leader, he was in command of the Republic's military forces.

Infuriated by that Republic's order, Governor McDougall began secretly to intrigue with the Ontarians at the Settlement. Anticipating his designs, young Riel, with 100 armed men, on November 2, 1869, marched through Fort Garry's wide-open gates to take command of the fort. (Was invited to take over, according to some authorities, by Hudson's Bay officials.) Next day, when the governor tried to force the barricade, *Métis* guards turned him back.

To British colonists these militant actions marked the *Métis* protest movement with the stigmata of rebellion. To quiet their fears and to show to Canada a united front, President Bruce and Riel invited every post in Rupert's Land to send delegates to a Red River Convention in mid-November to draw up a bill of rights. The convention met and adjourned with nothing accomplished. British delegates simply would not vote for French proposals, nor French for British.

McDougall's irate reports, meanwhile, combined with those of more moderate observers, had awakened Ottawa. Admitting that their dealings to date with Assiniboia had been a series of "egregious blunders," Canadian officials postponed the Day of Transfer. The idea would have been still better if someone had thought to notify Governor McDougall.

December 1 dawned. The Governor rushed across the Boundary to proclaim the transfer of Rupert's Land to Canada. To proclaim his own appointment as governor of North West Territory. And, for good measure, to announce *his* appointment of John Stoughton Dennis as deputy governor and Conservator of the Peace.

The Conservator of the Peace sped for Lower Fort Garry. Establishing headquarters there, he issued a general call to arms.

But neither British settlers nor half-breeds would take up arms against *Métis* "born and brought up amongst us." Only the Ontarians and a band of Indians in full war regalia, eager to fight anyone, anywhere, responded. Even Dennis dared not embroil the tribes.

The Canadians' enthusiastic drilling moved more *Métis* to fly to Riel's support. Within a week he had 500 armed men in his strictly disciplined organization.

Six days too late, McDougall received Ottawa's order to take no action about the transfer until further notice. Caught off base, he sent word to Dennis to demobilize his troops. The Ontarians merely reassembled about Dr. Schulz's storehouse in Winnipeg. Soon their loud threats to crush the "Rebellion" themselves, brought out a company of *Métis,* Riel at their head.

Now the Ontarians were willing to disband, go home. But the *Métis* had suffered too much at their hands to agree. Shortly, forty-five ex-Volunteers were occupying cells in Fort Garry's jail. Dennis—disguised as a squaw—was fleeing for Pembina. And Red River Settlement was in an uproar.

By this time even the stanchest British colonists had lost all respect for McDougall and multiplied their resentment for Canada. This change in public sentiment so strengthened Riel's hand that on December 2, he proclaimed a Provisional Government. Two days more, and the new Government's flag—a fleur-de-lis and shamrock entwined on a white background—floated over Fort Garry.

Barred from his own Territory, afraid to remain in increasingly hostile Pembina, McDougall abandoned the field. Returning to Ottawa and political extinction, he met en route another representative of the Canadian Government whose desire to bring peace to Red River was to place his foot on the first rung of the ladder to political fame.

After twenty years in Hudson's Bay service in Labrador, Donald A. Smith recently had been appointed to succeed Sir George Simpson as overseas governor of the Company. Immediately on his induction into office in Montreal, he had realized that the future of the Company depended on closest co-operation with the infant Dominion Government. To his chagrin, however, he found that in the eyes of both the Government and Canadian people the real instigators of Red River Rebellion were his wintering partners in Rupert's Land.

Though he never had been west of the St. Lawrence Valley, he promptly offered to pacify Assiniboia. His services were as promptly accepted.

He reached the Settlement on December 27, the very day the Provisional Government elected Louis Riel President. Three weeks later, in twenty-below-zero weather, with a strong wind blowing straight from the Arctic, he stood for five hours on a small outdoor platform to speak to more than a thousand colonists, representing every racial, religious, and political faction.

Wrapped in buffalo robes and Hudson's Bay blankets, while icicles lengthened on their beards and their faces turned blue with cold, they not only listened. For the first time in Red River history, they agreed to unite behind a central government that would direct Assiniboia's affairs.

Taking advantage of the unity Mr. Smith had achieved, Riel proposed the creation of a second Provisional Government. This time even the English-speaking settlers agreed, on condition that such a government would not impinge on the authority of Hudson's Bay Company or that of the Council of Assiniboia. Presidency of the new Government thereupon was offered to Governor Mactavish.

Very ill now, the old man refused, but urged, "Form a government, for God's sake! I have no power or authority." In his stead, Riel was elected President. And an English judge and a French priest were appointed delegates to Ottawa to negotiate terms for the annexation of Rupert's Land.

Bloodless Red River Rebellion now balanced on the very pinnacle of success.

Enter Thomas Scott.

This Irish-Canadian Orangeman, as passionate in his prejudices as he was ready with his powerful fists, had come to Red River in 1868 as a member of the Canadian road-building crew. Finding himself a white man among thousands of half-breeds and Indians, he assumed the superiority not unknown today among Nordics in the Orient, Latin America, Africa and other lands of darker-skinned peoples.

As one of Dr. Schulz's most zealous agitators for Assiniboia's annexation to Canada, Scott was one of the first to respond to Dennis' call to arms. And one of the first to be arrested when *Métis* troops tucked the forty-five Canadians into jail. Escaping to Portage la Prairie a month later, he joined a disastrous attempt to seize Riel and overthrow the Provisional Government.

Captured and imprisoned again, this time on charges of taking up arms against the established government, he incessantly voiced threats against Riel's life, attacked his guards, and incited other prisoners to do likewise. Fearing the infuriated guards might harm him, Riel himself went to the Orangeman's cell, first to persuade, then to warn him to behave. As confident as Robert Semple that no man of mixed blood would dare to touch a white man, Scott continued his defiances.

On March 3, 1870, a council of war, composed of seven *Métis*, found Thomas Scott guilty of treason, sentenced him to be shot. Though unconcerned for the man personally, leading men of all factions hastened to intercede with Riel. After conducting the Rebellion for seven months without spilling a drop of blood, they assured him, it would be suicidal to take a human life now.

But other malcontents, encouraged by Scott, now were inclined to disorder. To make both colony and Canada respect the authority of his Government, Riel denied clemency. At high noon, March 4, Thomas Scott died before a firing squad.

When his friends asked for his body, they were refused. Instantly rumors spread that the man still lived or had lived until a knife ended his tortures. In the darkness of that same night, a rude coffin, wrapped in chains, dropped through a hole in Red River's ice to sink into deep silt. There it doubtless remains to this day. But the secrecy of that burial fed still more alarming rumors.

Riel, however, had achieved his purpose. Overnight, Red River Settlement became a law-abiding community.

Archbishop Taché's return from a visit to Rome five days later eased the situation still more. With him he brought a copy of the Dominion Parliament's December Proclamation which declared that "no legal proceedings will be taken against any parties implicated in these unfortunate breaches of the law." He also had letters, one from the governor general, which left no doubt that Ottawa intended to grant amnesty to the rebels. Thus armed, the Archbishop assured Riel and other officials of the Provisional Government, on his personal word of honor, that all irregularities of the past would be overlooked or forgiven.

The Provisional Government then released all Canadian prisoners and disbanded its troops. Red River Rebellion was over.

It was Canada that now knew no peace.

Traveling by light rays apparently, accounts of Scott's execution swept the Canadian Provinces. Catholic Quebec was quick and hot to rise to the *Métis* defense. Protestant Ontario cried for vengeance on the "half-breed murderers."

At the height of this public frenzy, the two Red River delegates arrived in Ottawa. To accept them as representatives of the Provisional Government implied acceptance of that Government. Promptly the dead Scott's brother had them arrested, charged with murder.

But determined to make no more blunders, Canadian officials accepted their credentials, quashed the criminal charges.

The success of Red River's negotiators epitomized the needlessness and waste of Red River Rebellion. Fruit of their labors was the Manitoba Act which created Manitoba Province out of 11,000 square miles of British Red River Valley and provided for its admission into the Dominion.

The act also authorized a Provincial Government that was a nice mixture of appointed governor, nominated upper house, and elected assembly, with two senators and four representatives in the Canadian Parliament, and, to maintain equality of French and English languages, a dual school system. Above all, it assured Assiniboians that their land claims would be respected. And it set aside 1,400,000 acres for *Métis* and their children.

The title chosen for the fifth Province implied both Canada's and the delegates' hope that thereafter only sweet sounds would drift across the Wilderness between the Dominion and its new member. *Manitoba* is the name of the Chippewa Speaking God. In the stillness of the night from his abode on an island in Lake Manitoba, he speaks in tones sweet as those of distant church bells.

But it is the friction of waves rolling across beaches deep in limestone fragments under the north wind's urge that causes those sounds to drift across the waters. And waves of friction, continuing to roll between Red River and Ottawa, mounted to a roar. . . .

6. THE BATTLE OF PEMBINA

First discordant note to shrill above the incredulity and joy with which Red River hailed the Manitoba Act rose from the campaign O'Donohue and his Republican Party instantly waged for Assiniboia's annexation to the United States. Before long, it was whispered that funds—variously estimated at $250,000 to $1,000,000—had been offered Louis Riel to bring about that happy end.

If so, the president of the Provisional Government remained deaf to persuasions and offers. His leadership proved, he waited quietly in Fort Garry to surrender his authority to the incoming Lieutenant Governor, then return to civilian life.

As an ardent member of the Fenian Brotherhood, O'Donohue, however, had bigger fish than annexation to fry. For more than a decade the Brotherhood from its New York City headquarters had been trying to establish an Irish Republic in the United States. In various Canadian and American centers, notably in St. Paul, branch "Circles" operated to raise funds to arm Ireland and embarrass England.

Their failure to invade Canada through New England in 1866 had turned Fenian attention—and O'Donohue—to the western Boundary. As the first point where a land crossing could be made, Pembina appeared a natural base from which to harry England by stabbing Canada in the back.

O'Donohue's reports on Red River Rebellion and the aid Pembina's half-breeds were giving it, however, elevated the American frontier post to higher station in Fenian strategy. From Pembina, the Brotherhood could do more than harry England. It could seize and make Fort Garry the nucleus of a Fenian State from which, eventually, it could drive every Britisher out of Canada.

Forthwith, the Brotherhood called a Fenian Congress for March, 1870, in New York City. Circles were ordered to send as delegates only fit and reliable men, those with Civil War experience preferred.

Meanwhile, Canada's English-speaking Provinces long had been urging a military expedition to Red River to crush the *Métis*. Ontarian refugees from the Rebellion further insisted that military rule should be established in Assiniboia until sufficient immigrants from the Dominion could settle there to outnumber and outvote the original inhabitants. To them all, the Manitoba Act was nothing more than an apple-polishing concession to the French.

Canadian Government officials no longer saw need for a Red River Expedition against the *Métis*. But reports of the 1,500 troops the Fenians were arming to march on Red River in May gave them ground for believing that a federal force at Fort Garry might not come amiss.

Early in April, Parliament, consequently, authorized Colonel G. T. Wolseley to organize a Red River Expedition. To camouflage it and, incidentally, to make a little political hay, Ottawa permitted the British Provinces to think the expedition was a direct answer to their demands. At the same time it assured Quebec and Manitoba that the troops were going west on "an errand of peace."

Neither commander nor men of Red River Expedition looked on

it as a peaceful enterprise. Twice previously, hotheaded Colonel Wolseley had indicated his willingness to teach those *Métis* a thing or two. Now he assembled the latest equipment of modern war, as practiced in 1870, and for his professional troops, picked 350 men from the crack Sixtieth Regiment. He also called for 850 volunteers.

Technically, enlistment was open to all the Dominion. Actually, less than 100 of the recruits were French Canadians. The rest were British, largely Orangemen, bent on vengeance.

On May 2, the Expedition sailed. All went well until it reached Sault Ste Marie. American officials there permitted the first steamer, loaded with supplies and boatmen, to pass through the canal. The second, transporting troops and war equipment, was denied passage.

While Ottawa assured Washington of the expedition's peaceful purpose, the American press inflamed public opinion from east to west against "this crusade to crush and punish a people who merely had asked for their rights." The bored and impatient troops, meanwhile, whetted their vengeance for the *Métis*, particularly Riel.

Washington's consent finally came for the *steamer* to pass through the canal. The troops were obliged to walk to Lake Superior. Smarting under this humiliation, even neutrals among them began to anticipate Red River as an objective on which to vent their wrath. That wrath grew when they found that forest fires and heavy rains practically had closed the trail through primeval forests to the lake where they were to take canoes to Fort Garry. And grew again, after they'd broken their backs to clear it, when Colonel Wolseley used instead the rapids-ridden Kaministiquia River.

More weeks of paddling and portaging heavy equipment and horses, to the accompaniment of reports that both Canadian and American newspapers were ridiculing their slow progress, brought the expedition's fighting spirit to a peak. Wolseley chose that moment to pen and send ahead to Red River a Proclamation declaring that the expedition came in friendship.

Concurrently, a second and one-man British expedition was making a mettlesome progress to Red River. Until a few months before, Captain William Francis Butler, unable to rise higher in the British Army, had been the most discouraged young officer in London. Word of the proposed Red River Expedition revitalized him. Cabling Wolseley to hold a place for him, he boarded the first ship. But when he arrived, every post was filled.

To reach Red River he offered to do anything. Very well, said the colonel; make your way across the Northern States to locate possible points where Fenian forces might cross the Boundary to attack the expedition. At St. Paul, buy and ship supplies to Fort Garry.

To array himself for American travel, the captain bought a ten-dollar suit whose bright blue vest patterned with stars, bright blue trousers, with stripes, suggested the American flag. And to allay suspicions of any Fenians or Orangemen he might encounter, he topped this ensemble with a green and orange tie.

Chicago he found to be bursting at the seams to become distribution center for surrounding States. Milwaukee, a hodgepodge of German, Irish, and Scandinavian immigrants funneling through it to those same States. Duluth, the "sorriest spectacle of a city the eye of man could look on." St. Paul, the most raw and raucous of them all.

Nowhere could he find hide or hair of the Fenians. But everywhere the idiom of the country oppressed him. Not entirely because it consisted of the fewest possible dictionary words, a selection of Scriptural names, and a large percentage of "Git-up's!" and "Hi's!" Wherever he went he heard rejoicing over Red River Expedition's predicament and the belief that not a man—including himself—would reach Fort Garry. Red River Valley, one and all assured him, was a Valley of the Moon, without life or transportation.

Via stagecoach and horseback, he did reach Fort Abercrombie; via the S.S. *International*, Fort Garry. Thence he went north to the mouth of Winnipeg River to meet Colonel Wolseley and his tattered, battered, but intact Expedition.

Riel and the *Métis* were not ignorant of the expedition's size and temper. But in addition to the Colonel's own proclamation of friendship, they had the Canadian Government's repeated assurances that the troops came in peace. And Archbishop Taché's continued assurances that amnesty would be granted them before the expedition arrived. Confident that they had nothing to fear, they made no plans for defense.

On August 22, the expedition reached the mouth of Red River. While the main body of troops ascended in canoes, a mounted company rode overland to turn back anyone traveling toward Fort Garry.

Word of this roused the first uneasiness. *Métis*, colonists, Hudson's Bay officials urged Riel to flee. The Archbishop advised him to remain. His speech of welcome completed, the Fort's guards trained for the salute they would present to the friendly mission, Riel remained.

Within less than twenty-four hours, Colonel Wolseley had debarked his men at Fort Douglas. Preceded by skirmishers, he advanced in battle formation.

There was no time now to provide for civil authority to take over, to save records, even face. His speech of welcome in his pocket, Riel, with other Provisional Government officials, fled to Pembina.

At the head of massed troops, Colonel Wolseley marched through the open gates of a flagless, undefended fort. Within minutes, the Union Jack flew from the flagstaff and a royal salute from the fort's guns rolled across the prairies. Red River Expedition had indeed come in peace. It didn't remain there.

Winnipeg's numerous saloons soon were dispensing their homemade whiskies to one and all. With no civil authority to control them, many colonists joined in the excesses. Hastily, the colonel disbanded his troops. Within ten days, men of the Sixtieth Regiment were homeward bound.

Cheated of their revenge on Riel, the volunteers stayed to organize an Orange Lodge and "pay off all scores by shooting down any Frenchman even remotely associated with Scott's death." More serious was their wholesale seizure of *Métis* lands.

To defend lives and property, the half-breeds also organized. Shortly, several men on both sides were mysteriously dead.

The new lieutenant governor, arriving belatedly, found the Settlement on the brink of civil war. Sternly he warned the *Métis* that if they made one move against the Canadians, "it would be all up with them." Like the Boers in South Africa, the French half-breeds then began to trek west to seek freedom in the Saskatchewan Valley. The discontent of those that remained provided fertile soil in which O'Donohue and his Fenian cohorts sowed bitterness against the "treacherous misrepresentations of Red River Expedition" and rage against the Orangemen.

By December, however, Governor Archibald had Manitoba's affairs sufficiently organized to hold the first Provincial elections. Their returns refute the popular modern impression that Red River Rebellion was the work of ignorant *Métis*. With few exceptions, Manitoba's first officials were the same men, many of them British, who had held office under the Provisional Government.

Wider evidence of the importance of the Rebellion was the rapid rise of Colonel Wolseley and Captain Butler from the springboard of their "Conquest of Red River" to high social titles and military rank. Fifteen years later, General Wolseley and Lieutenant Colonel Butler, in Africa to rescue Chinese Gordon from seige at Khartoum, still were relying on experience gained during their respective Red River Expeditions.

To transport British troops over the difficult reaches of the Upper Nile, Wolseley imported two hundred French Canadian *voyageurs* of the caliber that so skillfully had powered his canoes through the Wilderness. And Butler sent for a steamboat like the *S.S. International* that could float on a moist sigh. With these they conquered the Nile. But again they arrived too late. Khartoum had fallen two days before. Gordon was dead.

Within three weeks after their flight to Pembina, Riel and fellow exiles were back in the Settlement to attend a meeting called by O'Donohue. The Fenian wished to petition the U.S. Congress to annex the British Northwest.

Riel refused to support the scheme and the *Métis*, without his approval, would not sign the petition. Instead, they prepared one of their own to ask President Grant to intercede with Ottawa in Riel's behalf. Undaunted, O'Donohue appended their signatures to his own petition to Congress, then undertook to restore the Provisional Government with himself as President. Now he was ready to foment the insurrection he would lead when the Fenian troops arrived.

To man his uprising he did not limit himself to Manitoba's French *Métis*. There were also the Indians, including many smoldering Sioux refugees. At Pembina were hundreds of resentful half-breeds and scores of thieves, cutthroats and other outlaws from American justice. Strung across the Northern States were thousands of unemployed railroad workers. By spring, in large or small groups, these tough, disgruntled men were drifting across Wisconsin and Minnesota toward Pembina.

On the aid of one man, however, O'Donohue counted too heavily— Senator Ramsey. Perhaps he forgot the close friendship between the Minnesota Senator and the new U.S. Consul in Winnipeg. James W.

Taylor, now congenially located for life in the land for which he had such wholehearted enthusiasm, did more than have the Fenian's petition to Congress tabled. He arranged with Washington that if Fenian troops crossed the Boundary at Pembina, American troops could follow.

Nevertheless, though only a handful of the railroad recruits arrived and less than that of the Fenians, on October 5, 1871, O'Donohue— *General* O'Donohue now—opened his campaign. By chance, James J. Hill was on hand to serve as war correspondent for the Battle of Pembina:

This A.M. at seven o'clock, a band of thirty Fenians under Generals Curley, O'Neill, Donnelly and O'Donohue, composed of 20 of the hardest looking roughs and ten Pembina loafers, made an attack on Hudson's Bay Post at North Pembina[1]. . .and captured it without resistance.

They at once set about clothing their half naked squad and loading up a wagon of provisions. Either the plunder had too much attraction for them or they thought they could rest on their freshly gained laurels for they remained in the post till eleven o'clock when they were surprised by Col. Wheaton and twenty-three men from Fort Pembina coming down the road in an army ambulance and a four-mule wagon. . . .

As soon as the Fenian leaders saw U.S. Troops coming over the Canadian Boundary, they at once dropped everything and fled. And such a flight! Some on foot and some on Indian ponies, with the wagonload of provisions scattering to the woody banks of Red River.

. . . .In about twenty minutes [Wheaton] returned with Generals O'Neill, Donnelly and Curley in the ambulance and about ten men on foot. . . .O'Donohue and the Pembina halfbreeds escaped. The whole thing was laughable in the extreme. . . .

About five o'clock that afternoon a French *Métis* brought word to Fort Pembina that O'Donohue had surrendered on condition he be delivered to American authorities. With other prisoners, he was tried before Colonel Wheaton. The trial was a farce. Unable to exert jurisdiction over Canadian citizens, the Colonel had to release them all.

The Battle of Pembina, however, was no laughing matter. As Governor Archibald reported to Ottawa:

When one considers the military potentialities of the *Métis* organization, the support which a general uprising might have obtained from the several thousand unemployed railway workers in the northern states,

[1] Emerson, Manitoba

we realize the great danger in which this little Province with its miniature army lay. . . . O'Donohue would have been joined by all the population between the Assiniboine and the Boundary, Fort Garry would have passed into the hands of an armed mob, and the English settlers would have suffered horrors it makes me shudder to contemplate.

Neither Governor Archibald nor Archbishop Taché now could compete with the influence O'Donohue held over the *Métis*. Only one man could do that. Traveling from *Métis* settlement to settlement, Louis Riel gradually won them away from the Fenian leader "to take a stand in favor of the Queen."

Peace assured, the governor reviewed the *Métis* troops and for their aid "in preserving Her Majesty's Dominions" promised them temporary amnesty for their participation in Red River Rebellion. To Riel, he presented a written promise of amnesty.

That promise so enraged an Ontario member of the House of Parliament that he posted a reward of $5,000 for Riel's capture. Hurriedly, Sir John Macdonald, Canada's Premier, borrowed from Hudson's Bay's Governor Smith, sufficient funds to enable Riel and Lepine, another *Métis* involved in the death of Thomas Scott, to live in the United States until Canadian emotions cooled.

Manitoba answered such tactics by electing Riel to the federal Parliament. Its Legislature condemned Ontario's interference, asked Ottawa to set at rest all questions concerning Red River troubles.

These "challenges" ripped wide-open the amnesty question. Rather, the amnesty question ripped wide-open Canadian unity to reveal the century-old cleavage at its root. After the conquest of New France, Britain did nothing to assimilate the French who remained in Canada. Now on the Dominion had fallen the task of reconciling two opposed nationalities, languages, religions.

Given time and no further cause for friction, it might have succeeded. But there was no time. And the execution in faraway Red River Valley of a loyal British Orangeman by order of a French-Catholic rebel not only brought the split into the open but deepened it incalculably. From all parts of the Dominion, petitions—252 of them—for and against amnesty poured into Ottawa.

To grant it in the face of Ontario's wrath was to commit political suicide. To deny it in the face of Quebec's wrath was to commit political suicide. Parliament, therefore, placed responsibility for the decision on the British Crown. The British Crown returned it to sender with the recommendation that Canada solve her own problems.

Finally, in February, 1873, Parliament granted amnesty to Riel and Lepine on condition that they leave Her Majesty's Dominions for five years. Everyone else concerned in the Rebellion received full and immediate amnesty.

Ottawa thrust Red River Rebellion into official limbo. And from British Red River Valley, as it had long since from the American Valley, the Old Order departed forever.

PART VII

The Empire Builders

1. GOLIATH AND DAVID

Like Alexander Mackenzie, Donald A. Smith, son of a storekeeper, had found the small seaport of Stornoway, Scotland, an unpromising field. In 1836, he sailed for Montreal, with but eighteen years and a few pounds as capital. What matter? Hadn't a score of his ancestors risen in the New World to traders, even partners, in the old North West Company? Hadn't an uncle, recently retired as chief trader in Hudson's Bay service, provided him with a letter to Governor Simpson? Not that he intended to use it. Business, not the fur trade, was his dish of tea.

Tens of thousands of British immigrants who had seen America first, he soon found, filled every commercial opening in the four maritime colonies. Hudson's Bay dominated all the rest of British America. Reluctantly he presented his letter to the Emperor of the North. And, watching the governor read, he tardily remembered that his uncle had retired in direct opposition to the will of the reader.

For the next two years, while counting beaver, mink, and other pelts at a small Quebec trading post, Donald Smith explored every facet of the governor's vicarious vengeance. Then as he was transferred from post to post to learn French before going to Rupert's Land, the prospect brightened.

But now he always was so close to Montreal that lonely Mrs. Simpson, to her husband's acute displeasure, often invited the youth to tea or to escort her on boating excursions. One Monday morning following a Sunday tea, the governor ordered Smith to leave within forty-eight hours for the distant junction of the St. Lawrence and Saguenay Rivers. Seven hard and lonely years there steeled the young Scot for his future role as "the little man from Winnipeg."

Overwhelmed by snow blindness one brillant winter day, he endured months of pain and an anxiety that became desperation when a weather-wise old Indian warned him he was doomed to lose his sight. Three times he wrote Governor Simpson for permission to return to Montreal for medical treatment. Receiving no reply, he boarded a southbound Company boat. On arrival, he went first to the governor's home.

Again he was kept waiting. When the Emperor of the North at last appeared, his own physician was with him. The doctor reported no danger of blindness. "Then," said the governor, "I will give you thirty minutes to leave for your new post."

The new post was Esquimaux Bay on the eastern coast of almost unknown Labrador. For a moment Smith thought to refuse. "Then I said to myself, 'If Governor Simpson can bring himself to give such an order, I can bring myself to carry it out.'"

Beyond Quebec, he and his Indian guide had to travel more than a thousand miles afoot. Before they had completed half the distance, the Indian was dead of cold, hunger, and exhaustion. Smith might have died, too, had he not stumbled into a Company post whose factor kept him there over the winter.

Even with a canoe and guides, it took three weeks to reach his destination in the spring. Unaware that he was exiled for life— Governor Simpson's life—he settled down in that vast, dreary, and lonely waste. Shortly, it became less dreary and lonely. A new chief factor arrived with his wife and family. In 1853, Smith married the older daughter, Isabelle Hardisty; the next year their only child was born.

In the 1848 of Smith's arrival, however, Labrador was little more than a minor fur preserve. During his twenty years there, he had plenty of time to study philosophy, political economy, medicine, history, and other subjects to such purpose that he became one of the best-informed and most independent thinkers of the time. To attain the intimate knowledge of Indian and Eskimo character that later made him a shrewd judge of all men. Above all, as he realized his exile was a test of his will against the governor's, to learn everything to be learned about the administration and development of the fur trade.

And there at his elbow was Labrador, a virgin field for demonstration of his abilities. As he rose in the service, he went into farming and stock raising, built salmon fishing into an export business, created a market for sealskin and seal oil, quartz, wild tea, developed other native resources into profitable supplements to the fur trade.

By 1860, his work was so well known that from Canada and the United States came tempting offers. He refused them all. His letter declining a lucrative Chicago invitation betrays his real ambition:

It is probable that settlement of the country from Fort William westward to Red River and even far beyond eventually will take place with
damaging effect to the fur trade generally. . . . I do not believe that those
in authority in London and elsewhere are well advised in shutting off
this country and disparaging its character. A Chicago there is just as
possible as in Illinois.

Nine years later he realized it when, in Montreal, he stepped into
Simpson's shoes as overseas governor of Hudson's Bay Company.
Because of the recent sale of the Company to the International
Finance Association and of the Company's imminent sale of Rupert's
Land to Canada, he took command at the height of both Company
and Dominion upheaval. In this he saw opportunity to retain Hud-
son's Bay's place and power by making its interests one with those of
the infant Confederation.

That, as a first step, he unified Assiniboia to accept annexation to
Canada has been said. But the most important outcome of his journey
to Red River dates from the moment when, on his way to Fort
Garry, he and his escort exchanged stagecoach for dog sleds at the
revived and growing settlement of Breckenridge.

Ottawa's primary grievance against the Company was that its
officials at Fort Garry made no effort to divert Red River Trade to
Canada. Now, as he descended Red River Valley, he saw why. Because of the Valley's north-south direction, that Trade funneled
logically into American hands. Only a railroad across British America
could divert it east.

Three months later, while fighting a blizzard south of Pembina on
his way back to Ottawa, he came face to face with the instrument
through which he was to get that railroad. At the time it appeared
merely to be a dynamic young man traveling north alone by dog
sled. Impressed, the governor asked his name.

"Jim Hill."

"Ah, yes," said the older man kindly, "you are the young agent who
so ably forwards Company goods to and from London. Norman
Kittson has told me of you." A little amused, a little puzzled, by the
intensity of the black gaze in the young man's one good eye, he
drove on.

Back in Ottawa, Governor Smith's knowledge of Red River country and people so impressed federal officials that they invited him to replace McDougall as Lieutenant Governor of Manitoba. That post he refused, but he did agree to serve as Manitoba's Conservative member in the Dominion Parliament. Then, both as head of the Company and as Provincial Representative, he ordered surveys made of Red River country's resources.

Its rivers, he learned, abounded with fish. Its forests, with good timber. Gold, coal, salt, granite and stone were to be had for the mining; limitless beds of clay, for brickmaking; horizonless prairies for cattle raising.

Forthwith, he began to canvass the possibilities for that Canadian railroad between Red River and the Atlantic. But meantime, to insure Company control of Red River navigation, he made Norman Kittson, now in St. Paul, Hudson's Bay transportation and shipping agent and authorized him to build another steamboat.

Just twenty years after Smith first debarked in Montreal, a black-haired, black-eyed young man arrived in St. Paul one late July day with a bizarre idea as almost his sole capital. Born eighteen years before in the farming village of Rockwood, Ontario, James J. Hill was obsessed by the thought of great business conquests to be made in the Orient.

Where he acquired that idea is uncertain. After four years at the rural school, four more at diminutive Rockwood Academy, he had ended his education to clerk in the village store. On what he saved from his few dollars a week during the next four years, he started for the Atlantic Coast to earn the necessary money to invade the Far East. Like Donald Smith, he found no opportunity waiting.

He turned west—for Fort Garry, where, while visiting boys from Red River he had known at the academy, he would find some way to reach the Pacific. He got no farther than St. Paul. Weeks before the last Cart Train of the season had left for the north. But Major A. E. Hatch was there, waiting till the following spring to make the three months' journey to the Rockies. Hill could go that far with him.

To tide him over the winter, Hill became a clerk for one of the three packet lines on the Mississippi. At that time, rivalry among the lines was so rugged that no device which would steal business from the others was barred. He proved a star pupil.

When spring came round again, he had decided on India as his field of conquest, its Hoogly and Brahmaputra Rivers as the means.

He even knew the type of steamboat he would place on them and how much business he could hope to win. However, as he also became absorbed in local conquests of Minnesota, his departure was postponed indefinitely.

From oil paper in his manifold book, he cut, in 1857, the stencil for the bags in which the first flour was exported from the State, proudly rode the dray that carried them to a waiting steamer. Construction, in 1862, of ten miles of track between St. Paul and Minneapolis by the St. Paul and Pacific, Minnesota's first railroad, held, in his considered opinion, great portent for the Northwest.

But nothing equaled his interest and curiosity for the freight the Cart Trains brought down each summer from Red River Valley. Undeterred by the fact that Norman Kittson exercised a virtual monopoly over the forwarding of Red River Trade, Hill moved in to induce one free trader after another to deal through him.

By 1863, when Kittson was obliged to return to Canada for a season or two, he feared he'd have no business left when he came back. But also convinced of young Hill's honesty and sagacity, he asked him to handle his agency during his absence.

This windfall, plus other traffic business turned his way, encouraged Hill to open his own transportation and shipping agency. On the side, he built up a thriving contract business in wood, coal, and half a dozen other products.

Within a year he was enlarging his warehouse to handle all the freight the St. Paul and Pacific Railroad brought in on the two lines it was extending toward Red River Valley. And now Kittson, forced on his return to choose between representing Hudson's Bay or the free traders, decided in favor of the Company. Hill became agent for all the independent groups and individuals in the Valley:

I received their furs and skins and sold them; received their merchandise and other goods from England; filled their orders for American merchandise, machinery or anything else they wanted to buy and held them in St. Paul or forwarded them as desired.

Feeling his feet firm on a ripening bonanza, the twenty-eight-year-old entrepreneur solemnly set out to accumulate what at the time seemed a major share of the world's wealth—$100,000.

A year later he married Mary Theresa Mehegan and organized his first J. J. Hill Company. Two years more, and still unable to decide whether to specialize in wood, coal or transportation, he enlarged his firm to handle them all. But by 1869, he had decided to concentrate on transportation.

Forming a new J. J. Hill and Company, he left to his associates the accounts of Minneapolis' seventeen small flour mills and other clients. His own personal capital and energies were devoted exclusively to the "merchandising and transportation business in Red River Valley." To further it, he also continued to handle the freight of the St. Paul and Pacific Railroad.

Like other Paulistas, Hill had seen in the launching of the *S.S. Anson Northup* a powerful medium for more efficient handling of Red River Trade. But Hudson's Bay's purchase of the *S.S. International* killed every hope. Even though the St. Paul and Pacific's rails now substantially shortened the Cart Trains' long haul, his days were a nightmare of confusion and frustration.

For every Red River client who sent him a draft for $25,000 to cover bonded goods from England, scores sent him orders like the clergyman's which listed, "two cases of gin, one cask sugar, two tuning forks, one copy each of the works of Tennyson and Longfellow." He had to cope with the high duties and innumerable restrictions Hudson's Bay placed on American goods. With the shortness of the shipping season. The time and risks involved in using Red River Carts as transport. When Red River Rebellion burst into the turmoil, his driving, single-pointed nature could tolerate no more.

About him exasperated St. Paul merchants long had been assuring one another that someone really must go to Fort Garry to study the situation at first hand. But still convinced, after thirty-five years of profiting from Red River Trade, that the Valley from which it came was a barren waste, no one went. Eagerly, Hill volunteered.

Late in February, 1870, he started by stagecoach for Breckenridge. Time after time, he had to tumble out to help shovel a road through mountainous snowdrifts. Several nights when the stage failed to reach one of its primitive stations, he slept in snow. Finally, he bought a dog team and sledge. No better. Caught in a blizzard, he and the dogs wandered in circles for hours, only by chance found shelter in a sod hut.

En route north once more along now exposed ruts Cart Trains had cut in western Red River Valley's deep, black loam, his farm-bred imagination flamed with pictures of thousands of farmers cultivating that soil. Of the railroad that one day would bring them there, of the business they would give that railroad. His original estimates, never low, of the future of Red River Trade doubled and trebled.

But neither he nor his Red River clients could wait for the distant day of a railroad. What they needed was a steamboat *now!* He was thinking of this when out of the murk of another blizzard came Governor Smith and his party, thinking of it as his one good eye searched the governor's face.

He continued north with the conviction, later confirmed at Fort Garry, that neither governor nor Company would reopen Red River navigation or suffer American steamboats to invade waters they considered so integrally a part of their own domain.

Riding or trotting behind his dogs, he pondered measures by which a thirty-two-year-old David like himself could challenge a Goliath like Governor Smith, backed by the Company's two centuries of experience and unlimited capital. The comparison did not displease him.

Back in St. Paul, he found his slingshot in an American law not yet applied to Red River Carts and steamboats. Forthwith, he commissioned Captain Alexander Griggs of Mississippi River fame to construct for him a steamboat.

2. THE STEAMBOAT ASSISTS ITS OWN DOOM

Fort Garry—all Manitoba—rocked on its foundations that mid-April day in 1871 when the *S.S. Selkirk* steamed in. Lining its rails were 115 passengers. In its hold, 150 tons of freight. And on Captain Griggs's lips, some very bad news for Hudson's Bay Company.

According to American law, the captain declared, all goods crossing American territory to Canadian ports must travel by bonded carriers. The *S.S. Selkirk*, he was happy to add, was bonded.

"Hill must be a very able man," said Governor Smith. "We must not be caught napping."

Promptly, he had the *S.S. International* bonded, placed in general passenger and freight service. And Manitobans, to show their disapproval of Hill's coup, boycotted the *Selkirk*.

Ensuing competition between the two boats was, by proxy, a battle between Jim Hill and Donald Smith. Soon, each convinced he had met his match, they met again. The outcome was Hill's public announcement that he had sold the *Selkirk* to Hudson's Bay. But privately, he and the governor had formed a coalition known as the Red River Transportation Company.

In command, ostensibly as owner and manager, was "Commodore" Norman Kittson. With three new steamers—*Dakota, Alpha,* and *Sheyenne*—added to *International* and *Selkirk,* and twenty barges, he and his silent partners raised passenger and freight rates to such a peak that discontent ran riot on both sides of the Boundary.

Inevitably appeared a rival line—the Merchants International Steamboat Company, organized in 1874 by several Winnipeg merchants. When they found they could not operate in American waters, they took in some equally dissatisfied St. Paul merchant-partners and incorporated under American law. The following spring their S.S. *Manitoba* and S.S. *Minnesota* appeared on Red River of the North.

Kittson and company at once reduced their rates below the cost of handling. Through Kittson's influence with the U.S. Customs at Pembina, the *Manitoba* was detained there indefinitely. Released, it was rammed and sunk by the *International* and all its valuable cargo lost. Raised and repaired at heavy cost, it was seized in Winnipeg against a trifling debt owed by the Merchants Line. On the American side of the Boundary, the *Minnesota* suffered the same fate. At this point, the inexpert merchant-owners were glad to sell out.

To warn other rivals off Red River, Kittson bought the hull of a steamboat a new company was building, left it to rot where it lay. And started rumors that the U. S. Government was going to tax flatboats heavily. The mere threat was enough for those one-voyage carriers. Thereafter, only small boats and barges for local, noncompetitive uses were permitted to operate.

The public learned of Red River Transportation Company's sweeping victory when it blandly returned to its monopoly rates and fares. While its defeated competitors licked their wounds, Kittson and company shared an eighty per cent dividend.

During these years on Red River's gumbo shores were repeated the colorful sights and sounds that characterized every pioneer river in America. Because of the short, five-month season and the vagaries of the River, however, they were many degrees more robust.

"Steamboat round the bend!" turned out budding settlements en

masse to add their cheers and laughter to the general pandemonium
of snapping flags, whistles, bells, shouts of "Mark twain!," "Mark
three!," "No bottom!" With popping eyes they gazed at first-class
passengers bound for Fort Garry—braided officers and blue-coated
soldiers, frock-coated and wide-hatted gentlemen elegantly promen-
ading upper decks with ladies garbed in the latest fashions. Audibly
they commented on the Mennonite immigrants below, the men with
dark, impassive, bearded faces, the women starkly unadorned and
shawled.

Winnipeg citizens rushed to the waterfront, so avid to claim their
printing presses, church organs, shoes and oysters that special police
had to be on hand to make sure that distinguished passengers reached
shore alive. Even schools were dismissed that the small fry might
behold and remember what appeared to be vagrant houses trun-
dling by under the drive of furiously threshing mill wheels at their
back doors.

Captains and pilots, with virile ways and lingo all their own, were
the real celebrities of the River. And rightly so, for they coped with
everything from mosquitoes to Indians, cholera to childbirth, fire to
man overboard, and the eternal hunger of their engines for wood and
more wood.

At first steamers stopped five or six times a day or night for their
crews to fell trees and chop them into logs. Later, Indians took over
the supply. They had only to watch a boat or two scorn a pile of cot-
tonwood to snap up another of red cedar to paint thereafter the ends
of every log red.

Accidents, fires, and hunts along the shores for elk, mink, otter, and
waterfowl, left passengers few dull moments. In three years, nine
people fell or washed overboard to drown. If the *Manitoba* weren't
on fire or a man overboard, a new Canadian or American citizen was
being added to its passenger list. Early freezes frequently forced
boats to tie up for the winter wherever they were. Then Winnipeg
lived on short rations. For lack of newsprint, its *Free Press* was reduced to half-size. Christmas goods didn't arrive till spring.

Topping all difficulties was the River that, in the printable words
of one roustabout, resembled "a reluctant and homesick pig being
driven on a straight road to market." Again and again sternwheelers
steamed for hours round bend after bend only to find themselves but
a few rods farther north or south.

But all was not sweat and swearing. On nights of full moon excursions were vogue. Then, American, British, and French flags flying, decks embowered with poplar branches, firebuckets stuffed with wild roses, fiddles squeaking, mouth organs wheezing, the River boats welcomed old and young aboard for festive dancing. Day or night a steamboat race might set the River agog. To maintain steam, rival captains ordered lamps emptied of kerosene, salon furniture burned, and ignored bends, sand bars, and shippers' prayers to stop at scheduled landings.

If the steamboat did nothing during its 1859-62 incarnation to people and develop Red River Valley, it now brought scores of settlers to Northwest Minnesota, thousands to Manitoba. (Dakota's share still belonged to the Sioux.)

Why immigrants, traders, officials, preferred to cross 1,500 miles or more of American soil to reach Fort Garry posed no riddle. Though built and maintained at great cost by the Canadian Government, the 500-mile Dawson route through the Wilderness, with its seventeen changes from steamboats to wagons, to open rowboats, to steam tugs, to stagecoaches, to say nothing of hardship, exposure and delay, was more than mortal man and fragile freight could stand. By the American route, they had only to change at Fort William to steamers for Chicago or Detroit, change there to trains for St. Paul, transfer there to stagecoaches for Breckenridge, and there wait the unpredictable convenience of a sternwheeler and Red River to carry them north.

But to the sternwheelers Fort Garry owes its transformation into the City of Winnipeg and many a village its origin. The day the S. S. *Selkirk* first docked at the fort, Winnipeg was a collection of 241 people, sawmills, saloons, skunky-smelling trading posts, and gunny-sack-covered rain barrels, sprawled along a crooked mile of Red River Trail. Two years later, incorporated as the City of Winnipeg, it was tossing up hotels, stores, homes overnight. Within a decade, it was the metropolis of the Canadian Northwest, its 8,000 residents confident it would pass the 100,000 mark before the century ended. To foil that ambition, die-hard Red River pioneers concentrated north of Lower Fort Garry to build the rival city of Selkirk.

To Captain Griggs's desire to turn an honest penny while he waited for the S. S. *Selkirk* to be launched, Grand Forks, at the junction of Red and Red Lake Rivers, owes its founding. The captain undertook to freight a fleet of barges to Pembina at the same time another ambitious pioneer, George B. Winship, set out with two barges loaded with kegs of beer for the same destination.

Griggs's barges, following Winship's, picked up a keg washed overboard during the night. By the time they reached *Les Grandes Fourches*, his boatmen so thoroughly had sampled the rescued beer that they literally were in no condition to navigate. The captain ordered the flotilla tied up to shore. Morning found them frozen in for the winter. Unloading his freight, Griggs used barge lumber to build a shelter. Before it was completed, he had decided the junction had a future. There and then he "squatted" on land that within two years was a rough and tough frontier town.

With Red River Trade from the beginning of the 1870's averaging more than $10,000,000 a year, the business the scarred and clumsy sternwheelers did was enormous. Their first two trips usually paid the cost of the boat. Each month Pembina's Customs House rang up more than $50,000 in duties.

But coming events already were casting long, mortal shadows over the bows of Red River's steamboats. After 1872, their passengers and freight no longer arrived by stagecoach, wagon, or Red River Cart at Fisher's Landing or other accessible points on Red or Red Lake Rivers. The Northern Pacific Railroad, from Duluth, and the St. Paul and Pacific now brought them directly to the forks of the Red and Sheyenne or of the Red and Bois des Sioux Rivers.

Within three years, River and residents were witnessing a prolonged and melancholy sight as steamer after steamer, nested among barges, toiled north with rails, ties, and other paraphernalia of their own doom. In two seasons, the *S. S. Selkirk* carried enough rails to lay 160 miles of track. And in mid-October, 1878, she again rocked Winnipeg, all Manitoba.

But this time, though her flags flew bravely, her whistle bellowed and bells rang, no one had eyes or ears for her. Riding the flatboat she pushed ahead was the "Countess Dufferin," the first locomotive to enter the Canadian Northwest. Its own steam up, smoke plume streaming, whistle piping, the Countess chuffed ashore to hysterical tears and cheers.

Some weeks later, to even greater fanfare, the rails of a line from Winnipeg were joined with rails of the St. Paul and Pacific at the International Boundary. Though Red River navigation flourished for

eight years more before dwindling to painful extinction in the next
century, on that memorable December 2, it officially died.

The *S. S. Manitoba, Minnesota,* and other serviceable survivors, in
whole or in part, moved on to sail the waters of Assiniboine and Saskatchewan until they entered the oblivion of the *S. S. Anson
Northup.*

3. THE RAILROAD CROSSES THE RIVER

Far from preparing Red River Valley to live happily ever after, the
coming of the railroads was preceded, accompanied, and succeeded
by turmoil and intrigue. When the tumult and the shouting died, the
same old battle pattern stood revealed. Whatever its charter, each
railroad was there for one purpose only—to capture Red River Trade.

The tumult began in 1853 when Governor Ramsey in his farewell
address to the Minnesota Legislature first breathed the magic word,
railroad. Immediately, to test the powers of a Territory to bestow
land grants, several eager citizens applied to the Legislature for
railroad charters. They got five! Within four years, Minnesota had
chartered *twenty* lines, whose directors, not knowing which one Congress would approve, "all had their plates ready should it rain pudding."

Shortly five companies were operating ten to twenty miles of track.
Each line began abruptly, ended casually in virgin timber or prairie.
No matter. Even a handful of miles of laid track entitled a railroad
company to a land grant on which to found and exploit into fortunes
favored town sites, terminals and way stations. The 12,000,000 acres
and $3,000,000 in subsidies Minnesota railroad builders garnered
kept them so happily occupied that Red River Valley remained at the
mercy of Cart Trains and stagecoaches.

With the end of the Civil War came the dawn—and the big operators. Among the thousands upon thousands of Americans who
started west was Jay Cooke of New York, whose high pressure sales of
U. S. Bonds to finance Union armies had made him the leading banker
in America.

In and around Duluth he invested heavily in lands. But lands will
remain idle unless fed. Looking about for an appetizing and nourishing food, he spied Red River Trade. To tap it, he undertook to act as

banker for the Lake Superior and Mississippi Railroad between Duluth and St. Paul.

Duluth was now hell-bent to become a great port. Looking about also, it spied the Northern Pacific Railroad which, though chartered in 1864, had failed to extract from Congress either land grants or federal subsidies for its construction. On condition that the paper-bound railroad make Duluth its eastern terminal, the "Zenith City of the Unsalted Seas" extended various practical aids, including Jay Cooke to serve as its banker-promoter.

On Red River Trade Mr. Cooke and Northern Pacific backers looked as through one eye. "They also appreciated," says E. V. Smalley, historian of the Northern Pacific Railroad,

the value of the then entirely undeveloped Red River Valley as a region likely to furnish heavy traffic in the future, and rightly considered that rich agricultural region a natural tributary to the Northern Pacific enterprise.

Those are niggardly words to express the degree of Mr. Cooke's enthusiasm. Before he agreed to promote the Northern Pacific, he had studies made of the Valley's soil, precipitation, and other features. These proved it so lavishly endowed for agricultural purposes that he retitled it, "Nile Valley of North America." And on that slogan he based such spectacular and continuous advertising that the wearied public dubbed the railroad's entire right of way from Lake Superior to Pacific Ocean, "The Banana Belt."

Though its charter required the N. P. to run straight west, with nary a glance to right or left, Mr. Cooke and the railroad's directors made control of Red River Valley and its Trade their first concern. As one means to this end, they chose the junction of the Red and Sheyenne Rivers as the point where their rails would cross from Minnesota into Dakota.

Here the main flow of that $10,000,000 freight could be diverted to Duluth. And here, to tranship it from steamboat to train, two lucrative town sites were founded. On Red River's east bank, Moorehead, named for Mr. Cooke's partner; on the west, Fargo, named for the head of the Wells-Fargo Express Company.

As another, they set out to gain control of the St. Paul and Pacific Railroad. By virtue of descending from one of Minnesota's original twenty lines, the St. P. & P. owned a charter to build a main line from

St. Paul to Breckenridge, with a branch line down the entire length of Northwest Minnesota to Pembina. On paper, it thus was ideally designed to catch and carry Red River Trade from end to end of the Valley.

On paper! In the sale of St. P. & P. bonds to credulous burghers in Holland, its backers found an even more profitable trade. Since no Dutch investor saw fit to visit the Valley, they all remained innocent that the last stretch of the main line's iron rails rested loosely on level prairie and that the Pembina branch failed to come within leagues of the Boundary. Within a handful of years the Hollanders sank some $13,500,000 in St. Paul and Pacific bonds. By 1869, however, the railroad had become the laughingstock of American investors. Even the Dutch would invest no more in it.

But it still owned two priceless assets. An excellent terminal in St. Paul. And that right of way through Red River Valley. By 1872, Mr. Cooke and associates secretly had bought sufficient St. P. & P. securities to reduce the line to a helplessly dependent feeder for the Northern Pacific. By June 6 of that year, when the first N. P. train crossed Red River to follow the speeding rails west, they were exercising in Red River Valley south of the Boundary the same all-inclusive monopoly Hudson's Bay Company so long had wielded to the north.

Now that all was ready for Jay Cooke to bring in the sheaves, the chameleon Valley put its worst feet forward. That summer of 1872 was so hot and dry that by August the prairies were burned a dingy brown, the soil baked to granite. September prairie fires turned the brown to dingier black and everywhere uncovered bleaching buffalo bones.

In vain, J. B. Powers, land commissioner for the Northern Pacific, and Joseph Dilworth, one of the vice presidents, drove back and forth across it in search of just one good feature to support Mr. Cooke's fulsome advertising. Not a foot of it appeared either cultivatable or habitable. Said Mr. Dilworth to Mr. Powers, "Uncle Sam made a smart deal when he exchanged such worthless country for a continental railway."

During the next fourteen months, despite Herculean effort, Mr. Powers and his staff sold but a few small tracts on the Sheyenne River in Dakota and the town site of Detroit Lakes, Minnesota. Mercifully, on September 30, 1873, a telegram from the New York office of Jay Cooke and Company ended their agony:

EXPECT NO FURTHER HELP FROM THIS END. TAKE CARE OF YOURSELVES AS BEST YOU CAN.

Having sunk $30,000,000 in 600 miles of Northern Pacific Railroad, America's leading banking house had closed its doors. Panic swept the United States, Canada, Europe. The Northern Pacific went into bankruptcy. Beneath it in irreparable ruin, lay the St. Paul and Pacific.

Jay Cooke could have survived his heavy loans to the N. P. if he had not also extended money and credit with reckless optimism in every other direction. But was he held responsible for the panic? According to Wall Street's financial experts:

It was the general opinion in the east that the principal cause of the collapse was the worthlessness of the [Red River Valley] land offered as security for Northern Pacific loans.

Holders of Northern Pacific bonds and stocks took any loss to get out from under. Closing the Fargo Land Office, Mr. Powers retired into the N. P. Building in Brainerd, Minnesota, to engage in prolonged and pensive doodling. Like a final curtain closing on a very bad tragedy, the following summer such a cloud of grasshoppers fell on Red River Valley that all but the hardiest settlers rose up and departed.

In all the country only one eye saw a silver lining in the catastrophe. It belonged to the young man who since making that 1870 trip to Pembina had progressed from the idea of a railroad in western Red River Valley to a railroad owned and operated by James J. Hill. Now with both the Northern Pacific and St. Paul and Pacific in bankruptcy, he had two arrows for his bow.

His preference, of course, was the Northern Pacific. But when, to save themselves, its backers sacrificed their holdings in the St. Paul and Pacific, he lost interest. The St. P. & P. still owned that Red River Charter.

Into the patient ears of Norman Kittson who, though twenty years his senior, was by this time his close friend and confidant, he daily poured his arguments pro and con. The St. Paul and Pacific, though valued at $20,000,000, now was so low in repute that no one would invest a dime in it. Still—if anyone offered its Dutch bondholders twenty-five cents on the dollar, say, $5,540,180, he felt sure they'd

jump at it. Before 1873 ended, he was informing the half-incred-
ulous, wholly awed Mr. Kittson that he was going to buy it.

But Jim Hill possessed less than a fraction of five million dollars.
No man in the Northwest with sufficient means to be interested
would listen to any idea of replacing so complete a wreck on its
rusted iron feet. The situation, Mr. Hill confessed to Mr. Kittson, was
hopeless. Yes, agreed his confidant, it was.

Since 1870, Donald A. Smith had learned that the outlook for a
Canadian railroad to contain Red River Trade and immigration
north of the Boundary was even bleaker. His own efforts to interest
British capital "might as well have been spent on a line to the North
Pole." The Dawson Route was useless. And just when he had re-
signed himself to depend on the St. Paul and Pacific, that undepend-
able line folded up. In desperation, he too turned to the Company's
St. Paul transportation agent.

Joyfully Mr. Kittson brought together the two minds obsessed
with but a single thought. In tireless energy, realism, business
acumen and ruthless efficiency, Hill and Smith were carbon copies
of one another. Both were experts on transportation. Both knew to
a penny the current value of Red River Trade and foresaw its even
brighter future. But with Smith determined to send that Trade east,
Hill to bring it south, they argued for two years to no effect.

By 1876, however, the Northern Pacific was back on its feet and
in no mood to have its monopoly over Red River Valley challenged.
Though it had lost control of the St. Paul and Pacific, it managed by
threats of litigation to keep its former satellite's affairs so hopelessly
muddled that no sane investor would consider its purchase.

Nevertheless, during the previous year, the St. P. & P. receivership
had made a tidy profit and now was voicing ideas about taking over
all Red River Trade. And Eastern capital, coming out of hiding, was
turning alert eyes and ears on the Northwest.

Jim Hill lived in a constant stew of alarm and suspense. Now or
never was the time to buy the St. Paul and Pacific!

With but two meager prospects in sight, he set to work. Though
past sixty and broken in health, Norman Kittson promised to back
him with every dollar of his modest savings. Governor Smith was a
harder nut to crack, but finally weakened to the point of inviting
his cousin, George Stephen, to meet and appraise young Hill and
his ideas.

George Stephen was another energetic, resourceful and financially acute Scot with a Horatio Alger history. Born in Scotland forty-seven years before, as the son of a carpenter, he had attended parish school a few years, then worked as herdboy until apprenticed to a draper in Aberdeen. There a prosperous relative from Montreal had found him, brought him back to Canada. In due time, Stephen not only became the cousin's partner, but extended his own interests into high finance. Recently he had been made president of the Bank of Montreal.

The banker was sufficiently impressed with the soundness of Hill's ideas to offer to interest British capital in the purchase of the St. Paul and Pacific. Smith then joined Hill and Kittson. A few weeks later the toss of a coin added Stephen to the partnership.

Together the four Scots went to New York to place Hill's offer before another Scot, John S. Kennedy, the banker in charge of the bondholders' tangled finances. Sure it was this offer or none, Mr. Kennedy promised to persuade his Dutch clients to sell.

He did. Only to have the deflated quartet, unable to raise the necessary five millions, withdraw their offer. But five Scots, all obstinate as roots, cannot be deflated long. Soon they were placing another proposal before the Dutch investors. Would they accept what money the four partners themselves could raise and seven per cent interest on the remainder until clear title was obtained? If so, the partners would pay the entire amount within six months in gold bonds of their own railroad company.

Handily for the partners, Congress recently had ruled that railroads must fulfill their contracts within ten years or forfeit their land grants. With the St. Paul and Pacific's incompleted contracts due to expire within less than a year, it was now or never for the Dutch investors also. On condition that the partners pay $280,000 down, they agreed to sell.

The partners didn't have $280,000 in cash or anything like it. But now, the goal in sight, Hill and Kittson tossed into the pot everything they owned, even the deeds to their homes and other personal possessions. If the venture had failed, as Kittson confessed later, he and Hill would not have had a dollar between them.

It didn't fail. On March 13, 1878, the sale was signed and sealed. Followed what is known in the history of the Great Northern Railroad, of which the reorganized St. Paul and Pacific was the seed, as the Breathless Year.

The partners had shouldered a debt of more than $5,000,000. They

had less than nine months to rebuild the disjointed fragments of the
St. P. & P. into a going system. In addition, they had to combat the
aggressive opposition of the Northern Pacific, of the Canadian Government, and of the men who had laid that Winnipeg line to the
·Boundary.

But with Stephen arranging credit, Hill built and equipped a mile
of railroad for each working day. Just twenty-four hours before one
contract expired, their St. Paul, Minneapolis and Manitoba Railroad was completed.

Hill had not worked with the strength of ten merely to save land-
grants. While finishing the gigantic task, he had grown acutely
aware that this little Red River Valley line was a woolly lamb entirely surrounded by blandly smiling tigers.

With only a St. Paul terminal, it was from the first little more
than a feeder for older, more powerful lines with Chicago terminals
and Eastern connections. Worse still! With the Dominion Government projecting a railroad across northern Canada, it now was but
a matter of time until the bulk of Red River Trade would be traveling east on the continental Canadian carrier Smith so ardently
desired.

Such frustrations were pygmy before another. In Dakota's Red
River Valley great events were taking place—to the everlasting profit of the Northern Pacific. And he, James J. Hill, the man who first
had conceived a railroad through that virgin land, was bottled up
in the eastern Valley, completing a branch line through a region
still devastated and depopulated by a grasshopper plague!

4. BONANZA!

By courtesy of the one source from which by this time no one expected anything but trouble, great events *were* taking place in Dakota's Red River Valley. Red River soil had fulfilled every prediction
made for it since the days of Verendrye.

This, at what, in all reality, was a crucial hour! Crop failures in
Europe had created an imperative demand for American wheats.
Improvements in flour-manufacturing machinery had created, among
American millers, specifically, an imperative demand for hard wheats.

In August, 1874, from one of those little forty-acre tracts on the

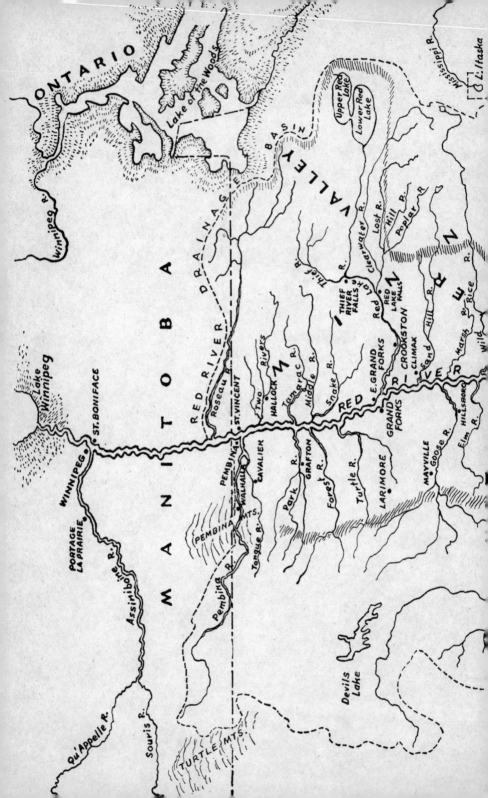

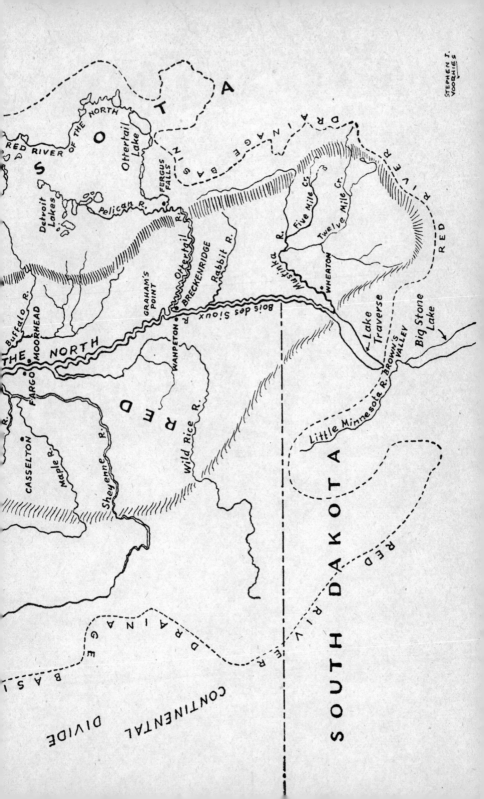

Sheyenne River that Mr. Powers and his staff had sold with such effort, a farmer drove into Fargo with 1,600 bushels of No. 1 Hard. It sold for the unprecedented price of $1.25 a bushel.

Forty bushels of No. 1 Hard from a single acre? Two thousand dollars from little more than a vegetable patch? Out came pencils. From 160 acres, that would mean $8,000; from 640, $32,000. Red River soil was more productive than California's gold fields!

As word of more and more such harvests flashed across the country, a tidal wave of inquiries broke over Mr. Power's desk in Brainerd. Everyone wanted to own a farm in Red River Valley. *To own a farm.* That was the rub. No one had the slightest intention of cultivating it himself.

But merely to transfer Northern Pacific lands into inactive private hands, as the land commissioner knew too well, would do the bankrupt railroad no good. What it needed was business, something to carry. If he had a few small farms, already broken and equipped, to sell, perhaps he could start the ball rolling.

Hurrying to New York, Mr. Powers tried to persuade some of the N.P.'s directors to advance the necessary funds. General George W. Cass, president of the Northern Pacific, and Benjamin F. Cheney, one of the directors, shook their heads. What the N.P. needed, said they, was capital on a grand scale. Well, then, why not equip a demonstration farm on a grand scale?

Mr. Powers returned to Red River Valley charged with finding for them eighteen sections—11,520 acres—of land and an able man to farm them. Near Casselton, an N.P. siding about fifty miles west of Fargo, he chose the land. And, in St. Paul, the man.

Some years before, Oliver Dalrymple, a onetime Pennsylvania farm boy, had arrived in Minnesota, armed with a Yale diploma, to practice law. There was almost no law to practice, but the demand for farm loans was incessant. Soon he had 2,500 defaulted acres on his hands. Planting them all to wheat, he had realized $40,000. From then on that diploma was one more scrap of paper. He had just sold another 3,000-acre farm and was looking about for a bigger and better location when Mr. Powers came upon him.

Before agreeing to take over the Cass-Cheney acreage, Mr. Dalrymple insisted on seeing the land. But in winter Northern Pacific trains didn't run west of Fargo, and it was then March. Nevertheless, by pumping a handcar that fifty miles and back and burrowing under

. deep snow, he did see the land and excavated a sample. Its analysis filled him with such enthusiasm for Red River soil that he became a partner of Cass and Cheney and increased the acreage to 13,440.

On the success, in 1876, of his first harvest from less than 2,000 acres, Red River Valley rode to international fame. So did the instantly coined phrase, Bonanza Farm, and Oliver Dalrymple as the world's first Bonanza Farmer.

Now the land that at forty to sixty cents an acre couldn't be given away leaped to five dollars, from then on rose steadily. Wheat raising in Wisconsin died a sudden death as more than 4,000 of its most experienced wheat growers departed for the Valley. From New York came 2,000. From Pennsylvania, Ohio, Michigan, Indiana, Illinois, Iowa, thousands more. From Minnesota alone, more than 7,000. Almost every State sent at least a small contingent. Together they poured millions of dollars into Northern Pacific Land Offices.

Among them were J. L. Grandin and his brother of Tidioute, Pennsylvania. Word of their ex-neighbor's exploit reminded them of the great block of Northern Pacific stock they had tossed as worthless into some vault. Exchanging it for ninety-nine sections of land along Red River north of Fargo, they established the second successful Bonanza.

By the time all lands within range of the N.P.'s right of way through the western Valley were taken up, Jim Hill had brought the St. Paul, Minneapolis and Manitoba across Red River at Grand Forks. Racing his rails north to the Boundary and so to Winnipeg, he opened up the Lower Valley and founded his own Bonanza on thirty-six square miles of Pembina County.

By 1879, the Great Dakota Boom was on. Within three years, immigrants in score after score of thousands had broken the prairies into a checkerboard of homesteads. Within a year, from their virgin fields, streams of No. 1 Hard were flowing into the rivers of wheat from the bonanzas to create a veritable Amazon of production:

	Population	Acreage	Wheat Production
Western RRV, 1879	27,828	81,896	1,629,755 bushels
Eastern RRV, 1880	21,123	103,363	1,692,180 "
Canadian RRV, 1883	65,954	209,674	4,549,093 "

In their turn, these millions of bushels of No. 1 Hard transformed Minneapolis into a grand-scale flour manufacturing center; Duluth, into a grand-scale Great Lakes terminal. More: this new and doubly valuable volume of Red River Trade already had become an important factor on the grain markets of the world.

But it was not the myriad small farms and homesteads that held universal attention. Dakota's "Valley of Two Thousand Bonanzas!" was the wonder of the world.

Farmers in the western Valley snorted scorn. True, there were 2,000 farms of more than 500 acres, several hundreds of them of more than 1,000. But the proud title of bonanza by their definition applied exclusively to less than 100 holdings whose boundaries embraced 3,000 to 50,000 and more acres.

Soon the names of several were household words. The Mosher, 19,000; Amenia and Sharon, 38,350; Antelope, 17,300; Clarke, 9,900; Spiritwood, 19,700; Steel and Troy, 10,000; Carrington and Casey, 35,700; Cooper, 34,000; Grandin, 61,250.

Writers and reporters from every State and almost every foreign country arrived with pencils hot to describe the phenomena of their one-crop, multiple-machine system. Their medical and nursing services. Private churches and ministers. Private racecourses and race-horses. The steamboats, each with its four-barge convoy, the Grandins built to carry their own wheat to their own elevator in Fargo.

Both as the pioneer and, when increased to 75,000 acres, the largest farm in the world, the Cass-Cheney-Dalrymple Bonanza naturally roused greatest curiosity and interest. With Yellowstone Park and Niagara Falls, it became a *must* on every globe trotter's American itinerary.

All manner of dignitaries, from the President of the United States, foreign diplomats, world-famous scientists, industrialists, artists, down to mere Northern Pacific vice presidents escorting investors and advance agents for large bodies of European immigrants, traveled those 1,500 miles west to see it. And daily the Northern Pacific sidetracked its de luxe transcontinental train that passengers might descend to "Oh!" and "Ah!"

One hundred and fifty gang plows moving down the fields were something to see. Or 150 self-binders, their white wings gleaming in the sun like a flock of gigantic seagulls in flight. Most impressive of all was the threshing in the fall when twelve extra-large steam outfits, attended by hundreds of men, horses, and wagons harvested enough wheat to fill two trains daily for Minneapolis, a steamboat every other day for Duluth.

Small wonder that with the eyes of all the world upon them bonanza farmers forgot that wheat failures overseas and improved flour machinery had set the high prices they received. Forgot that the invention of the John Deere Plow, the McCormick Reaper, and other modern farm equipment, and the advent of the railroad in Red River Valley coincided with their own arrival. Forgot the low prices they had paid for their hard-wheat-growing lands, the high prices asked for Eastern acres that could grow only soft varieties. Except to exploit it ruthlessly year after year, they forgot the very soil that produced those millions of bushels and millions of dollars.

Even to obtain sufficient seasonal labor for their remote fields caused them no headaches. From Minnesota and Wisconsin forests came hundreds of lumberjacks, free from early spring till late fall. From every Northern State young men flocked to the Valley to earn "college money." From towns and cities came hundreds more to earn the capital to go into small businesses of their own or to recoup losses suffered during the panic. And from Europe came the immigrants to work and save for their own Red River homesteads while they learned the language and ways of the country.

Among these industrious, ambitious, law-abiding laborers, the occasional exception, like Knut Hamsun, received short shrift. This soon-to-be-world-acclaimed Norwegian writer was so fascinated by the isolation, magnitude and beauty of the prairies that, happily riding his Dalrymple plow, singing like a meadowlark, he forgot the furrows corkscrewing off to right and left behind him to wreak havoc among the rest of the brigade.

Swift elimination of the inefficient was but one measure employed by the bonanza farmers to extract the utmost return from men and soil. Because they bought everything from tacks to threshing machines in quantity, they secured their equipment wholesale. To concentrate on No. 1 Hard, they indulged in no supplementary production, imported all foods, even butter and eggs. On the tremendous freight they shipped in and out of the Valley, they received huge rebates from the railroads.

Following the lead of Oliver Dalrymple, they evolved a combination of army organization and factory mass production. While Eastern farmers debated the wisdom of continuing to grow wheat that cost them one dollar a bushel, bonanza farmers by this combination system reduced their own production cost to *thirty cents!*

As their pride in their lands, methods and wealth accumulated, bonanza farmers placed managers in charge and left the Valley for greener social pastures. In Minneapolis and St. Paul, Chicago, New York, and other distant cities, they built luxurious homes and lived with all the display of the old North West partners during their palmiest days in Montreal. Their children, attending Eastern schools and colleges, going to Europe for the Grand Tour, sent French maids and other exotic "presents" back to relatives and friends in the Valley but lost all touch with it themselves. Every fall, however, when it was time to harvest the fields and the profits thereof, the feudal lords returned.

Traveling in state, again reminiscent of the Lords of the Lakes and Forests returning to Fort William, they arrived in their private railroad cars on their own railroad spurs, accompanied by retinues of guests, servants, and imported foods and liquors. Shortly, their riding and hunting parties were galloping at will over any field or garden that crossed their path. And scandalized whispers were whipping up and down Red River. Of dinners that cost from fifty to one hundred dollars a plate. Of unbelievable dissipation. Of gambling by night and horse racing by day, with fortunes in money or sections of land won or lost on the turn of a card or the nose of a horse.

From the small farmers about them, murmurs of discontent and uneasiness long had been rising. Now these amplified into howls of protest. Unable to buy their equipment wholesale or to obtain rebates from the railroads, they couldn't compete with the cheap, mass-production wheat of the bonanzas. And these absentee landlords, they complained, viewing the Valley as a bottomless reservoir of dollars to be squandered elsewhere, made no contribution to its schools, roads, churches, government. The bonanzas, in short, were a menace.

Eastern States, dismayed to find that the wheat-growing center of the United States had shifted to this obscure Valley, heartily concurred. Magazines like the *Atlantic Monthly* solemnly warned that, if not curbed, the bonanzas would destroy American agriculture. To discourage more Eastern farmers, capital and labor from moving Valleyward, Eastern newspapers employed nth degree adjectives to picture Red River as a plague spot of floods, blizzards, and first-cousin catastrophes.

Springing to arms, Red River editors rearranged the adjectives into what was known as a "Western Roarback":

Snow one hundred feet deep. . . .There will be no more immigration to Dakota. Railroads will take up all tracks west of Chicago. Everybody, including oldest inhabitant, dead. Wind tearing up great crusts of earth, terrible, horrible, terrific, awe-inspiring. . . .Grim death hovers over all the land.

The forests that supplied the newsprint for all this might well have remained standing. The bonanzas' own success was bringing on their decline. To compete with them, the small farmers, forced to improve their own methods, began to make substantial profits. And the fabulous legend of the bonanzas, exploited and re-exploited in America and Europe, induced such a stampede to the Valley that land values rose sixty- and seventyfold.

Red River millionaires now found it more profitable to incorporate as land companies to divide and sell their acres as small farms. Falling wheat prices after 1886 and the beginning of a three-year drought in 1877 accelerated the movement. Though some bonanzas continued to operate into the twentieth century, by 1890 their sun was sinking.[1]

During their brief and florid existence, they had done much more than make a few men rich. They had made Red River Valley known throughout the world and brought more than 200,000 Americans, Canadians and Europeans west to people it. Once more they had demonstrated that outsize farming is economically and politically unsound. (A lesson one day soon to be relearned as the Valley's current potato kings, increasing their holdings, production, and wealth, embark on the familiar cycle.) They had vindicated forever the prowess of Red River soil. And they had stimulated immigration to push on west to open up the great plains and, in time, to add eight more States to the Union. If one must speak only good of the dead, that can be said.

Using the bonanzas as bait, the Northern Pacific and the St. Paul, Minneapolis and Manitoba Railroads had advertised the Valley too well. Like the proverbial mustard seed, that pinch of 1880 figures, within a decade, had swollen to:

	Population	Acreage	Wheat Production
Western RRV, 1890	89,859	1,676,858	('91) 37,883,156 bush.
Eastern RRV, 1890	71,190	600,000	('90) 8,000,000 "
Canadian RRV, 1891	150,000	916,664	(91) 23,191,599 "

Yet this production represented but twenty-five per cent of the Valley's arable land. Optimists estimated that in wheat alone, the

[1] A few, like the Larimore and Dalrymple estates, still operate, some of them increased in area, as Bonanza holdings.

Valley, when fully opened, could yield 200,000,000 bushels. With Dakota's share accounting for more than half the total production, it was, indeed, as the railroads proclaimed, the Breadbasket of the World.

For Jim Hill and the St. Paul, Minneapolis and Manitoba Railroad, it was a basket of continuously renewed gold. Early in the 1880's, he had maneuvered the Northern Pacific into an agreement to keep out. Now while that shortsighted line had but two main right of ways running east and west across it, his four north-and-south lines, plus one east and west, all with ever-spreading branches, annually harvested the victor's share of freight and immigration.

But now rivals rushed in. By 1882, a dozen railroads had paper plans to make Grand Forks a terminal. That dream faded, but some did materialize elsewhere in the Valley. Like the Soo, which crossed it from northwest to southeast. Like the Milwaukee and Northwestern, which sent up branches from southern Dakota. Like the Canadian Pacific which, during the infancy of the bonanzas, was born of Red River Trade, old and new.

5. "DUE WEST FROM RED RIVER . . ."

For lack of a transcontinental railroad, the three widely separated segments of the Dominion of Canada by 1880 appeared on the verge of disintegration, if not annexation by the United States. Maritime Provinces were dotted with "secession societies." Manitoba and North West Territory were rife with threats of secession. British Columbia had made a Canadian Pacific railroad the condition on which it would join the Dominion. Tired of waiting, it had passed resolutions to secede.

Failure to provide that railroad had tossed first the Conservative, then the Liberal, Government out of Ottawa. Now back in power, Prime Minister Sir John Macdonald and his Conservative Party knew that unless they built that road their political number was up.

Yet even granting that the implacable opposition of England, the Maritime Provinces, Grand Trunk Railway, other interests and conditions could be overcome, remained two obstacles that were unconquerable. The physical barriers imposed by Rocky Mountains and the Wilderness. The titanic task of peopling such terrain to support a railroad.

The Prime Minister had reached but two conclusions. The railroad route through northern Canada on which the Liberal Government already had spent $30,000,000 must be scrapped in favor of a southern route through Manitoba. Private capital must build the road.

But private capital needed only one glance at the problem to run for its life. And the Canadian Parliament was irrevocably opposed to placing in private hands either the responsibility or power a transcontinental railway would bestow.

Parliament suddenly changed its irrevocable mind when Sir Charles Tupper rose in the House to summarize "the marked and wonderful success . . . of the syndicate that had purchased the St. Paul and Pacific Railroad." Another legislator reminded the Prime Minister that of the four members of the syndicate, Governor Smith and George Stephen were Canadian citizens, Jim Hill and Norman Kittson Canadian-born Americans. "Why not get some of those millions," he suggested, "before they invest them elsewhere?"

Resulted an invitation to the syndicate to submit its terms for building a Canadian Pacific Railroad. Though influenced to accept because they all were Canadian by birth or adoption, the partners managed to control their emotion before it blinded them to the fact that the Dominion's need was so urgent it was in no position to quibble. Their terms were stiff:

A cash subsidy of $25,000,000, plus important loan guarantees. A land grant of 25,000,000 acres. A twenty-year exemption from taxation. A twenty-year monopoly over the 100-mile-wide territory between the Canadian Pacific's new southern right of way and the International Boundary. An assortment of free gifts that totaled millions more, including the $30,000,000 worth of rails and equipment sprawled over northern Canada.

The moment the terms were announced, the Liberal Party hit the ceiling. Nevertheless, they were accepted. In February, 1881, a new syndicate of four partners agreed to build a 2,905-mile railroad across southern Canada by 1891.

Only three members of the new syndicate—George Stephen, James J. Hill, and R. B. Angus—signed the agreement. From the seed of that long unpaid loan Governor Smith had advanced at Sir John Macdonald's request to induce Louis Riel and Lepine to leave Canada, a bitter political enmity had grown between the two men. Though throughout the construction of the Canadian Pacific, Donald A. Smith was the power behind pickax and piledriver, his signature was omitted.

While Stephen handled the financing and Smith raised funds, Jim Hill chose and surveyed the new route and handled its construction. In the mutual interest of both the CPR and of the St. Paul, Minneapolis and Manitoba (which hauled mountains of equipment across the Boundary), he established his headquarters at Winnipeg, began work on the line to British Columbia first.

Opposition rode again. The syndicate intended to make the CPR the tail for its own Red River Valley kite! Any day now its headquarters would be transferred to St. Paul! Thoughtful Canadians and Americans feared that with three of the same men building parallel lines under two different flags, the end result would be monopoly. Within a few years their agitation culminated in the U. S. Interstate Commerce Act.

Hill, Smith and Stephen also began to suffer misgivings. One day the two railroads inevitably must become competitors. When that day broke, joint control would be impossible. Accordingly, in May, 1883, Hill resigned from the CPR board of directors and from directing its construction. Two months later, Smith and Stephen resigned as directors of the St. Paul, Minneapolis and Manitoba.

To succeed himself, Hill recommended another American of similar energy and resourcefulness. William Cornelius Van Horne and the reorganized CPR syndicate worked together so successfully that five years before the scheduled 1891, Canada had its transcontinental railroad. Not, however, without encountering transcendental difficulties in which Red River Valley and its people continued to play leading parts.

In fact, from the moment the new CPR route was made public, Manitoba was in there fighting. The original plan called for the right of way to cross Red River at Selkirk. Delirious Selkirkers first celebrated the coming demise of Winnipeg, then mapped out an ambitious program calculated to extract the last dollar from every blessing their railroad terminal could confer. Winnipeggers settled down to some ominously quiet finagling.

Neither town had a bridge across Red River. Winnipeg immediately projected one. This it spread, like a veritable Sir Walter Raleigh's cloak, before the CPR's unreluctant feet. In addition, it guaranteed, "in perpetuity," tax-free exemptions within the city limits.

Thus it was that Winnipeg became central Canada's transportation, industrial, and distribution capital; Selkirk, the quiet little fishing and farming village, they are today.

CPR's conquest of the Canadian Rockies was arduous and costly enough. Even more so was that of the Wilderness, where an army of men attacking rock, muskeg, hill, hollow, lake and river, laid line after line only to see it sink from sight. In one muskeg area, seven layers of railroad and two locomotives are buried, one above the other. One specific mile cost $700,000. Several cost $500,000.

As loan after loan was needed to finance such construction, the Canadian Parliament's resistance hardened. So did the antagonism of the Maritime Provinces as Grand Trunk, Northern Pacific and other competing railways fed them propaganda on the waste and stupidity of building a railroad through a region icebound for six months of every year, uninhabitable for twelve.

But nothing now could discourage the "little man from Winnipeg." Though to guarantee one loan, Governor Smith (with Stephen, Van Horne, and others) pledged his possessions down to household linens and cuff links, he succeeded in keeping the rails moving. Until 1885. Then with but $35,000,000 needed to finish that 2,905-mile undertaking, Parliament refused to disgorge one more penny.

Another little man from Red River Valley completed the Canadian Pacific Railway. Recalled from the United States to lead another "rebellion," Louis Riel brought Canada face to face with civil war. Only one thing could prevent it—immediate arrival of troops. Although the CPR line to the east was incomplete, with one gap of ninety miles, it transported 4,000 troops to Manitoba and North West Territory within four days. The rebellion was crushed. So was all further opposition to loans or anything else the CPR wanted.

On June 29, 1886, the first transcontinental train left Montreal for British Columbia, and Donald A. Smith was able to say of his own brain child:

This great national work has consolidated the Union of the Dominion . . . . It has given outlets on the Atlantic and Pacific and has provided an imperial highway from the United Kingdom to Australasia and China and Japan.

He didn't remain Donald A. Smith long. For his part in the achievement that in Canadian history ranks second only to the Confederation of the Four Provinces, he became Lord Strathcona and Mount Royal.

Red River Valley, however, is no respecter of titles. From the first, postage-stamp Manitoba had refused to be bound by that twenty-year monopoly clause in the CPR contract. Now, taking advantage of a clause in her own constitution, she chartered line after line of competing railways. Each time Canada exercised its superior rights to disallow them. Mad to the roots of her prairie grass, Manitoba set about building her own railroad—the Northern Pacific and Manitoba —to the Boundary.

As her mass meetings stirred up the Canadian Northwest, the midget Province's cold war against continental Canada grew exceedingly hot. And this time Ottawa could not place responsibility on "*Métis*, Indians, nondescript white men and Americans." By October 20, 1888, the day the Northern Pacific and Manitoba tracks were scheduled to cross the CPR's right of way, "Fighting Joe" Martin, attorney general for Manitoba, numbered the Provincial Cabinet, the Mayor of Winnipeg, and other influential citizens among the 300 warriors under his command.

The CPR also was prepared. Its "Fort Whyte," named for the superintendent of construction, was a locomotive stalled on the right of way at the point where the rebel rails would cross. Beside the "Fort," two more locomotives, fires up, long hose attached, and hundreds of "constables" waited to throw live steam and scalding water on the embattled Manitobans.

Only the inability of the tracklayers to reach the battlefield before darkness fell averted actual conflict. But each day for two weeks more, while awaiting a decision from Ottawa, the two forces faced each other. The Conservative Government, already tottering to another fall over this and other Manitoban challenges, did nothing. At last, the exasperated CPR sought an injunction against the upstart railway. The courts refused to grant it. Northern Pacific and Manitoba tracks went through.

Heady with triumph, the Red River Province now burned with the same fever that Territorial Minnesota had suffered. Within a dozen years more than a dozen railroads were conceived and cradled in Winnipeg. Some remained merely paper projects. Several material-

ized to endure a sad existence until gathered to the capacious bosom
of the CPR. Those that lingered beyond the turn of the century were
swallowed alive when the Canadian National Railways arrived to
make Winnipeg its terminal and add one more transcontinental line
to the swarm now feasting on Red River Valley honey.

No three sons of the same mother ever were more unlike than
this trio of railroads Red River Valley had nurtured. Having learned
little from its first failure, the Northern Pacific, again the dashing
prodigal, was rocketing west to waste its substance on constructing or
acquiring small lines that had to be operated at a loss. Though still
a mere skeleton, the CPR moved steadily east and west, confident that
because of the tremendous political responsibility it carried, the
Dominion would insure its future. The St. Paul, Minneapolis and
Manitoba remained on the prairies where it was born, but it no longer
bore the faintest resemblance to a little woolly lamb.

While directing construction of the Canadian Pacific, Jim Hill had
matured his own dream of developing the St. Paul, M. & M. into a continental railroad. To this end as soon as he was free from further responsibility for the CPR, he concentrated on Red River Valley. During the next three years, he webbed it with threads of gleaming steel.
And to people every mile of that web, he brought in from eastern
America and northern Europe thousands of farmer-converts to his
gospel of intensive farming.

(Here it should be said that it was the Empire Builder's success in
well-watered, fecund Red River Valley that later deluded him into
leading tens of thousands of credulous immigrants to tragic disaster
on the high, dry plains west of the Missouri River. But that sad chapter in the development of the American Northwest happily is beyond
the range of this book.)

By 1886, the torrent of wheat and other products pouring out of Red
River Valley, plus the torrents of flour and lumber rolling out of
Minneapolis' mills, woke Eastern capital to the magnitude of the trade
on this Northwest frontier. Already three Eastern railroads had extended trunk lines from Chicago to St. Paul. Now these and other lines
sought to cross the Mississippi into Minneapolis. There was only one
way to do it. Over the stone bridge and tracks of the St. Paul, Minneapolis and Manitoba Railroad.

To a subsidiary of the Chicago, Burlington and Quincy Railroad,

Mr. Hill was pleased to extend the courtesy of his facilities. Having accepted, the Eastern line could do no less than reciprocate. Presto! The St. Paul, M. & M. had a right of way into Chicago and, via this terminal, to the East Coast.

Next, he laid his rails to the very doorstep of the Northern Pacific's home grounds at the head of Lake Superior. Before 1888, with his own elevators, docks, and Northern Steamship Company, he had provided his transcontinental-railroad-to-be with an unobstructed Great Lakes route to the Atlantic.

All might have been well if the Northern Pacific had accepted with Christian meekness these inroads on its domain. Instead, it competed so strenuously, both with the St. Paul, M. & M. and with the CPR, that in 1889 Mr. Hill was compelled to write Mr. Stephen:

The more I think of it, the more I am convinced that the thing for us to do is to. . .get control of the Northern Pacific.

Accordingly, just eleven years after its harrowed birth, with a paltry $15,000,000 capital, the St. Paul, Minneapolis and Manitoba was reborn as the Great Northern Railroad, with a capitalization of $105,735,000. Now, riding comfortably on its profits from Red River Valley, it started west.

In January, 1893, it reached the Pacific. Eight months later, the Northern Pacific again was bankrupt. But *this* time, Wall Street experts—and Siemens, representative of the N.P.'s German stockholders—found it had collapsed because

it had neglected to cover Red River Valley where the Great Northern by a constant extension of its system clearly had demonstrated how much was to be gained in this rich wheat district.

And the Interstate Commerce Commission, reporting as of June, 1894, that no less than 192 railroads were in the hands of receivers, seconded the motion. The Great Northern, whose "most important territory is the wheat district of Red River Valley," was not among those present in the bankrupts' corner.

Mr. Hill himself led the Valley downstage to take a deep bow when he wrote his banker, Mr. J. P. Morgan:

Now we have them all—Northern Pacific, Union Pacific, and other competitors—in bankruptcy for more than a year, while. . .we have not only met their competition but that of the Soo and Canadian Pacific. In addition, we have met the worst conditions of business and still hold our own.

The Empire Builder and Mr. Morgan forthwith completed plans for a merger by which the Great Northern would absorb the Northern Pacific in a mighty traffic monopoly over the whole American Northwest. But the American public would have none of it. Its howls of "Octopus!" and similar epithets for Mr. Hill, in fact, almost put the N. P. out of business permanently. Wiser heads knew that unless he were given a voice, the Northern Pacific never could regain its feet. By a compromise, Mr. Hill and his friends were allowed a substantial though not a controlling interest.

Before the fiftieth anniversary of his arrival in St. Paul came round, James J. Hill, with terminals and steamships on the Pacific, had realized his boyhood dream of conquest in the Far East. And in time, all three of Red River's transcontinental railroads had realized for Verendrye, Duluth, Mackenzie and all the rest of America's pioneer Western explorers their common dream of reaching—and crossing—the Western Sea by a route due west from Red River.

PART VIII

The Great Migrations

1. THE PIONEERS

During the nineteenth century, some 30,000,000 Europeans abandoned the Old World for North and South America, Australasia, South Africa. More than two-thirds of them headed straight across the Atlantic for Canada and the United States.

As one of the largest mass and class movements of all time, the exodus largely was composed of peasant farmers who'd wrested a precarious living from less than five dearly bought or rented acres. Of laborers who, depending on their skill and native land, had earned from ten to seventy dollars (*sic*) a year. Of young men faced with the prospect of three to five years' compulsory military service. Of men, women, and children, whose lives from birth to death were organized and dictated by their own State and Church or those of their conquerors.

By the mid-1850's, the first waves had occupied all available space on the Canadian and American seaboard. Quickly to lure the migrant hordes to newly opened regions further west, Dominion and United States Governments, immigration bureaus, land companies, railroad and steamship lines, combined to chorus, "Free Land! Free Land!" To the soil-starved Europeans it was a siren song.

Between eastern Canada and Red River of the North, however, the Wilderness, plus 165 miles of open prairie unblessed by steamboat or railroad and jealously guarded by Hudson's Bay Company, barred passage to Manitoba and beyond. But nothing obstructed passage across the United States.

Turning south, the Canadian migration joined the American to flow and settle over North Central States until the Civil War called a temporary halt. Peace restored, and their numbers augmented by restive Canadians, Americans, and sons of established immigrants in quest of land of their own, thousands upon thousands moved west once more.

Into Chicago, if they came by water, into Milwaukee, if they came by train, flowed this hopeful, travel-weary river of humanity. Wearing every style of native garb. Speaking every tongue. Eating all manner of sausage, bread, pickles and cheese while they sagged among their

221

iron-banded trunks, gaudily painted wooden chests, and shapeless
bundles.

Group by group, they were sorted into freight cars, coaches, wagons, for their final destination in Wisconsin, Iowa, southern Minnesota or Dakota Territory. The occasional rugged handful that claimed
Fort Garry as its goal was ticketed for St. Paul and consigned to the
hands of God.

But after 1871, when the *S. S. Selkirk* reopened navigation on Red
River, each summer found from 2,000 to 6,000 Manitoba-bound immigrants added to the melees. Canadians, chiefly from Ontario.
Scotch, Irish, and English refugees from the aftereffects of the agricultural and industrial revolutions. Clutching their clocks, candlesticks,
teabaskets, and pride about them, they eyed askance their "foreign"
fellow passengers:

Small groups of Scandinavians, plus a rare Russian or Pole, all set to
conquer the prairies with scythe and spinning wheel, accordion or vio-
lin. A few Yankees, surrounded by featherbeds, saddles, Dearborn
wagons and, inevitably, some sort of small machine. Large clots of
German Mennonites, among them few with more than Peter Penner,
whose wife, child, and two dollars and fifty cents comprised all his
worldly wealth when he reached Red River.

After a century of practicing their life of renunciation under the
protection of Czarist Russia, these one hundred per cent pacifists had
been confronted with a new edict that required every male to fight in
the imperial army or navy. Migrating to western Red River Valley,
just north of the Boundary, they thought to be forever protected from
wars, all earthly distractions. Alas, never having known prosperity,
they failed, in undeveloped Manitoba of the 1870's, to recognize the
symbols of its coming![1]

Whatever their nationality and philosophy, in Canadian Red River

[1] Within seventy-five years, some 130,000 Mennonites were spread from
Manitoba and northern counties of Dakota's Red River Valley all over the
Northwest. Not only were they prosperous. Their faith was in danger of disintegration. Their younger generations, educated in public schools, were marry-
ing outside the church, leaving Mennonite communal villages for towns and
cities. There they engaged in worldly businesses and professions, even the
specifically forbidden field of the law, took pride and pleasure in modern homes,
dress, automobiles, radios, motion pictures and other vain devices. Orthodox be-
lievers saw but one hope of salvation. In the summer of 1948, more than one
thousand of the faithful, including a few pioneer members, now grandparents,
of Manitoba's original colonies, migrated to an isolated section of Paraguay to
begin all over again.

Valley the European newcomers either merged with or were sub-
merged under the Scotch, Irish, and French-Canadian basic stocks to
evolve the telephone books of today, paged with Macdonalds and Mc-
Donalds, McKays and Mackays, McKenzies and Mackenzies; with Le
Blancs, Desjardins, and De Gagnes.

But south of the Boundary, there were as yet no basic stocks. With
Minnesota and Dakota Territory exclusively concerned to develop
their southern halves, the two to three hundred settlers in Northwest
Minnesota, the less than one hundred squatters along Red River's
western bank were there without benefit of record and at their own
risk. It was the pioneers arriving during the decade of the 1870's
who sketched the first racial patterns of the American Valley.

By 1852, seven of the emigration that before the century ended
would place more than a million Norwegians on farms in the northern
states, had reached St. Paul. Fifteen years later, their countrymen,
having overflowed southern and eastern Minnesota, were spilling over
into Iowa and Nebraska. Filled with tales of the perils and hardships
of Red River Valley, into Northwest Minnesota they refused to go.

Unwilling to lose such hardy, industrious settlers to rival States,
Minnesota's Immigration Bureau in 1869 commissioned Paul Hjelm
Hansen to search the eastern Valley from end to end for any possible
habitable areas. Before he even reached Red River, Hansen was a convert to the now familiar gospel:

God gave to the people of Moses the fertile Valley of Canaan. To
us sons of Norway, He has given the greater, more fertile Valley of Red
River of the North.

Hansen's conversion came at an opportune moment. In Norway, a
collapsed land boom had dispossessed small farmers and merchants of
all they owned. And along the western coast small fishermen-farmers
had waked one morning to find that the herring had caught the migrating spirit, too, and departed to return no more. To them all, Hansen's call for Norwegians to occupy Red River Valley came as an
answer to prayer. By 1871, the first small bands were crossing Red
River to take up land along the Northern Pacific's proposed right of
way.

In midsummer of that same year, two footsore Bohemians—Albert
Chezik and Mathew Lorenz—having walked almost the entire dis-

tance from the Mississippi, arrived at the junction of the Red and Bois des Sioux Rivers. Finding work with a farmer on the east bank, they used every free hour to scout surrounding territory.

On the west bank, but one white man was living in a dugout.[2] A glance at the soil he had broken for his small gardens, and they staked out claims near by. Before snow flew, the stranded Bohemian colony they had left in St. Paul was putting down stakes around them, never to return to their Austria-ridden homeland.

Since pre-Revolutionary times, Swedes had been living in America, but it was not until 1840 that the emigration which was to cost Sweden one-fifth of her population got under way. Then, skeptical of the laudatory descriptions in Stockholm's newspapers of life in these United States, several young adventurers started out to see for themselves.

All wrote such glowing letters home that relatives, friends and friends of friends soon were America-bound. But one, Peter Cassel, outdid Marco Polo. And when, in 1845, he discovered Iowa, he outdid himself. Via ever-widening repetition, fragments of his bulging-eyed epistles reached the ears of a beggar girl in Kisa on the eve of her departure to ply her trade in the rural districts. As she went, she cannily improved what she'd heard. Who would turn empty-handed from their doors the bearer of such tidings as:

In America, the hogs eat their fill of raisins and dates that everywhere grow wild and when they are thirsty, they drink from ditches flowing with wine.

"Surely it is better," deduced her listeners, "to be a hog in America than a human being in Sweden." Like migratory blackbirds, they began to gather on sailing days in the seaports.

From the farms the fever swept into towns and cities. "Why wear ourselves to catmeat for a pittance," said the small merchants, "when the United States is a land where gold is cut off with a caseknife?"

By 1852, Swedes were settling in Minnesota, spreading across it as fast as new lands were opened. In 1872, they too followed the Northern Pacific through Northwest Minnesota into western Red River Valley.

The panic of 1873 stopped immigration for four years. If an iron

[2] Dugout: a cellar-like excavation, roofed with branches and sod. Habitable, even comfortable, if occupied after frost hardened the ground in the fall, vacated before the spring thaws.

curtain had dropped from the sky to Red River, the Norse, Bohemians and Swedes west of it could have been no more isolated.

Yet, despite huddling in dugouts or in tiny soddies whose two-foot-thick walls had to be hewn sod by sod from the surface soil, on prairies that can reduce a square mile of trees to the dimensions of a scatter rug . . . sleeping on icy, packed earth floors . . . using tree stumps for chairs and tables, tightly twisted bunches of prairie grass for fuel . . . living on potatoes and turnips, infrequently varied with antelope or wildfowl . . . enduring cold and storms in winter, prairie fires and threat of fires in summer. . . .

Despite breaking virgin soil with implements hand-made, like their crude carts, from trees . . . cutting hay and grain with scythes, gathering and stacking it with wooden rakes . . . threshing it with flails . . . cleaning it of weed seeds with stiff and aching fingers . . . pounding it into a passable flour or hauling it thirty to fifty miles to be ground. . . .

Despite all this and the cruel loneliness and remoteness, they survived. Bohemians hauled freight from Georgetown to Fort Garry. To the aid of Norwegian and Swede came the uncounted tons of buffalo bones covering the prairies. Bones of earliest herds had enriched the Valley soil; now, tiring Eastern acres needed that same nourishment. From ten dollars a ton, the price leaped to twenty. To this last service of the vanished bison many a pioneer owed his existence.

Even before survival was assured, these pioneers took pen in hand to exhort the folks at home to make this Promised Land a New Norway, Sweden or Bohemia:

God by His Grace has brought us away from both material and spiritual slavery. . . . In like manner did He bid you receive the same grace and goodness, yet ye did not heed His Voice. What will the Lord render to you now? He will allow you to be deprived of all this during your entire lives and in future to repent bitterly for your negligence. We have the word of prophecy. . . .

Bonanza farmers were not the only ones to rush into Red River Valley on the heels of headlines that blazoned word of Oliver Dalrymple's first harvest in 1876. Hundreds of Eastern business and professional men, ruined by the depression, set up shops and services in villages along Red River. Disillusioned goldseekers, having failed to extract a quick fortune from the Black Hills of South Dakota, arrived to find a slower but sure one waiting for them in the Valley.

Discovered by the Norse in 874 and peopled by them, Iceland shared the history of its mother country, including more than three centuries under Danish rule, until 1814. But when Norway gained her independence to join Sweden, little Iceland was left behind. The combination of fierce Arctic winters and harsh trade monopoly Denmark imposed soon brought the mass of landless peasants to the brink of starvation. Some years many did die of hunger. But less than half a dozen had sought the American mainland when in 1871 four young rebels discovered Wisconsin.

Hundreds immediately followed. Another 365, also Wisconsin-bound, were persuaded to remain in eastern Canada. Unhappy there without a waterfront of their own, they moved to the western shore of Lake Winnipeg to found, in 1875, the "Republic" of New Iceland, as parent colony for the thousands of their countrymen who later spread all over the Northwest. While erecting Gimli, first of their long, narrow villages, they sent a call to the Wisconsin colony for a Lutheran minister.

Arriving a year later by way of Red River of the North, the Reverend Paul Thorlaksson found his flock in the depths of despair. To poverty of funds, equipment and experience to clear and cultivate their timber-covered lands, a death-dealing smallpox epidemic had been added. Now, to survive the winter, the proud Icelanders had been compelled to accept charity in the form of a federal subsidy.

As they listened to Thorlaksson describe what he had seen of Red River Valley, many colonists wanted to leave at once. In the spring of 1878, about half of them did follow him south to the fertile prairies west of Pembina. There prairie fires destroyed their first small buildings and when the young minister borrowed $400 to obtain supplies, fires destroyed them, too. Ridden with pity and responsibility for his desperate people, Thorlaksson plunged deeper into debt to carry them through the winter.

That ordeal behind them, the rest was steady if heavy sailing. Leaving the women to cultivate the fields, the men walked 100 miles south to earn on Bonanza Farms the money to pay off Thorlaksson's loans and to start them all on the road to a prosperity that exceeded their wildest expectations.

That winter of 1878, Christen Westergaard, Danish publisher of a small, radical newspaper in Illinois, received a fan letter from Fargo.

Having read with regret, wrote his subscriber, that for lack of support, *Light of Day*, was to be extinguished, he would be glad to advance a loan for traveling expenses if Mr. Westergaard would consider moving to Red River Valley. Mr. Westergaard would. By mid-June, he, his brother, and a third Dane they had met en route, were putting down stakes on Maple River southwest of Fargo.

Hardly had they arrived when small Danish farmers and artisans began to trickle in from the Old Country. Most of them came from Jutland and Schleswig, where land was so scarce a peasant could not buy so much as an acre, living so high that wages of fourteen to sixty dollars a year served as a one-way ticket to starvation, and the disintegration of families while the men served long years in the army was too painful to think about.

What with high wages and free land, another battle for Red River Valley now broke out. Norwegians and Swedes not only exhorted by letter their respective countrymen in Europe and America to make haste to this Promised Land. They met steamships in Quebec and New York to proselytize among incoming immigrants. They went in person to the Old Countries to display their American wealth and ways and win recruits.

Peter Polda of the Bohemian settlement supplied paradisiacal descriptions of the southern Valley to foreign language newspapers in the United States. Paul Thorlaksson, whose efforts already had increased his one poor colony to four thriving ones, so bombarded Iceland that annually hundreds of small farmers left the island, several to walk from the Atlantic mainland to Pembina. The Westergaards did more than crusade for Danes. They turned their settlement into a receiving center where their compatriots might live until they, too, had learned and earned enough on the bonanzas to take up land of their own.

By 1881, Red River Valley had no need of promotion agents. Its soil had demonstrated its productivity beyond all challenge. Its bonanzas were paying harvesters the unprecedented sum of two dollars and fifty cents a day. And every day main and branch lines of the St. Paul, Minneapolis and Manitoba Railroad were making more acres accessible. Best of all, the United States Government, after almost a century of disillusioning experience elsewhere in the distribution of public lands, had evolved a policy both wise and generous.

Free land now was available only to American citizens who would make it their permanent home. No citizen could acquire more than 480 acres, and to accumulate that much, he had to exercise three different rights. Homestead. Timber culture or "tree claim." Pre-emption.

Germans, Austrians, Russians, Poles—first citizenship papers in hand—now swelled the flood of Scandinavians. Even to canny Scots, already wealthy or at least well-to-do from their years in fertile valleys of eastern Canada and the United States, this was too ripe a plum to ignore.

With their sons and sons-in-law, they took up adjoining lands for a dozen or more square miles along Red River's tributaries and, with their livestock, modern machinery, carpets and grand pianos, settled down to the business of becoming the landed gentry. Other Scots came as ministers, teachers, bankers, lawyers, doctors, to growing villages. And many of nonexistent means arrived from Scotland to confound the confusion of tongues on the bonanzas with the rumble of their burrs till they also could join the landowners.

So great was the rush, via train, steamboat, prairie schooner, hayrack, cart, foot and horseback that the rivulet of Canadians slipping in from Manitoba and North West Territory hardly had been noticed. But by 1881 the Canadian migration was numerically impressive. Why they came is a later story. Here it is sufficient to say that they joined the battle for lands in the Valley's northern counties (Britishers west of Red River, French Canadians east), and when those were gone, moved on to people the northern tier of all Dakota Territory.

They did not have a clear field. From the Icelanders in the north to the Bohemians in the south, the Valley's national fronts were advancing west. The Norwegians, having gained dominance in all but two Red River counties, sped their recruits into every corner of the Territory. Beside, ahead, or on their heels marched the Swedes.

Statistical reports of immigration agents shortly began to read like war bulletins:

The Norwegians have gained Foster County and lost Dickey, La Moure, and Pierce. The Canadians have lost Foster and Kidder while the Austrians have wrested Billings from the Canadians and Irish. Germans do not lead in any county now.

2. "US AMERICANS"

The coming of the pioneers from '71 to '79 resembled a motion picture slowed down for minute study of every detail. The next six years, while the Great Dakota Boom rolled to crest, were a film speeded up until its action was a whirling blur.

In May an entire county might display unbroken green, spangled with violets. In June, a tracklaying crew would hew a broad black swath through massed wild roses. Before their pink and red faded, a "mixed train" would jerk to a stop at one of the sidings arbitrarily placed every five miles. From its open doors, scores to hundreds of men, women, and children from Niagara, New York; Edinburgh, Scotland; or Oslo, Norway, with their cattle, horses, sheep, dogs, cats, household furnishings and farm equipment, would spill out to trail immigrant or land agent to tracts chosen, divided and assigned in advance.

By mid-July tiger lilies and bluebells were disappearing by the millions before the inexorable bite of plows. Within one to three years, mile-square fields of wheat in which low soddies had given way to substantial homes and barns were centered about a Niagara, Edinburgh, or Oslo, Red River Valley.

Was the overall effect a scene of pastoral peace and industry? In Red River Valley! Began then the Battle of the Town Sites.

To the aid of most promising combatants, land sharks rushed reinforcements in the form of a carload of buildings made up in sections. In two hours as many men could erect a one-story structure with a one-and-a-half or two-story façade. In a day six men could set up a block of buildings, including one with a fancy scroll or two about tall black letters that proclaimed its function as OPERA HOUSE. To give the traveling public an impression of sizzling growth and enterprise, all faced across the rutted strip of prairie known as Main Street to the railroad. When and if the town folded up, the buildings did, too, to be be freighted away overnight to the next potential "New Chicago."

However innocent their knowledge of American life and language, Europeans grasped as readily as Americans and Canadians the elemental principle that where the county records were, there perforce was the county seat. Followed intrigues, raids, and battles by dead of night in which not only the records but sometimes the matchbox structures that housed them were spirited across the prairies. Such "wars" continued until one village, like the No. 1 Hen in a barnyard, had proved its claims by might and main. Frequently the defeated villages picked themselves up to settle down again with one or another of the victors.

Incoming American settlers, restless as chickadees during the first snow, saw no novelty in owning land. If a Valley homestead offered high adventure or profitable speculation, they remained. If not, they moved on, sure they always could find good land farther west.

But, steeped in the tradition of living on the same land in the same community for generations, the Europeans had torn up their roots only temporarily. Come hell or high water, where they put down their stakes, they put down their roots again—to stay.

Men and women, all of them, whom the weight of centuries of political, social, economic and religious autocracy had crushed into enduring molds of brawn and spirit, they were custom-made to the Valley's specifications. Mistakenly, they thought the Valley custom-made to theirs.

Free land! they cried when they beheld the 160 acres of their own homestead. Free land! and they hurried to plant to trees the ten acres that would entitle them to 160 more. And as they acquired means, many purchased still another quarter-section by right of pre-emption. In their exultation at owning as much or more land than the richest gentry in their Old Countries, few identified the bitterness that seared their mouths as the taste of slavery.

Freedom! they cried when they found no social castes in the Valley. Freedom! when they learned that every man had a vote and that Ole Olson's was as good as Oliver Dalrymple's. Freedom! when they discovered they could live with their own nationals, speak their own language, read or even publish newspapers in their own tongues, erect their own church, enjoy their own native dress, traditions, festivals; above all, send their children to public schools.

Forthwith, each national group set up its own community behind steadily enlarged frontiers. Within them they created a land autocracy wherein no "foreigner" could penetrate. Their own Church. Their own political hierarchy, with Norwegian voting for Norwegian, Swede for Swede. Sometimes it was not understood till the second or third generation that freedom for oneself implies freedom for others. Sometimes still it is not understood.

The truth was that during the first years, except as a word to roll on the tongue, they were afraid of freedom. When they found in Red River Valley no laws, officials, pastors, landowners, elders, to tell them what to do, they felt lost, hopelessly separated by more than land and sea from "Home." As rapidly as they could, they recreated what they always had known.

Though with the high wages and high prices for wheat, it was cheaper and easier to buy American clothes, they spun, carded, wove and knit wool from their own sheep to duplicate the costume of the homeland, even shaped shoes from sheep- and hogskin. In a Valley alive with wild game, fish, fruits, they clung to their native curds and breads, bannocks, pancakes. Holding religious services in one home or another until they could build their own house of worship, they tried to live as though the Church of their forefathers were right next door. With reading societies, libraries, Old Country newspapers, chanters who went from farm to farm to recite sagas and ballads, they struggled to retain their native speech. On birthdays and days of homeland festivals, they danced the old dances, sang the old songs, performed legendary rituals to Thor.

And now freed from the oppression of Church, State and landowner, they created prairie symbols of privilege and authority to fear and hate. (Not without reason, sometimes, it should be said.) The railroads, for one. The bonanzas, for another. The elevators that bought their wheat, for a third. "O Lord," they prayed in home and church,

protect us against false inspection at the elevators. Thou knowest the price of wheat, O Lord, and we beseech Thee to see that Brother Smith's men do not misinform us. We know the value of the wheat, O Lord, but we pray Thee to tell us what we should receive when we deliver it. Thou knowest all that is done in the elevator, O Lord, but we do not, and we pray Thee inform us that Thy Name shall have all the glory for ever and ever, Amen.

Nevertheless, to the stamina and resource which Sioux, explorer, and fur trader had bred into Red River Valley life, the pioneers added a quality conspicuous until their coming by its absence—continuity of effort. Because of their respect for law, the Valley was spared the lawlessness that characterized frontier life in western Dakota and Montana. Whatever their origin, they were alike frugal, industrious, deeply religious, extremely sociable, devoted to music and dancing, mad about education for their children.

These virtues are reflected today in the fatness of the Valley's bank deposits and annual reports, in the plethora of schools, colleges, churches, in the high percentage of college graduates, in the extraordinary numbers of organizations, in the astonishing response of any group, unhampered by Anglo-Saxon inhibitions, to rhythm.

From this reservoir one day must come composers and musicians to enrich not only the Valley but Canada and the United States with their gifts. Must come also writers, bred of the long tradition begun with the interminable narratives of hunt and battle told by the Sioux, of the detailed journals the fur companies required annually of every trader, of the diaries into which the pioneers poured their hopes, fears, and struggles against the violent physical facts of the wide open spaces, of endless letters to the folks at "Home," of the ever-continuing mystic relation between soil and people.

That day, though perhaps near, is not yet. Too strong still is the ingrained influence of the Old Countries, where teacher, banker, minister, doctor, lawyer, ranked next to the aristocracy. Into such fields, Valley young men and women still turn for careers. From their children or their children's children must derive the creative artists of tomorrow.

By that time, alas, the scenes and speech that so vividly colored pioneer life will be lost memories. Who then can recreate the annual candle-making when patient women dipped, one by one and again and again, scores of short strings into pots of melted fat and hot water? Or scenes about candle and lamp when men carded and women spun while one member of the family read or recited saga and tale? Or the tremendous funeral feasts to which each guest, there by formally written invitation, contributed? Or the summer days when the Danes, from replicas of boats built to withstand the North Sea's storms, fished with homemade nets the shallow, placid waters of Maple River?

Who then can catch the light and shadow playing over a thrifty Icelander as he retrieved, with the aid of homemade windmill and grindstone, sharp knives from broken pieces of his scythe? Or over the anxious faces of Swedes as they placed lamps backed by mirrors in their windows on nights of maniac storm to guide a lost stranger to safety? Or on the first small fields, where men and women, toiling side by side, might have posed for Millet's reportorial brush? Or on the song fests and dance fests in home or woods when men whirled and stamped all night long in wracking tests of endurance?

Still remain the afternoon coffee clatch of the Scandinavians, the afternoon tea of Scotch and Canadians. Not only remain but engage most of the Valley's population whatever one's national descent. At Christmastime, the village school or church party, complete with tree, gifts, Santa Claus, and assorted small fry rendering "pieces," first introduced by the Scotch, still continues. Winter or summer, word of a dance in hall, barn, grove, brings out young and old for counties round.

Today, the Valley again is experiencing an era of ambulating villages. This time it is due to the automobile and paved highway demonstrating to whole communities that it is just as easy to reach the country from the town as vice versa. In brief migrations, families *and* homes move on wheels to larger centers where, relocated side by side on new streets, they can live within range of each other and of shops, churches, schools, clinics, theaters.

How, within the span of man's three score years and ten, could Red River Valley life pass from hand-tilled to mechanized fields, from soddies to modern homes, from the homogeneous colony to cities housing thirty to forty nationalities and only God knows how many blends? Because for State, Church, and landowner of the Old Countries, the Valley substituted an equally vigilant and stern American authority. Its name was Competition.

No matter how European farmers drove themselves and their families from dawn to dark, their Old Country tools and methods could not compete against John Deere Plows and McCormick Reapers. No matter how they fulminated against railroads, bonanzas, elevators, words availed them nothing. Willy-nilly, they were forced to abandon scythe and rake, to grind their own wits to invent easier, quicker methods. Willy-nilly, they had to learn about world conditions and markets, take an active interest in local and national politics, sink their distrust of every other nationality, compromise and co-operate, to elect the candidate who would fight for laws, rates and prices they wanted.

Once they began to question and to act independently, they found no end to it. The Church, particularly, came under their scrutiny. Before they were done, the Valley was peppered with churches representing, theologically, every point of view in every pioneer language.

If to learn the use of economic, religious and political freedom made pioneer blood boil and heads ache, the reverse was true of social freedom. Never, under any condition, in their home countries were they permitted to employ the singular *you* to any member of the upper classes, even to a babe in arms. What a delight then to find in Red River Valley that "a man can say 'you' even to Jim Hill!" Never was a three-letter word so overworked!

Still better was the discovery that the Valley harbored not a single germ of "title sickness." To men accustomed to stand, hat in hand, before every Mr. Banker, Mr. Lieutenant, Mr. Gardener, Mr. Barber, Mr. Coachman in the Old Countries, the pleasure of keeping one's head covered on Red River's Main Streets was something to write "home" about:

> The finest thing I can say of this country is that when I meet anyone on the street, be he rich or poor, pastor or official, I never tip my hat. . . .

> My cap is not worn out from lifting it in the presence of gentlemen. . . .

> When I meet the banker on the street, I do not lift my hat. I do not even tip it. Instead of "Good morning, Mr. Banker Gylvensans," I say, "Hi, Pete!"

On the other hand, what a thrill to be addressed oneself as Mister!

Consider the women when they learned that in Red River Valley they all were either Mrs. or Miss. That they no longer need wear heavy shoes and coarse clothing in keeping with their low social position. That they were not expected to work in the fields. That a man could be *put in jail* for lifting a hand to his wife! That on the street a wife must not walk behind but beside her husband and on the *inside*, at that. That she must not heave a 100-pound sack of flour to her own back that her husband might walk with empty hands. No! Dear God, can this be true? *He* must carry the sack, *she* walk with empty hands.

Consider the young women who, as maids in the Old Countries, would work the clock around, sleep when they could, in the kitchen. They flocked to Valley towns to "live like a lady," with a room of their own, with regular hours for work and *Thursday afternoon off* to go buggy-riding with Peder Pedersen or, if they could speak English, with John Smith. Ah, to be seen out with the owner of an American name! Ah! *ah!* to marry such a one!

To the pioneers, democracy was a formidable word, seldom voiced and even more rarely understood. But its symbols were both plain and easily described to their ever-widening circle of Old Country readers:

The hired man, maid and governess eat at the husbandman's table. "Yes, sir," says the master to the hand. "Yes, sir," says the hand to the master. "If you please, ma'am," says the lady of the house to the maid. "Yes, madame," says the maid to the mistress.

On the street the maid is dressed exactly as the housewife. Today is Sunday and at this very moment what do I see but a housemaid dressed in a black silk hat, green veil, green coat, black dress, carrying a bucket of coal! This is not an unusual sight—and it is as it should be. All porters and coachmen are dressed like gentlemen. Pastor, judge, and banker carry market baskets.

Having savored the delights of literary license, such authors invariably worked up to a peroration that concluded:

We hope and pray the Lord may open the eyes of Sweden's [or Norway's, Iceland's, *et al.*] people, that they may see their misery; how the poor workingman is despised and compelled to slave, while the so-called better classes live in luxury. . . . We believe all the workers had better depart and leave the lords and parasites to their fate.

Ten years under Valley discipline, of seeing more, thinking more, experiencing more, so changed an immigrant, even in facial expression, that it became a truism to say, "Even your best friends in the Old Country never would know you." Hundreds did visit their homelands to return to boast that such indeed had been the case. Others sat down more soberly to appraise themselves and to record their findings:

What a newcomer from Europe will first notice in "us Americans" is the change in our language, and next our good manners, the respect shown the women, the small class distinction between rich and poor, high and low, and finally our quickness and practical insight into work and business.

3. MR. RIEL AND MR. SMITH RISE AGAIN

By this time the reason why Canadians and *Métis* were moving south of the Boundary had become plain. In Manitoba (and North West Territory), history was repeating itself. Whites, half-breeds, and Indians again were as desperate and uncertain as in the Assiniboia of 1869; Ottawa, as absorbed in more important matters. And again, the crux of the trouble was land.

With the opening of CPR headquarters in Winnipeg and the joint campaign of Dominion and railroad to draw one million homesteaders to Northwest Canada, land and immigration booms had burst into flower. Winnipeg became one enormous speculation. Along the CPR's right of way, "a town had sprung up at every siding; a city, at every siding plus watertank."

Rising in one of the worst floods of his career, Red River of the North in 1882 washed out both booms. But even his enraged waters were powerless to end the Canadian Pacific's monopoly or Ottawa's land regulations.

Following the American system, the federal Government had had Manitoba and North West Territory divided into townships. Each township included 36 square-mile sections; each section, four square quarters. Of the 144 quarter-sections in every township, however, only eight, widely separated tracts were available as "free land." All the rest, earmarked as Government, Hudson's Bay Company, or CPR lands, had to be purchased.

Many immigrants, confused, had proved up on reserved lands. All of them were denied the opportunity to form the mutually helpful communities homesteaders south of the Boundary enjoyed. To white settlers, the last straw was their failure, after fulfilling all conditions, to secure from Ottawa the necessary papers to guarantee them permanent title.

In Manitoba, the *Métis*, of course, had the 1,400,000 acres set aside for them in 1870. But within a few years, either the Government's incompetent administration, as *they* charged, or their own inability to co-operate, had moved hundreds to sell their grants for a song and depart. Following the lead of uneasy French Canadians, scores crossed the Boundary into Northwest Minnesota. The majority followed the 1870 exodus into the Saskatchewan Valley.

Profiting by the mistakes of the United States, Canada had evolved a much wiser policy for its Indians. Through a series of treaties, it took title to all but approximately 11,000 square miles of tribal territory in the Northwest. Those 11,000 square miles were divided into reservations located where the tribes themselves chose to live.

In Manitoba the policy had worked out fairly well. But in North West Territory, misunderstandings angered the Indians into refusing to occupy the reservations. When at last they consented, Ottawa refused to send them the promised supplies to see them through the winter. Out of the ensuing turmoil, two Cree chiefs, Poundmaker and Big Bear, had risen. Each was resolved to unite and lead all Canadian Northwest tribes against the Government.

Lest Saskatchewan Valley experience the horror and pillage Minnesota River Valley had suffered under the Sioux outbreak, Canadians in Manitoba and North West Territory organized Settlers' Unions to bring united pressure to bear on Ottawa. When their petitions were ignored, more and more families moved into Dakota's Red River Valley and other northern counties. Those remaining in Saskatchewan joined forces with the *Métis*. Their one topic now was the need for a leader.

Outcome of the discussions was the departure of a delegation, financed by the Canadians and led by James Isbister, a British halfbreed, for Sun River, Montana. There they invited the schoolmaster of St. Peter's Mission to aid the people of Saskatchewan and Manitoba to win the desired reforms from Ottawa.

On condition that he be allowed to return to Montana in time for the opening of the new school year in September, Louis Riel accepted. But the man who accompanied them back to the Saskatchewan was not the Louis Riel of 1869.

After spending his compulsory exile in the United States, he had returned to Quebec. But five years of brooding over his success as president of Assiniboia's Provisional Government and his downfall through what he considered the treachery of Colonel Wolseley and Ottawa had left him torn between illusions of grandeur and persecution. For almost two years he had been confined to mental hospitals. Released, he had drifted out to Montana.

But he still retained his quiet voice and gentle manner. Impressed, the Canadians in Saskatchewan formed a new organization, with Riel as leader. And under his direction, they employed every legal means to obtain from Ottawa more liberal treatment for the Indians, immediate issuance of land titles, and other reforms.

Alarmed by the intensity and unanimity of public sentiment, the Catholic clergy, commander of the North West Mounted Police, Northwest newspapers, and the *Toronto Globe,* all warned Ottawa of the

thorough understanding between French and English halfbreeds and the Canadian settlers. All are pledged to unite in one common brotherhood until all common grievances are redressed.

Convinced the unrest was purely local, the Dominion government did nothing.

His work completed, Riel tried three times to return to Montana, only to be overruled. Big Bear sought him out to assure him of the support of all Northwest tribes. British and French *Métis* organized to demonstrate their united support of his leadership. Canadians, both in Manitoba and North West Territory stepped up their threats of secession and annexation to the United States.

Sure now that he held all the winning cards, Riel decided that if a Provisional Government could bring a Federal Government to terms in 1869, it must do so in 1885. Once proclaimed, with himself as President, he need only take over Fort Carlton, headquarters of the Mounted Police, as once he had taken over Fort Garry. Ottawa then would send out a new Donald A. Smith to unify all factions, and everything would proceed as before.

It was the dream of a madman. But, again alternately exalted by the adulation of the crowds and frustrated by Ottawa's indifference to just demands, legally presented, Riel no longer was sane.

The Canadians, however, realized that in 1869 Assiniboia had not been an integral part of the Dominion. The North West Mounted Police had not been organized.[3] Nor had a Canadian Pacific Railroad been laying rails at a frenzied pace east and west of Winnipeg. Refusing him further financing and support, they fled to a neutral corner. Quickly, the British half-breeds followed.

Desertions and denunciations excited Riel to do for them what they wouldn't do for themselves. On March 19, he proclaimed a Provisional Government, appointed a Council and a military commander, and opened enlistments in his "Army." This time, despite the increased numbers of *Métis*, less than five hundred signed up.

Even so, they outwitted the Mountie defenders of Fort Carleton. Seizure of that federal fort was, of course, a declaration of rebellion. And just what Big Bear and Poundmaker had been waiting for. On April 2, their red warriors captured a Hudson's Bay post, killed eight white men. Before the month ended, they practically controlled Saskatchewan Valley.

Crowded into improvised stockades at Prince Albert and Battle-

[3] On his return from Red River to Ottawa in 1870, Mr. Smith had recommended that a military force large enough to police all the Canadian Northwest be organized. Three years later, the North West Mounted Police established headquarters in Winnipeg.

ford, the terrorized whites cursed Riel. While they cursed, he again achieved what he had set out to do.

Within eleven days after he proclaimed his Provisional Government, Ottawa acknowledged the justice of his every demand. Ordering all land claims investigated, the necessary proofs of ownership issued, it rushed carloads of supplies to the Indians and promised immediate consideration of every other grievance.

Yet once more, Louis Riel's was a Pyrrhic victory. Eastern Canada again howled for his blood. And instead of a Donald A. Smith—came troops.

Today it is the fashion to link the disturbances of 1869 and 1885 under the common epithet, "Riel Rebellions," and dismiss them as negligible local uprisings created and led by a negligible man. And it is true that had this son of Red River Valley died on the battlefield, these revolts against social, economic and political injustice might now be forgotten.

But Louis Riel was taken prisoner on May 15, hanged six months later. The scourging blasts of religious and racial fanaticism fanned to fury during his trial and execution left wounds in the Canadian commonweal that ache and burn hotly under stress to this day. They again brought the Dominion to the verge of division into two bitterly antagonistic nations. Though that disaster was averted by a hair, the consequent realignment of Conservative and Liberal Parties altered the whole course of Canadian politics.

Most immediate effect was the disintegration of the "New Nation" which, against great odds, slowly had been rising to higher social and economic levels. Some of the *Métis* moved to Peace River. Others, by virtue of their Indian blood, sought social oblivion on the reservations. Hundreds crossed the Boundary to become American citizens and make the northern half of Northwest Minnesota peculiarly and picturesquely their own. Outside the usual exceptions, those that remained in Manitoba and North West Territory slipped back to the status originally defined for them as hewers of wood and drawers of water for the white man.

The situation of the white man after 1885 in Manitoba, all the Canadian Northwest, was not much better. The entire region suffered almost the same utter stagnation Upper Red River Valley had known after the Sioux outbreak.

Though the great European migration now was at its height, its millions of landseekers, viewing Manitoba and North West Territory as twin caldrons of continuous trouble, settled south of the Boundary. That American Red River Valley, though starting almost sixty years later than the Canadian, now was forging decades ahead, heavily underscored Manitoba's unhappy plight.

By 1896, all Canada knew that without federal aid, the Northwest never could recover from that second rebellion. To the rescue, Ottawa again called onetime Donald Smith, "the little man from Winnipeg," now, at seventy-six, one of the most powerful men in the British Empire.

More than patriotism impelled Lord Strathcona to accept appointment as High Commissioner of Immigration. As overseas governor of Hudson's Bay, he believed the fur trade doomed. The Company's true wealth, in his opinion, was the hundreds of thousands of acres, including the commercial core of Winnipeg, it had retained from its sale of Rupert's Land to the Dominion. And as father of the Canadian Pacific Railroad, he was concerned for the 40,000,000-acre land grant still unpeopled along its right of way.

But now European countries, drained of ten to forty and more per cent of their most productive citizens, had set up stern laws and police systems to prevent further migration to the New World. South of the Boundary lay the greatest obstacle of all.

During the past half-century, so many millions from Northern Europe, notably Scandinavia, had taken root in American soil that emigrants who did succeed in getting away from their homelands preferred to join their countrymen. Besides, snooty now, they all wanted to travel by the newest, fastest ships. The United States had these.

Undaunted, Lord Strathcona devised an irresistible combination offer of free land, free transportation, plus, if necessary, loans. In Europe, he organized a network of immigration agents, paid as in the days of Lord Selkirk, "by the head." But primarily he beamed his fire on the United States.

During the next fifteen years, almost 800,000 Americans, among them thousands from American Red River Valley, moved into Manitoba or spread over the Canadian Northwest. Some 900,000 citizens of the British Isles joined them. And from Belgium, France, Poland, Greece, Rumania, Spain, Serbia, Palestine, India, Bohemia and other less exploited nations came more than half a million. Overflowing the "free land," they eagerly bought up Hudson's Bay and CPR acreage.

From a town of less than 40,000, Winnipeg leaped to a city of more than 200,000. And throughout the Northwest, Europeans and Americans, concentrating about fur trading posts, built up young towns and cities. Some of these, sad to say, duplicated the dingy gentility of the provincial towns from which they came.

Northwest pioneers rose in wrath. They had not endured years of travail to be smothered now under Old World ways and tradition. Nor were the fur traders, their trade ruined, themselves neglected or forgotten, reconciled to carry on as best they could. And thousands of Winnipeggers and other Canadians feverishly speculating in lands were outraged to find Hudson's Bay agents their most aggressive competitors. From Red River of the North to most remote reaches of the Saskatchewan, a cry went up: "What has Hudson's Bay Company ever done for Canada?"

Again as in 1857, the Honorable Company read the handwriting on the wall. In northern Canada, Hudson's Bay continues today, but from Red River Valley and other populated areas, it removed the last vestiges of a regime that since the advent of Henry Kelsey had affected Valley history for good or ill. Replacing its trading posts with great department stores, it set the pattern for modern life in modern cities. Only the historic name, blazoned on their façades, remains to deny total victory to its ancient enemy, agriculture.

PART IX

The Golden Door

1. BEHOLD—THE VOTE!

As a bridge between the United States and Canada and between eastern and western Canada, Red River Valley grew steadily in territorial, provincial, state, national and international importance. Yet though now permanently partitioned into three political units, it persisted in functioning as a single economic entity.

Via the Valley, immigrants, as well as supplies, mail, and other things and services, by 1881 had funneled through St. Paul to Winnipeg to swell the population of the Canadian Northwest from 12,000 to 118,000. And the competition for their products and trade, funneling through Winnipeg to St. Paul, continued to be one of the primary factors in the development of the American Northwest.

While taking full advantage of this flow and counterflow, the Valley spun some fine dreams of enterprise of its own. Of Red River as the head of a continuously channeled waterway that would carry the products of both Northwests through Lake Winnipeg and the Nelson or Hayes River to Hudson Bay and the markets of the world. Of Red River as the source of enough electrical power to supply Valley and surrounding country on both sides of the Boundary. Of a canal from Great Lakes to Red River, thence upstream and down, to develop Grand Forks and Winnipeg as important inland ports.

Red River's unco-operative waters, now too low, now flooding the prairies with two to six feet of clay-saturated liquid, were dampening enough. The economic stagnation in Northwest Canada following the second rebellion added its dead weight. But after 1886, political barriers raised by International Boundary and State lines became rigidly defined and observed. So many political bodies now were required to act in concert that few men with the longevity had the temerity (and vice versa) to propose any improvement that would engage the entire Valley.

How best to control that recalcitrant problem child, Red River of the North, is but one of many multifaceted cases. Until 1950, the Canadian Valley was concerned merely to discipline him sufficiently to prove useful for industrial and sanitary purposes. Its drinking water is brought in from purer sources and the floods that periodically scourge the Valley south of the Boundary dealt tenderly with the north. The American Valley uses his waters for every purpose and, in addition, at least once in every generation since records have been kept, has had to cope with a bankrupting flood whose cost, averaged annually, is $1,400,000.

Consequently, though since 1872 Jim Hill and others continuously have urged joint federal action, not until recently, following years of negotiation, did the United States and Canadian Governments, the Provincial Government of Manitoba, the State Governments of Minnesota, North Dakota and South Dakota, to say nothing of the International Joint Commission (a U.S.-Canadian body set up to make sure that what one country does on mutual waters won't hurt the other), the U.S. Army, and multitudinous lesser local bodies involved, agree on what should be done.

And that agreement broke in two at the Boundary. Canadian authorities continued to consider ways of regulating Red River to prevent water pollution and, during dry years, drought conditions. And for the same purposes, primarily, the U.S. Army Corps of Engineers in St. Paul began work, in 1949, on a $17,000,000 system of dams, dikes, reservoirs, dredging and channel straightening here and there.

Came 1950. Contemptuous of that idea or any idea of controlling him, Red River rose in floods second only to those of 1826, to bury progressively hundreds upon hundreds of square miles beneath his dirty waters and keep them that way from early April till mid-June. The public heard of his depredations when he finally reached Winnipeg, forced more than 100,000 of its residents to abandon homes and city, and wreaked property damage estimated at $17,000,000.

Because Red River Valley slopes north at the rate of six inches per mile and Red River at his dizziest speed attains a velocity of less than four miles per hour, he is one of the few rivers in the world that can run amok while practically standing still.

At such times, he resembles nothing so much, says Ralph Allen, a Canadian observer, as a heavy, sluggish, many-fingered giant squid groping languidly for vulnerable spots into which to ooze. Since his Valley is level as a table top, most of it is vulnerable. Over it he oozes, fat, flat, and flaccid, to remain inert week after week, or, meeting natural or man-made barrier, to lean against it with a seedy, aimless air.

Horrified by the repulsive creature and their helplessness to deal with him, Manitoba politicians and susceptible lay voters suddenly roused to the need for the United States Government to bridle Red River from source to Boundary. But Red River's rampages, both American and Canadian hydrologists agree, cannot be controlled by American or joint federal action or even by good works.

Cities like Fargo, Grand Forks, and Winnipeg can be protected to a degree by permanent dikes. Winnipeg further can be safeguarded perhaps by the proposed 22-mile pass around the city. Elsewhere the front is too broad, too thinly held for diking to be economical. While watching future floods creep toward them, smaller towns, villages and farms on both sides of the Boundary must find what consolation they can in the fact that since they represent the inhabitants on four out of five miles of Red River's Valley course, they are not alone in their misery.

Political co-operation toward the solution of devious physical and economic problems is not the only headache Red River Valley's trio of political divisions suffers in common. Another is the psychology of Red River voters. As an outgrowth of their early history, they share, both north and south of the Boundary, an easily irritated sensitivity toward anything that smacks of "bossism." This cockiness at times has carried them too far; at all times, makes politics, whether municipal, county, state, or national, a very personal affair.

When conditions are good, Red River voters are willing, as individuals, never collectively, to ride with the band. But when conditions are bad,—ah, then, what political -ists and -isms, budded in some obscure mind, can grow to startling flower!

From this it follows as immutably as night the day, that though the political history of the three divisions is as diverse and unrelated as that of three different countries, temperamentally it is the same old embattled pea dodging about under a trio of shells.

NORTHWEST MINNESOTA

If, politically speaking, Northwest Minnesota is the eldest of the three divisions, in its own bailiwick it is the youngest and least considered. By the time it attained stature as the Ninth Congressional District of the State of Minnesota, eastern Red River Valley was expected to echo, "Me, too."

Never was a political blueprint more mistakenly misread. Even in Territorial days, Norman Kittson and Jo Rolette, as Pembina County's representatives to the Legislature, first dazzled St. Paul with their spectacular arrivals by pomponned dogs and sledges, then settled down to upset as many applecarts as the time allowed. For this St. Paul should have been eternally grateful. To "King Rolette," specifically, it owes its permanent possession of the capital.

By 1848, when Minnesota applied for Territorial status, devout Red River French Canadians and *Métis* had beaded the Cart Trails from St. Boniface to St. Paul with camp sites and hamlets named to honor Vincent, Joseph, John, Thomas, and a host of other saints. In the belief that when the Territory became a State, its citizens might prefer a capital with a mundane name, Congress granted St. Paul but temporary title.

Notwithstanding this prejudice, St. Anthony (Minneapolis), St. Peter (Mendota), and other towns whose founders included Red River emigrés, battled to secure the prize. It was St. Anthony's all-out efforts in 1851 that engendered the enmity that today lies at the root of the rivalry between the Twin Cities.

Six years later and five days before the Territorial Legislature was due to adjourn, the struggle reached its climax. When the Speaker called for the Capital Removal Bill that would rob St. Paul to reward St. Peter, even the most pertinacious Paulistas had abandoned all hope. But though Mr. Speaker called again and again, day after day, no bill appeared.

As chairman of the Committee on Enrolled Bills, Jo Rolette had secreted the document with his banker and himself in an attic room in the Fuller House. There he spent a delightful five days among the cobwebs playing poker with old cronies. Meanwhile, Minnesota's lawmakers, cots beside their desks, hampers of food scattered about the Chamber, remained in continuous session for 123 hours. At the exact moment when the Speaker's gavel had adjourned the session, the redoubtable Jo marched in with the bill.

Second redoubtable citizen of Northwest Minnesota was Oliver Hudson Kelley. As founder of the National Grange of Husbandry, he further strengthened the bones of Red River Valley's individualistic political tradition.

After the Civil War, the elevator, miller, and meat packing combine perfected its policy of paying the farmer as little as possible for his products. And the farm machinery, lumber, and other corporations that supplied him essential equipment and services joined to charge him all the traffic would bear. Not to be outdone by combine and trusts, Minnesota's five little railroads exacted maximum rates for minimum services. The goose that laid their golden eggs was left only enough to survive.

All this so riled young Kelley, struggling to cultivate virgin acres near Red River of the North's headwaters, that he organized the Grange as a secret fraternity through which farmers could unite against their enemies. But not until the 1880's, when no more free land remained in the Valley, and bankers, viewing Red River farms as gilt-edged securities, had further enmeshed its farmers with enticing loans, did the Grange attain effective strength in Minnesota.

Then it established the principle that railroads must submit to State regulation of rates and taught the greatest individualists on earth to co-operate—a little. Not enough. After a brief existence, the Grange died. But thereafter, whenever economic conditions rubbed too raw a sore, farmers on both sides of Red River remembered.

Either as originators or supporters, they promoted the Greenback Movement, Populist Party, Farmers' Alliance, Non-Partisan League, Farm-Labor Party, and so on and on to the Farmers Union and Farm Lobby of today. As the last stronghold of the Farm-Labor Party, Northwest Minnesota as late as 1942 sent a Farm-Labor Congressman to Washington.

Rising with or leading one movement or another, many eastern Red River Valley politicos gained state or regional attention. One, Knute Nelson, during twenty-eight years, first as governor of Minnesota, then as United States Senator, became a giant in the earth of the nation's political forces.

The passionate lengths to which Red River voters will go to support the candidate of their choice are typified in the campaign of 1882 when Charles F. Kindred and Knute Nelson fought to occupy the same seat in the U.S. Senate.

Having made a fortune out of Northern Pacific lands in Red River Valley, Mr. Kindred dedicated $100,000 of it to victory. While arranging for a series of county caucuses at strategic points, his henchmen took the precaution of hiring every horse for miles around each meeting place and organizing strong police forces to make sure no Nelson supporter gained admittance. Afoot, on skis, and snowshoes, Nelson's men not only arrived. They battled their way into the meetings to win delegates for Knute.

For the final convention in Detroit Lakes, Kindred money engaged every hotel room, brought in police from surrounding towns to insure an ironclad defense of the convention hall until Kindred's nomination was secure. Nelson's cohorts erected a circus tent across the street, held their own rump convention and nomination.

When election day came round, Red River voters, traditionally on the side of "a man of the people" versus "Wall Street," sent Knute Nelson to Washington. What is more, they kept him there until he died.

SOUTHERN MANITOBA

Canadian Red River Valley similarly was conditioned to become the stormy petrel of Dominion politics. This is all the more remarkable since its founding Scot and Irish peasants, conditioned by centuries of submission to upper class rule, had accepted the authority of governors appointed by Lord Selkirk and Hudson's Bay Company.

Sixty years of coping with every physical and man-made crisis the Valley could devise were, however, more than enough to insure that when Assiniboia became Manitoba, Assiniboians became voters short on diplomacy but long on fighting qualities. These they sharpened on rebellions and minor upheavals during their first quarter-century under provincial and federal governments to attack with surer aim the Manitoba Act.

Resenting the 11,000-square-mile boundaries that quickly earned their Province such subtitles as "Postage Stamp" and "Cinderella," they began the fight that, stage by stage, enlarged Manitoba to today's 252,000 square miles. Resenting the fact that their natural resources had been placed under control of a newly created Department of the Interior, they began the fight, not won until 1930, to regain them.

Such prolonged and complicated procedures were most distasteful to a new fighting element added to the population after the Rebellion of 1885. Though the expected influx of French-Canadian settlers from Quebec did not materialize, more and more Ontarians, still unappeased by the death of Riel, did. Their numbers added to those who had come west since 1868 gave the British Canadians a clear majority.

Throwing out the Manitoba Act's provision for a dual system of Protestant and Catholic schools, they established a system of nonsectarian schools. Similarly, they disposed of French and English as the official languages in favor of English.

This second slap at the French, following so closely on the heels of Riel's execution, soon had all Canada in turmoil. It was the chief cause of the downfall of the long-lived Conservative Party, the rise of the Liberal. As a reward, the new regime permitted Manitoba to direct its own educational affairs.

Now, too, the decision to bring the Canadian Pacific Railroad south, possibly the most important event in Manitoba's history, began to bear fruit. By changing the course of immigration and settlement, the CPR's new right of way made Central Canada the granary of the British Empire, and Manitoba the keystone province between Great Lakes and Rockies. And as the bottleneck through which all transcontinental traffic and communication passed, Winnipeg became the spokesman for all the prairie provinces.

During these transitional years while trading post gave way to modern villages and towns, buffalo to domestic cattle, Red River Carts to railroads, the "Old Northwest" died. The Midwest was born.

To the white man this was a time of growth and adventure. To *Métis* and Indian, of decline and disaster. The thousands of foreign immigrants spreading over the prairies fared somewhat better. But their assimilation and the reconciliation of French Canadian and British Canadian are two problems stated by this period that, like similar issues in the United States, await the healing hand and social enlightenment of the future.

In some fields, however, Manitoba pioneered. It was the first Canadian Province to grant woman suffrage, the first to award pensions to widows and dependent children. With the aid of John W. Dafoe, farsighted editor of the *Winnipeg Free Press*, it either led the fight to secure better terms for all the Western Provinces or bent a strong shoulder to achieve such National victories as that which won Canada Dominion status in fact as well as name. Following the depression of 1929, it embarked on a new campaign in behalf of all the provinces for revision of Canada's confused tax system and for needed social reforms.

Manitoba's demands for such legislation, unforeseen and unprovided for by the Constitution of Canada, moved Ottawa in 1937 to create the Royal Commission on Dominion-Provincial Relations. After conducting the most thorough investigation of Canadian economy ever made, the commission presented its recommendations. If and when realized, every Province will be able to carry out its normal functions of government without heavy taxes. A most important provision—removal of domestic tariffs that favor the Maritime Provinces—will free Western Provinces to develop their own industries.

To achieve this industrial changeover, Manitobans for once have curbed their inalienable right and instinct to do battle. Since 1940, they have supported a coalition government. The rewards, they say, justify the supreme sacrifice.

RED RIVER VALLEY (NORTH DAKOTA)

Hardly had Congress created Dakota Territory out of all the odds and ends west of Red River of the North than it was realized that the halves north and south of the forty-sixth parallel were about as compatible as a pair of man-eating tigers.

As capital of the Territory, Yankton, particularly, was first startled, then annoyed to discover it must serve unseen and unknown Red River Valley. When, time after time, Red River votes, arriving months late by dog sledge, unseated already functioning official or measure, its annoyance deepened to surcharged suspicion. By the end of the 1870's, the two tigers were incessantly at one another's throats.

The vastness of the Territory, with its lack of communication services and of railroads running north and south, no lack at all of great, unpeopled distances, was the real troublemaker. For business or pleasure Red River residents sought Winnipeg, the Twin Cities, or one of the burgeoning Valley towns. Their legislators, returning more dead than alive from lawmaking sessions at the capital were not persuasive travel agents.

If they set out for Yankton by horse and wagon over open prairies, they endured a month of unbroken exposure to the elements and to clouds of mosquitoes that reduced man and beast to nervous skeletons. If they went by horse or dog sledge to Breckenridge to entrain for St. Paul, thence by way of Sioux City, Iowa, spent fifty hours of train and change, they lost a week. Either way, by the time they reached the capital to consider Territorial affairs, they were in neither mood nor condition to exude sweetness and light.

Besides, as Red River voters themselves, also hardened by the Valley's natural and man-made rigors, they did things their own way.

Once determined on a course of action, they could not be turned from it. And politically they were not amateurs.

During their years in Territorial Minnesota's Legislature, Norman Kittson and Jo Rolette had set the pace. Now, in Fargo, Grand Forks, and other ports up and down the west bank, Jud La Moure, George Walsh, and other clever young lawyers and newspaper men were carrying on. Among them were many budding political strategists and a few with real statesmanship qualities. By inciting southern Dakota's politicos to fight over a bone while they ran off with it themselves, they made Red River Valley known "as the place where the balance of power was weighed and not found wanting."

They were not alone in the struggle for political power and plums. If Dakota's first carpetbag officials were too indifferent to the public weal, those that followed were too enthusiastic. Into every financial and political deal they sank such sticky fingers that the reek of ensuing scandals spread from coast to coast. And when the railroads came in, their backers, also, plunged predatory fingers deep into politics. After 1878 Washington no longer appointed Dakota's officials, but by that time the mold for Territorially elected candidates was set.

Almost every election and session of the Legislature gave the Territory a black eye. Candidates hurled such bitter personalities at one another that fist fights and cut faces were commonplace. Once lawmakers' tempers flared so high that a ballot box containing the votes on one measure was hurled through a window to be lost in the gaping crowd outside. Details of the murder of one official by another titillated the nation for months. Accusations against the infamous intrigues, boodle gangs, plots and frauds of "northern rings" or "nefarious southern combinations" also were run of the mill. But when fraud was proved against one side, opposition papers sped the news east and west.

The example of the Territorial capital did nothing to refine life in the raw little towns along the Red and Upper Missouri Rivers. Respectable citizens complained that the drunken brawls, night shootings, tar-and-featherings, occasional lynchings, kept them awake, deplored the men with bashed heads sprawled untidily across sidewalks in the mornings.

On street corners, Eastern "skippers" from entangled business or matrimonial affairs frequently encountered irate pursuing employers, fathers, or other Nemesis, horsewhip, pistol, or cane in hand. Notorious women, pitiful young girls, penniless men, jumped from bridges, drank laudanum. From every corner of the country sharpers and thieves flocked in to prey on bonanza harvesters, tracklayers, River roustabouts, Minnesota lumberjacks who clotted Red River towns on Saturday nights.

To the ill fame distilled from all this was added Dakota's ballooning reputation as a divorce mecca. Cases heard during that legislative session of 1862 had blazoned the word that here freedom from undesired spouses could be had within ten days. No sooner had the Sioux gone and railroads come than opportunistic Eastern lawyers flocked west to open offices in Sioux Falls, Fargo, Grand Forks. Their extensive advertising in national magazines attracted to the prairies not only garden varieties of Canadian and American divorce seekers, but a very plush assortment of the "Newport Set" and the European peerage.

Even the law passed to require divorce hunters to spend ninety days in the Territory failed to stem this new thundering herd. As prima-facie evidence of such residence, applicants were required to file their receipts for room and board when they filed their case. By supplying those receipts themselves, lawyers spared their clients the discomfort of arriving in Dakota until the day they appeared in court to receive their decrees.

As no papers were filed until lawyer, applicant, and witnesses assembled for the hearing, the many citizens who desired secrecy had it. Their cases were heard in remote county courts where no one concerned was known. It was the few who sought publicity that won Dakota Territory international renown and fed the impression that hundreds of divorces were granted daily.

One was Madame DeSueurs who no sooner secured release from a French marquis than she married Count Zborowski. Another was Freddy Gebbhardt who divorced his wife to marry Lily Langtry, only to learn that the celebrated beauty had decided to marry Sir Hugo de Bathe. Mrs. William Rhinelander Stewart found Dakota just the place to get rid of her husband, so that she could marry multimillionaire "Silent" Smith, so that he could settle enough wealth on her daughter, so that she could marry Prince Bragança, pretender to the throne of Portugal.

Most flagrant sensation was the case of Mrs. Bob Fitzsimmons. Immediately on her arrival in Sioux Falls, she employed a press agent to headline her wrongs to the world. Soon appeared her prize-fighter husband to do likewise with his publicly shed tears and remorse. When they could wring no more newspaper angles from their emotions, they staged a dramatic reconciliation in a hotel dining room. The next night they re-enacted their maudlin story in a playlet, written *before* either of them came to Dakota.

Though Washington was fully informed, the divorce scandal blinded the public to the bitter struggle going on between north and south. Claiming the name of Dakota as its own, the southern faction again and again applied for Statehood, with a recommendation to Congress that the north be made Lincoln or Pembina Territory. To frustrate such treachery, northerners plotted to "remove" the capital from Yankton.

By 1883, with 5,000 immigrants pouring daily into the Territory and every boomer town eager to house the capital, conditions were ripe for what is still considered the greatest coup ever perpetrated by Red River politicos.

Aware that a capital on Red River of the North would be no more accessible to Dakota in general than Yankton, Valley strategists joined hands with Jim Hill and officials of the Northern Pacific Railroad to make Bismarck on the Upper Missouri the chosen site. Aware also that if such a motion were put to a vote of either Legislature or people, defeat was certain, they waited till the close of the 1883 session to push through their Capital Removal Bill.

Among its double-talk clauses was one that ostensibly placed the capital on the auction block, available to any town in the Territory that would guarantee $100,000 and a suitable location. Another that empowered a commission of nine men with final authority to select the winning bidder. Taken by surprise but automatically scenting a rodent, Yankton's supporters inserted a third that required the commission to organize *in the capital* within a very short time after the Legislature adjourned.

Yanktonians placed far too cheap an estimate on Alexander McKenzie of Bismarck, audacious and ingenious young henchman of the Northern Pacific. As chairman of the commission, he not only named its members, but shortly assembled them in Sioux City, Iowa. There after dark on an early April night, he shepherded them aboard a special train composed of an engine and one coach. En route to Dakota's Territorial capital, the nine gentlemen prepared all the necessary papers of organization.

At five o'clock in the morning, as the train entered the city limits, they removed their hats, unanimously elected officers, carried all motions, and adjourned until May 1. While Yanktonians all too symbolically slept at the switch, the commissioners, hats again in place, were on their way out of the capital-that-was.

By May 1, eleven towns had qualified as bidders for the capital-to-be. Dutifully, the commissioners visited them all. Then, returning to Red River Valley, they staged in Fargo a farcical if suspenseful series of ballots, favoring first one aspirant, then another, until Bismarck emerged the victor.

The furor over this "steal" intensified north and south Dakota's willingness to separate as soon as possible. But since 1819, Congress had been viewing with alarm the day when a "hotch potch of wild men from the Red and Upper Missouri Rivers" might wedge themselves into House and Senate "to manage the concerns of a seaboard 1,500 miles, at least, from their residence." Now, disgusted with the political shenanigans of both factions, shocked by the notoriety they had accumulated, and motivated by some extremely eccentric political reasoning of its own, Congress six times denied Statehood to North and South Dakota.

And now the Territory, holding Red River politicians responsible for all its woes, united against the Valley. Feeling ran so high that when some forty legislators left Bismarck to inspect the university and other institutions Valley towns had extracted from the patronage bag, the acting chaplain of the House felt it high time to take the matter up with God:

Oh, Lord, bless this House. Of course, there are not many here. Thou knowest their motives in going. If it is in the best interests of this country, Thou wilt bless them, but if it is for the wayward pleasures of this world, Thou mayest do with them as seemeth best. They have gone to the land of the boomer and the flush, to the land of Jud La Moure. . . .

Meanwhile, both north and south concentrated on framing Constitutions that would win Congressional approval. North Dakota revised its divorce laws to require a bona fide twelve-month residence of every candidate for a decree. After harrowing campaigns in which national suffragist leaders even petitioned President Cleveland to remove the governor, it granted women the vote. And by dint of a mixed team's double play, it placed itself in the dry column.

To induce the Territorial Legislature to insert a Prohibition clause in the future State's Constitution, Elizabeth Preston Anderson, national leader of the antiliquor forces, arrived in Bismarck. So did a dedicated group of men from exceedingly wet Northwest Minnesota. Success won, Mrs. Anderson belatedly thought to ask Dan Sullivan, spearhead of the Minnesota battalion, why he had served so devotedly as her right arm. "Ma'am," he said, "I own a saloon in East Grand Forks."

Saloonkeepers from Grand Forks and other towns on Red River's west bank at once entrained for Bismarck to battle *against* ratification of that Prohibition clause. The night before the Legislature was to vote, they wound up their campaign with a royal entertainment for the lawmakers. The next morning their guests of honor woke with such raging hangovers that they marched into the capitol to vote as one man *for* ratification.

These issues and others satisfactorily settled on both sides of the forty-sixth parallel, Congress at last relented. On February 22, 1889, North and South Dakota were admitted to the Union.

One of the first bills considered by North Dakota's first Legislature made it immediately apparent that Red River Valley, as the oldest, most populated, and most productive section would direct the State's political destiny.

At this time the charter of the Louisiana Lottery Company was due to expire. Neither Louisiana nor any other established State would grant it a new one. After canvassing all the recently admitted States, lottery officials picked on North Dakota, with its small and poor population, its heavy debt, and need for high taxes to support numerous and costly State institutions, as the ideal prospect. Before a Legislature already feeling the pinch of the new State's poverty, they spread a seductive offer.

In addition to paying fabulous taxes, they promised to liquidate the State debt, finance annually its entire school system, supply every needy farmer with seed and machinery. And they secretly assured

both Fargo and Grand Forks, as the two main centers of political
influence, that each would be made the site of the architectural
masterpiece they would erect to house their hundreds of clerks.

Seduced, the Legislature passed a bill to authorize the charter. Red
River Valley voters rose to protest. The governor used his veto.

With but few interludes thereafter, the Valley, as continuously the
oldest, most populated and productive section, has influenced, when
it did not dictate, the political fortunes of North Dakota.

2. THE WHITE KID GLOVE ERA

No corner of the modern world is as inaccessibly isolated from all
contact with civilization as was the junction of the Red and Assiniboine Rivers in 1812. Not only isolated. Captain Miles Macdonell
brought his nineteen unlettered Scots and Irish rustics to their New
World destination at the moment when the ruthless and degrading
warfare between the fur companies was mounting to a climax. For
the next ten years, its was to degrade the Selkirkers also. Yet seventy-
five years later, Winnipeg was edging into its corner as one of the
four leading social and cultural centers of Canada.

That metamorphosis was surpassed by another. From an almost
standing start in 1872, American Red River Valley simultaneously
was attaining, notably in Grand Forks, an elegance and cultivation
that equaled, when it did not excel, Winnipeg's. By 1886, men and
women on both sides of the Boundary were old hands with white
kid gloves.

Officially, the White Kid Glove Era was inaugurated one March
night in 1848 when officers of the departing Sixth Regiment of Foot
entertained the elite of Red River Settlement at a sumptuous Farewell Ball. Though the feet that carried a certain Mrs. Cowan onto
the floor of Fort Garry's ballroom were moccasined, her hands were
sheathed in shimmering white kid, right off the last boat from London.

But little by little, following the merger of Hudson's Bay and
North West Companies, reorganization of the colony on higher
ground after the Great Flood, and the exodus of the discontented
to Fort Snelling, comparative peace on both banks of Red River had
encouraged social amenities. Shortly, from early November to early
April, winter was tamed into a social season.

Weddings became such community affairs that two weeks were necessary to encompass all the ceremonies, dinners, dances centered about the bridal couple. Three weeks of feasting, dancing, singing, church services, and, crowning event, a Hudson's Bay Ball, welcomed the New Year. On Christmas Eve, Good Friday and Easter, Catholics and Protestants alike attended impressive masses in St. Boniface Cathedral. "Surprise Parties," when twenty carioles of merrymakers descended on some unwarned farmhouse, sleighrides, races, and skating on Red River, gala dinners to honor Lord This or Sir That, and other notable Hudson's Bay guests filled in round the edges.

Perhaps because of the colony's many lean years, food was the key to social success. Weddings always were scheduled for Thursday that men might begin on Monday to cook over open fires the king-size beef and mutton roasts for the wedding dinners. Women prepared plum puddings; *de croxegnols,* finger-length bits of fine-buffalo-tallow-and-water pastry, twisted into fancy shapes and fried in boiling fat; *poutine dans le sac,* a suet pudding also made of fine buffalo tallow, big raisins and nutmeg, boiled in a bag, served with a sauce stiffly laced with brandy; many other delicacies.

Even wedding feasts bowed before the dinners staged by Hudson's Bay Company officials at Fort Garry. Their guests sat down to oyster soup, whitefish, roast beef, roast prairie chicken, home-grown vegetables, stewed gooseberries, plum pudding, blancmange, raisins, nuts, coffee, port, sherry, brandy, punch and cigars.

Men and women rose from such menus to wear out more than one pair of fancifully beaded moccasins while dancing away a night of jigs, double jigs, reels of four and eight—Strip the Willow, Tucker's Circle, Drops of Brandy, Rabbit's Chase. At Home Sweet Home, a Handkerchief Dance continued until every guest had received a good-night kiss.

Top favorite was old Red River Jig. Everyone could dance it, almost every man fiddle it. But to dance or play it well was considered the highest form of terpsichorean and musical art. With the violinist sawing and stamping madly, everyone shouting, "Ho, ho, ho!" two dancers "stepped it up" faster and faster until one dropped—sometimes literally—out. At that moment another was on the floor and on the beat. And so it continued for hours.

French Canadians and *Métis* never stopped singing—at home, on the hunts, on the Trails, on rivers and lakes. Indians, too, loved to sing. The best singing in the Settlement, in fact, was heard in the Indian Missions. But neither was any British gathering complete without its session of Old Country songs, *voyageur* chanties, hymns.

Long before the advent of the Selkirkers, letter-writing had become a prime recreation of the fur country. When Hudson's Bay transferred its headquarters to Red River Settlement's Fort Garry, its main post office came, too. Here, during the year, all outgoing mail for Company posts in southern Rupert's Land collected, to be sorted out for London or for the posts in northern Rupert's Land.

Departure of the Northern Packet on or about December 10 for Norway House, mail center for the North, accordingly was celebrated as a very red letter day. Then in great style, mail runners, gay in blue and red, their sledges drawn by magnificent dogs whose harness also was gay with yarn and feather pompons, atinkle with little bells, set out on the eight-day journey. Again on their return with mail from the North, expectant correspondents gave them a hero's welcome.

By this time, the spring departure of the York boat brigades for York Factory with the winter's pelts and mail; even more, their safe return in the fall with a year's supplies and mail from Home, had assumed dramatic proportions as community festivals. Rowing as one arm, singing as one throat, the vividly costumed crews brought the heavy craft, all aflutter with flags, upriver to cheers of thanksgiving.

Like the Biblical leaven in the three measures, the influence of Governor Simpson, notably of his and Mrs. Simpson's three-year residence at Red River, gradually revamped this naïve, democratic social structure. His regal arrivals and departures, and the grandiose annual meetings of Company officials he conducted each summer at Norway House, delighted the French-Canadian love of drama, the British respect for dignity. And the council and court, Forts Garry and Stone, the private schools for sons and daughters of Company officials he established at Red River, restored and heightened social barriers between peasant and gentry. Finally, the color line he drew for his wife's benefit narrowed to a handful the circle of Red River's elite.

Later, as more and more Company officers and traders were transferred to Fort Garry, the circle widened. During their years in the "interior," such newcomers had put up with most primitive conditions. Not at Red River.

Annually, they imported books and magazines from England. All manner of foods, wines, liquors, cigars. Violins, flutes, bagpipes and other small musical instruments on which they rapidly learned to play with "a certain ghastly facility." And reassured by Mrs. Simpson's onetime residence, they also imported the wives and sweethearts they had left behind them. These young, gay, resourceful British women delighted Company guests and such American visitors as Major Long and Governor Ramsey with their good looks, charming manners, and homes.

Arrival of the gallant and urbane officers of the Sixth Regiment of Foot acted like a shot in the arm on Red River's social set. Dress and manners were further refined, waltzes, polkas, cotillions, inserted among the jigs and reels, formality given to balls and dinners. From then on society took unto itself a capital S.

Orders lengthened on London for whole wardrobes of watered silk dresses and fine merinos, of bonnet shapes and fripperies for the women and, for the men, frock coats, dress coats, cravats and toppers, all "in the fashion most used." For melodeons, pianos, harps, silver cups and spoons, household linens, Drawing Albums, Musick Albums, and the famous white kid gloves. Letters went, too, to sons and daughters in British schools to instruct them how to comport themselves "to maintain their position and prestige" when they returned to take their places among Red River's aristocracy.

Inauguration of Red River Cart Trains to St. Paul and opening of navigation on Red River, enriched homes of the smart set with brocaded wallpapers, glass and marble lamps, bathtubs, the first apples and—luxury of luxuries!—tin pans to replace wood and stone utensils. Books, magazines, pipe organs, art and news of the world provided physical and mental equipment for more schools, reading clubs, singing societies, charades and home theatricals.

While the gentry enlarged its social horizons, farmers, free traders, and others engaged "in trade" had not been standing still. They, too, now ordered "store boughten" clothes from London. Not without mishap. One poor man, year after year, ordered a cloak, only to receive, year after year, because of deficient handwriting or spelling, a clock. Their children now went to school, their wives rarely worked in the fields. As plows and other machinery, stoves to replace open fireplaces, and similar time-saving conveniences increased, they too had leisure to look about and think about what they saw. What they saw brought Canadian Red River Valley to another memorable date.

In the summer of 1857, Henry Youle Hind, Canadian engineer,

went out one morning to inspect the prosperous fields of John Gower. Later, when the farmer took his guest to the house for the noon meal, they found that Mrs. Gower had laid but one place. And when her husband asked, "Where is my place?" she exclaimed in shocked protest, "Oh, John, you would not think of sitting at table with *gentlemen!*" John looked from face to face of his son-in-law and children watching silently from a far corner, came to an historic decision. "Am I not a gentleman, too?" he said. "Is not this my house, my farm, my food? Give me a chair and a plate."

Step by step during the seventies, the Canadian Valley's social pattern continued to evolve. For their biennial balls, Manitoba's new Government House officials, looking with disfavor on men and women in elaborate evening dress but moccasined feet, made cold fact the American quip, "It's formal; wear shoes." Completion of the St. Paul, Minneapolis and Manitoba Railroad, arrival of Canadian and American shops and services, removed the last obstacles. And a social structure, happily balanced between the whaleboned formality of the British system, the ever-changing, consistently informal features of the American, took final form.

South of the Boundary, meantime—came the revolution!

Technically, the pioneer period in American Red River Valley ended on December 31, 1879. By that time, railroads, actual or projected, to embryo villages and towns had declared unnecessary the tree-stump furniture, one-post beds, and other ingenious makeshifts. The way was clear, the day had come, when civilization could arrive in safety. It did—with white kid gloves.

Though the Great Dakota Boom was less than two years old and still to reach full stride, began then from Boston, New York City, Philadelphia, Richmond, Atlanta, New Orleans, and other centers depleted of man power, capital, and opportunities by the Civil War and the panic of 1873, a migration of personable and ambitious young Brahmins.

Seeking a mount that, though saddled with a shoestring, could be ridden to fortune, if not fame, doctors, lawyers, college professors, bankers, land and grain brokers, flour, wool, and sawmill operators, wholesale and retail dealers in everything from farm machinery and bricks to hand-painted lace fans, swarmed up and down Red River to appraise "immigrants" and new boomer towns. In Fargo, and particularly in Grand Forks because of five-starred plans to make it another Chicago of land and water transportation, they concentrated.

Well educated professionally and socially, many still proudly wearing their military titles as major, colonel, general, they lived in what for lack of any words at all were called hotels and boarding houses, opened offices and shops in the barnlike one- and two-story frame buildings strung along a chewed-up half-mile of prairie known as Third Street. But one glance at the crowded saloons, brothels, gambling houses, and rickety log and frame shacks was sufficient to convince them that Grand Forks was no place for their wives and children.

South of the raucous frontier town, however, Red River moved in a wide bend below a high and wooded ridge. On the ridge, they built duplicates of the Victorian homes they had known. Set back in deep lawns, dripping with wooden lace and pillared porches, bug-eyed with bay windows and cupolas, these mansions further were embellished with stained glass, tiled fireplaces, parquet floors, mahogany and oak paneling. And behind each, rose a miniature replica for the family horse and buggy and "hired man."

Here they installed their families and armaments against the social wilderness. Haviland and Lemoges china. Versaille and other ornate silver services. Flowered carpets. Leather-bound libraries. Pianos. Lush lace curtains and velvet draperies. And here arrived buxom, able, and willing "hired girls" from the farms, eager to care for house and family for two dollars a week and Thursday afternoon off.

To Fargo, Grand Forks, and other towns came also well-educated, socially endowed young women who, to escape manless New England and other such hapless areas, artlessly or artfully had disguised themselves as schoolteachers. In man-full Red River Valley, they seldom clung to that disguise long.

By 1881, a self-anointed group of men with imported wives, newly-weds, and a corps of eligible bachelors were primed for Grand Fork's first social season. Dinners, receptions, progressive euchre parties, home theatricals, horses races on River ice, spangled winter and spring. On May 25, to the strains of an imported orchestra, men and women in formal dress, moving through waltzes, Newport heel-and-toes, raquettes, Saratogas, Montabellas, and the latest college steps closed their calendar with a Grand Ball.

Followed then a "little season," largely theatrical. For now Georgia Minstrels, Jubilee Singers, traveling stock companies, tent shows, magicians, acrobats, had scented the filling purses on the prairies. Even the racing season on the new track north of town, where blooded pacers and trotters competed for ratings on the Northwest Circuit, concluded with an opera. With thirty-inch-high Jenny Quigley as prima donna, the Lilliputians presented *Jack the Giant Killer.*

Picnics, boating, excursions to celebrate the St. Paul, Minneapolis and Manitoba's arrival at some new town, feting of visiting celebrities and marriageable sisters, sped the days till July 4. Then with a parade and sports by day, another Grand Ball at night, the socialites retired to their vine-curtained porches to sit out the hot months and make new plans.

Shades of long-suffering Verendrye! Of the Selkirkers! Of every European immigrant who crossed the seas to break virgin Valley soil! In the cool seclusion of their River retreats, these newcomers beheld themselves as pioneers. No, upper case: PIONEERS.

Within half a decade, their Pioneer Club in its resplendent modern clubhouse, their Pioneer Riding Club, Pioneer Polo Club, Pioneer (Ladies) Reading Club, had proclaimed them the First Families of Red River Valley.

Balls in their clubhouse and in the handsome new Hotel Dacotah, with orchestras and flowers by the carload imported from Minneapolis, were the ultimate in elegance. Gowns of the women, copied in Chicago or New York from Paris models worn at Presidential Inaugurals in Washington or the opening of the Metropolitan Opera in New York, were described in tongue-rolling detail in the *Grand Forks Plain Dealer.*

On one thing the newspaper's eye-rolling readers could rely. If the Pioneers with White Kid Gloves wore diamonds, pearls, rubies, emeralds, those jewels were genuine. If they trailed skirts of Spanish or Chantilly lace, that lace was real. Their cut glass, crystal, paper-thin china, silver services, heavy, polished, six- or nine-yard linen tablecloths with enveloping napkins to match, needed neither candle-light nor wit to make them dazzle. Possessions, like their owners, if one may say so, were solid.

Other ladies' reading clubs from end to end of the Valley might peruse Stoddard's *Lectures* or Dickens' novels during snowbound months. With the exception of one or two weeks in summer when the temperature hit one hundred in the shade, Pioneer Ladies confronted without a tremor Metternich's *Memoirs,* Rambouillet's *His-*

tory of Russia in six volumes, Wilkerson's *Egypt*. Other groups might discuss Swinburne's poetry or Shakespeare's heroines. *They* grappled with everything from Swiss Heroes to Dutch Art to the Differences between American and English Locomotives. Their Thursday Musical Club embarked on programs that would turn today's Traubels, Heifitzes, Rubensteins a trifle pale.

Perhaps in a sense these Mr. and Mrs. Johnny Come Latelys were justified in considering themselves pioneers—wherever they lived in the Valley. The women had only their fragile Royal Worcester bouillon cups, their afternoon rounds by carriage to leave one of their own, two of their husbands', heavily engraved cards at carefully approved doors, their boned and bustled gowns and white kid gloves to bulwark their solid-gold faith in themselves and their way of life. The men had only their meticulously groomed mustaches and Vandykes, Prince Albert coats, pin-striped trousers and canes. Yet resolutely and courageously they set out to define and conquer a new frontier.

3. THE LIFTED LAMP

Long before the first trader in Red River Valley wrote his first letter or journal, the Sioux had founded its literary tradition. If collected today, their narratives of hunt and battle, their detailed explanations, now called legends, of every natural phenomenon as the work of the gods, would fill a library.

The journals required annually of every fur trader were merely a continuation of an already rooted art. Those of Alexander Henry and Daniel Williams Harmon, a Vermonter, are remarkable both for content and style. Writings of James Hargrave, a trader stationed for years at Fort Garry, highlight the period following the merger of Hudson's Bay and North West. But Archbishop Cochrane and the Reverend David Jones of the Anglican Church, Archbishop Taché and Bishop Provencher of the Catholic, even Cuthbert Grant, John Tanner, and many more used the leisure of their later years to tell of life in Red River Valley.

The list is, in fact, so long that modern researchers find themselves more grateful to the few who didn't write than to the myriad who did. Following Red River Rebellion and the founding of Manitoba, no sheet of paper was safe. Even newcomers caught the fever.

Ernest Seton Thompson, arriving in rural Manitoba from Pennsylvania, with a crate of chickens as capital, took one look at the wild life about him and began the stories about the *Sandhill Stag, Mother Teal, Bingo, the Dog,* that were to make his name a household word. In Winnipeg, the Reverend W. V. Gordon, as "Ralph Connor," wrote *Sky Pilot, Parrot of Sundance Trail,* and other novels that, translated into almost every language, circled the globe. Many others carried on. Despite the fact that, to live, modern writers must appeal to American readers rather than to the Dominion's limited market, Canadian Red River Valley is arattle with typewriters transmuting ore from the mine of the past into every literary form of the present.

In little, old Red River Jig, the Winnipeg Symphony Orchestra, Manitoba Music Festival (of some 15,000 participants), hundreds of musical clubs and choruses, Celebrity Concerts, Winnipeg Light Opera Company, the Ballet, all the activities that make the modern capital a city of music and music lovers, have a common ancestor. The charades of the forties, home theatricals of the fifties, amateur dramatic societies of the sixties and seventies, pyramided naturally to today's Little Theatre of Winnipeg and the commercial playhouses.

If proof is needed that north of the Boundary (and south), the arts stem from the past, witness the fact that among the books and musical instruments imported by traders and colonists, neither brush nor chisel found place. For all its handsome public buildings, Winnipeg has produced no painters or sculptors of notable stature. *To date.* Few cities in North America are doing more to preserve and develop the arts and crafts of their foreign immigrants. On this filling reservoir, artists and sculptors of tomorrow may draw for inspiration.

Given such a heritage, the moving belt of evolution alone must have carried to fruition not only the arts but sports, education, religion, love of home and garden, all the ingredients that, blended together, form the culture of Winnipeg. That in seventy-five years it approached equality with eastern Canada's four times older capitals is due to three supplementary generators.

The physical bottleneck the Valley represents between Boundary and Lake Winnipeg, by concentrating population, industry, transportation, communication, government, finance about the junction of Red and Assiniboine Rivers, made the Manitoba capital a modern version of the old city-state. Unable to compete economically and politically with Winnipeg, smaller, younger St. Boniface on the east bank sank many a spur into the metropolis on the west while making itself second only to Quebec as a treasure house of French-Canadian tradition and culture. Most important of all were the blueprints of British-Protestant and French-Catholic civilizations laid down by earliest explorers and fur traders for Canadian Red River Valley to follow.

Though no historic date or event marked its transition from Pioneer to Modern Period, by 1890 its basic structures were complete.

American Red River Valley, on the contrary, had a date and event, but no such stimuli. With the greater part of its population flooding in between 1879 and 1885, the arts had no more chance to function than an unconnected electric switch. Level as a floor, the American Valley has no bottlenecks; one square mile is much the same as another. Though by 1885, most of its population was made up of English-speaking Americans, Canadians, Britishers, its minority—a composite of European tongues, traditions, traits—set far in the future the welding of a community of background necessary to a community of culture.

What impulses then powered the Valley south of the Boundary to lift its lamp before the golden door contemporaneously with Winnipeg? Two. The first was Prohibition; rather, until 1889, the lack of it. The second was the rising tide of wealth, stabilized by the imminence of Statehood for North Dakota.

Though even before North Dakota became a State, most of the Valley's people were temperate, every crossroads had its saloon or saloons. Some sold the meanest liquor ever brewed. Some catered to Indians, the most degraded business, it was considered then, a man could enter.

Up and down Red River, the respectable, God-fearing majority fixed stern faces on the Demon Rum. The churches through their clergy, services, Ladies Aids, box socials, Christmas parties, song fests, sleighrides, hayrack rides, were a power in the land. So were the schools, with their evening lyceums where many a Dakota and Minnesota legislator gained confidence and fluency, spelldowns, Christmas parties, harvest home festivals, dances and song fests. So, above all, in a land where men outnumbered women ten to one and a wife was as essential as a roof or a plow, were the marriageable young ladies who pledged themselves never to wed or even "keep company" with any liquor-lovin' male.

Came Prohibition. Now into Fargo and Grand Forks, as twin mouths of the cornucopia, flowed widening streams of Eastern capital to finance banks, office buildings, stores of brick and glass. And streams of residents from the rural districts, grain checks crackling, to purchase fine machinery, furniture, feathers, and fine fun.

But to them also came wealthy, gorgeously wardrobed Eastern women seeking divorces and, often, the wealthy men, many of them titled, who were to marry them the moment their decrees were won. Came remittance men, like Lord Thursby to Grand Forks, to build expansive homes and entertain on a lavish scale. Came large parties of rich "Sports," from east and west, for the hunting, fishing, and wide-open freedom in wide-open towns. Came the armies of harvesters, lumberjacks, tracklayers, roustabouts, their wages burning holes in their pockets, and the predaceous tribes, male and female, who feed on them.

Using the west bank as their address, these transient pleasure-seekers swarmed across the pontoon bridges to the east bank to spend their time and money on what was known conservatively as riotous living.

For to Red River's east bank in Northwest Minnesota, saloons, gambling houses, bordellos and dives of all North Dakota had moved, to take over existing settlements or found new ones. From the junction of Red and Bois des Sioux to the Boundary, every west side Hyde soon had its east side Jekyll.

In less than a year, East Grand Forks, with a population of 200, boasted twenty saloons; shortly, forty-two compressed, wall to wall, within two blocks of the bridge. Beer at five cents a glass rolled between eight and nine million dollars annually across their counters. Whiskies rang up about half that. Neither gentleman nor *hoi polloi* wasted time on other liquids.

Orchestras, entertainers, costly paintings, carved mahogany interiors, expert bartenders and other features ranked two of them among the finest bars in the United States. Others ranged from good to bad to clubfooted, hunchbacked "Little Harry's" hole in the wall where a gang of arsonists relaxed between excursions to burn down, for a price, anything, anywhere.

Above or behind most saloons, poker rooms operated day and night, week after week, year in, year out. So unending was the supply of victims, so astronomical the profits, that dapper little Billy le Praik was able to indulge his taste for books to the tune of a library valued at a quarter-million dollars.

When the eastern approach to the bridge burned, cutting off the west side clientele, enterprising saloon and gambling house keepers quickly erected a street of frame substitutes on Minnesota's share of Red River ice. Though simple outside, a few were most luxurious within. In these the divorcees, their escorts, and the sports left thousands of dollars nightly. Profitable also and even more convenient were the makeshift structures. Now undesirable customers could be shoved through a hole in the ice, not to cause trouble again until their bodies floated downriver in the spring.

At a discreet distance, on the "Point" between the forks of Red and Red Lake Rivers, rose the five sprawling mansions, also bedecked with wooden lace, pillared porches, flowered carpets, velvet draperies, known as the "Houses in the Hollow." Here lived Irene, Madame Harriet, Mabel, and other extremely expensive ladies of the evening. Periodically, representatives of New York couturiers brought trunkloads of gowns, plumed hats, handmade lingerie and jewels for their selection. On Sundays and pleasant afternoons, their complexions and finery protected by fragile lace parasols, they took the air in open carriages, perversely finding it freshest along Grand Fork's most exclusive residence streets.

Good hunting for elk, moose and deer in near-by Minnesota forests, for prairie chicken, pheasant and duck on the prairies, good fishing in innumerable streams and lakes were perennial attractions. To these, East Grand Fork's own sports lovers added their quickly organized Sportsmen's Association to equip grounds that contained the only mile track in the Northwest. There and, in winter, on Red River ice, racing meets in which their own registered thoroughbreds competed against those from east and west drew thousands of bettors and customers.

Because of their trigger tempers, East Grand Fork's leading citizens never locked their homes or places of business. As a warning to all whom it might concern, they early had suspended from the nearest bridge, without benefit of trial, two suspected evildoers (one of them innocent). What happened to harvesters, lumberjacks and other unrefined characters didn't count.

So much happened so often that the *Minneapolis Tribune's* almost daily recital of robberies, assaults, and murder roused a local judge to threaten suit for libel. Within forty-eight hours after a *Tribune* investigator arrived, the judge himself was dead, shot by robbers on the open street.

The *Minneapolis Tribune* was not the only broadcaster. Newspapers all over the United States and Canada enlarged every sensation emanating from east-bank Jekylls, then linked them up with tales of the bonanzas, political scandals, railroad and other land grabs. To the shocked gaze of the Victorian Age, Red River Valley became Sodom multiplied by Gomorrah.

In vain, to disclaim some villainy, the *Grand Forks Plain Dealer* headlined to the world at large:

NOT FROM GRAND FORKS
From East Grand Forks, If You Please, Sir

In vain, residents of Dakota's Valley assured friends and relatives, east, west, south, that they were living with the same decorum as Boston's Back Bay or Atlanta's Peachtree Street.

Worse still was the prospect of the effect of the east bank's example on the west bank's growing young, and the hint that trade might seek Winnipeg, Minneapolis or developing towns to the west. Tension heightened as the old watchword, "What of it? Millions in it!" fell before the bolder, "The Sky's the Limit!" *Something had to be done!*

Thus east-bank towns, serving the same function as grains of grit in oysters, rapidly brought culture to a fine finish in western Red River Valley. Again, and logically, as the largest bivalve, suffering the most painful irritant in its side, Grand Forks produced the largest, purest pearl.

Not through organized campaigns alone, but stirred by the same spirit that motivated Londoners as individuals to outlast and outfight the Blitz, its solid citizens co-operated to elevate Grand Forks as the "Little Athens" of the prairies.

Though a town of but 5,000 people, it had the men and money to do it. Because of the lucrative divorce colony, more than thirty of its professional men were lawyers, several of them known far beyond the Valley for their brilliance and learning. Among the ex-captains, majors, colonels, generals were many able men, including a portly, florid gentleman of punctilious Old World manner. Though now the owner of a drugstore, in his youth he had been for years in Denmark companion of the Danish prince who ascended the throne as Christian IX and of the three young princesses later known as Alexandra

Queen of England, Marie Dagmar Empress of Russia, and Thyra Duchess of Cumberland. Another citizen and descendant of one of the signers of Norway's Declaration of Independence, was a lover and connoisseur of the arts. From his many European voyages, he had made his Grand Forks home the setting for one of the most valuable collections of paintings and marbles in the Midwest.

Among the clergy were three or four most dedicated and cultivated men. Among the University faculty, a number of recognized scholars, so devoted to furthering learning in the new State that when an agricultural-minded Legislature refused them funds, they served without compensation. And if all the prominent fathers of families and pillars of the church were not tall, handsome, well educated, and all the rest, they made up in zeal for any social or cultural lack.

To grace and dignify banquet halls and church auditoriums in Grand Forks and erase the onus of a Red River Valley address, they imported world-renowned artists from stage and concert hall, lecturers, writers, heroes, Cabinet officers, even a President of the United States. They brought in dancing teachers, music teachers, art and "elocution" teachers, set up libraries and art exhibitions, parks, sports, new schools, and blazed the travel trails to every corner of the world annually followed today by a large percentage of Red River's population.

They painted and refurbished homes and shops, removed the open barrels of dried and salted fish that rimmed the exteriors of many stores regardless of their interior merchandise. They replaced the short lengths of boom logs mounted on low stilts with wooden sidewalks. They aisled the treeless streets with quick-growing box elders, and dislocated many a vertebra producing soft green lawns where wild and matted buffalo grass had reigned so long.

They made Grand Forks so refined that harvesters, tracklayers, lumberjacks, roustabouts patronized the thoughtful haberdasher who filled his window with celluloid collars fitted with snap bow ties. For a quarter, these could be worn during a day in town, discarded on the way out. They made it so refined that many ex-fur traders, steamboat captains, stagecoach station owners and other hitherto untrammeled characters hastily sought respectability in marriage—some of them to wives secured through matrimonial agencies and Lonely Heart columns. Incorrigibly freedom-loving spirits took off for the uncensored liberty of the Black Hills.

One thing the culture crusaders achieved in all innocence. They welded the love of adventure, courage and high pride, the exhilaration of gambling everything for high stakes, bred into the Valley by Prairie Sioux, explorer and fur trader, with the solid virtues of the European immigrants and American and Canadian homeseekers.

It was this combination of enterprise, daring, vision and pride that carried American Red River Valley to the date and event that sums up and symbolizes its history and the aspirations, if not the realization, of all its people as they moved from Pioneer to Modern Era.

4. EXIT, BOWING

Early in October, 1890, George Broadhurst, then as manager of the Hennepin Avenue Theater in Minneapolis, on the first miles of the road to fame and fortune as Broadway playwright and producer, received a letter. To his bewilderment, it invited him to take over the management of a new theater in Grand Forks, North Dakota.

Faintly, he recalled the signer, George Batchelder, as a dynamic young man who a year or so before had whirled in and out of the Minneapolis theater. More curious than interested, he entrained for the "obscure burg," Twin City newspapers pictured as an unpretentious trading post, stagecoach station, and steamboat landing.

Arrived, he did catch more reassuring impressions of brick and stone buildings rising above frame, shoebox shops, of decorous townsmen and women arriving by foot or carriage before their doors. But he only had time for glimpses. His escort, young Batchelder, hurried him straight toward the massive brownstone structure towering over midtown.

"That's it," Batchelder told him. "That's the Metropolitan Opera House. We just got her named the other night. She cost $150,000 to build—only $26,000 of it subscribed yet—but she's up."

Aghast, its prospective manager exclaimed, "You don't expect to make it pay, do you?"

"Of course not. But she's there. No matter what happens, they won't pull her down."

Once inside the high, locked bronze gates that sealed the arched foyer against any hint of what lay beyond reaching public knowledge, Broadhurst swallowed his intention to suggest that a less grandiose name than that of New York's opera house might be more fitting.

The interior was a gem of ivory, blue and gold baroque décor. With its well-proportioned auditorium, two curving balconies, luxurious draperies, upholstered seats, especially designed loge chairs, spacious and well-equipped stage, "it was in fact," he admitted, "Metropolitan." It was, in fact, almost a duplicate of Chicago's famous Auditorium.

"That's right," Batchelder agreed. "When a bunch of men here decided more than a year ago to do something to put Grand Forks and Red River Valley on the map, they wanted nothing but the best. So I scouted Minneapolis and Chicago. Picked you as the best manager. The Auditorium as the best theater. And signed up the Emma Abbott Opera Company as the opening attraction."

Broadhurst rocked back on his heels. "But that's the most important organization of its kind on tour. What night will it appear?"

"Night, nothing! We've booked them for three nights and a matinee."

Such a thing was unheard of, impossible. Even in Minneapolis and Chicago, No. 1 road companies played to one-night stands. Drawing a deep breath, Broadhurst asked, "And what percentage do they play on?"

"No percentage. We're paying them $4,000, or $1,000 a performance."

That did it. "You won't play to half that," Broadhurst said flatly. "I'm taking the next train back to Minneapolis."

Batchelder laughed at him. "Maybe you don't know it but you're in Red River Valley, the greatest grain country in the world. Wheat this year panned out forty bushels to the acre, at one dollar and fifty cents a bushel. People's pockets are bulging with money and their breasts with local pride."

"But $4,000," the theatrical manager protested. "Can't you realize that that means you've got to take in $1,000 a performance, including the matinee, before the house gets a cent?"

"We'll play to $5,000—maybe $6,000. Don't you worry. You're here now. Give it a whirl." From a pocket Batchelder dug out a crumpled bit of paper. "Here's a list of the first half-dozen men to see about subscriptions for the opening night."

More to please the ingenuous young man than with any hope of success, Broadhurst finally consented to give it a whirl. His first prospect was a red-bearded giant of sixty, square, wide and erect as a barn door.

"If I get ten dollars out of this character I can qualify as a confidence man," he thought as he began to expatiate on what a powerful advertisement a magnificent opening in the new opera house would be for Grand Forks and Red River Valley.

The giant listened impassively, then rising to his full height, boomed in a seagoing voice, "Young fella, I guess you don't know who I am. I'm Captain Alexander Griggs. I drove a dog team between St. Paul and Winnipeg before a railroad up here even was thought of. Part of Grand Forks is on my original homestead. I captained the first steamboat Jim Hill put on the River. I was at the first wedding here. I was at the first christening. I was at the first funeral. And I'm sure going to be at the opening of the first opera house. Put me down for three hundred dollars for two seats for the first performance, and if anybody sees me, I'll raise him fifty."

Broadhurst tottered over to his next prospect, "Billy" Budge, one-time proprietor, with George Winship, of the opera-bouffe-run stagecoach station just north of Grand Forks. Before he was well started on his opening sentence, his listener interrupted, "Seen the Captain? How much did he give?"

"Three—three hundred dollars."

"I'll see him."

With $650 subscribed for four seats in two interviews, Broadhurst rushed back to Batchelder to learn whether he had been the victim of Red River Valley's idea of good, clean fun. That young man was delighted, but not surprised.

Then and there the two conceived the historic souvenir program of white satin on which the names of all who subscribed $50 or more for two seats for the opening night would be printed in gold.

Now Broadhurst had only to shake the tree. With that program the equivalent of a social register, no married man who had or could raise the necessary $50, dared refuse. In no time, with no name down for less than $200, Grand Forks citizens alone had bought out the first night to the tune of almost $7,000.

From Winnipeg to Breckenridge, from Detroit Lakes to Larimore, subscriptions poured in from every corner of the Valley for the remaining performances. From all Manitoba, North and South Dakota, and Minnesota came more, to swell receipts beyond $10,000.

Now rose the issue of what to wear to do the Valley proud. Among the pioneers were many accustomed to evening dress, but the decision that formal dress would be obligatory for the opening night boomed the tailoring business from St. Paul to Winnipeg.

For weeks the *Grand Forks Herald* had titivated Emma Abbott's fabulous jewels and $25,000 wardrobe, all made by Worth and Felix in Paris, for the delectation of the Valley. "Her garments for *Rose of Castile* alone are paralyzing to a woman," it warned, then added hastily, "Clothes, of course, do not make an opera, but they certainly help." It quoted long excerpts from New York and Chicago rave reviews of the performances of the eighty-member troupe and its twenty-piece orchestra. It summarized the librettos of *Martha, Rose of Castile, Fra Diavolo, Il Trovatore.* But not one word did it print about the interior of the theater.

On November 10, 1890, when the opening of the Metropolitan came round at last, not only ticket holders, but the Valley at large were bowstrings of pride and suspense. Hardly had the great bronze gates swung back on the dot of seven-thirty than carriages and "hacks" converged on the entrance that ladies and gentlemen might enjoy a leisured preview of the hidden wonders.

But promptly at eight-fifteen the footlights flickered. Beneath the muraled dome, the great electric sunburner dimmed until it resembled a galaxy of a thousand remote stars. One by one the incandescent lights and gas flames cradled in frosted crystal cups went out.

Though the theater was packed to the roof, when the footlights signaled again, the proverbial pin could have been heard falling from the dome. In the pit the orchestra smoothed the overture to a close. Gold hangings across the carved and gilded proscenium moved to loop and lift. Behind them the muraled curtain on which a beauteous maiden reclined against crusted gold tapestries in a flowered and languidly powered gondola, quivered. And in the wings, Manager George Broadhurst, truly foreseeing the immediate future when Broadway's brightest stars and No. 1 road companies would include this little frontier town on their Chicago—San Francisco—New Orleans circuit, mopped an astounded brow.

But neither to the breathlessly still audience nor to the surrounding country was that curtain rising on *Martha*, the Metropolitan Opera House, or Grand Forks. It was rising on Red River Valley.

After twenty thousand years of exodus and migration, of trial and error, of tragedy and triumph, of isolation, of battle, of hidden abundance gradually revealed, the land through which *Red River Runs North* was ready to begin.

BIBLIOGRAPHY

Until this century, Red River of the North and his Valley have suffered from too many part-time Boswells. Bits of their story are scattered through English, Scotch, Irish, French, Swiss, Norwegian, German, Danish, and many more European literatures; through American and Canadian, and widely, of course, through those of Manitoba, Minnesota, North and South Dakota. Twentieth-century pens have been too busy with World Wars and other cosmic events or with the re-creation of the story of more familiar regions to engage in a study of Red River's affairs.

Because of the trigger-quick national, regional, and personal prejudices characteristic of the eighteenth and nineteenth centuries, their writers rarely sought access to other literatures and points of view to explain the reverse side of the coin of history. Thus French versus British accounts of the same Red River event, British versus Canadian, Canadian versus American, Manitoban versus Dakota-Minnesotan, even North Dakotan versus South Dakotan, uniformly interpret motives and actions of their own nationals or citizens with sweet reason. To the machinations of the villains operating outside their own physical and political jurisdictions, they apply a stiff mixture of ink and acid.

The result is that names, dates, personalities, circumstances, even spellings, selected by writers of opposing origins for a common theme often bear little resemblance to one another. As the first attempt to co-ordinate the story of the three political divisions of Red River Valley, this book picks a precarious way from official records to firsthand accounts to so-called histories and other sources, hoping for the best, but guaranteeing nothing.

The irony of the mountain of words about Red River preserved in libraries, archives, and family records is that it rests on shifting sands. Only in recent times have documents basic to its story come to light. Many more, if they remain extant, are yet to be revealed. Many may be lost forever. Others are so rare that, guarded closely by their custodians, they are inaccessible to the general reader.

Radisson and Groseilliers, Henry Kelsey, the Verendryes, and Peter Pond logically might be grouped as the founding fathers of Red River Valley. Yet all died in poverty and obscurity, their claims to fame discredited, ignored, and later covered over by those of more literate newcomers who not only wrote books but secured for them early and wide acceptance.

Radisson's account of his "travels and experiences," now considered the most absorbing document of early mid-North American history, though prepared in the 1680's, did not reach public notice for almost two hundred years. When Charles II of England finished with it, his ingratiating Secretary of the Admiralty, the diarist, Samuel Pepys, wangled it for his personal manuscript collection. After Pepys's death in 1703, it was sold with the rest of his collection to London tradesmen for practical uses in their shops. Rescued by another collector, Richard Rawlinson, it eventually was interred in the manuscript collection of the Bodelian Library at Oxford University. There it remained until 1880, when the Prince Society of Boston published it in a limited edition.

The 1690-92 journal of Henry Kelsey lay in the archives of Hudson's Bay Company in London until 1749, when it was dug out temporarily to serve as evidence in a court case. In 1926, it turned up among the documents found in Castle Dobbs, Carrickfergus, Ulster. Presented to the Public Records Office of Northern Ireland and published three years later as *The Kelsey Papers,* it now ranks second only in interest and importance to Radisson's narrative.

No considered, comprehensive account of the life and work of the Verendryes was available until 1927, when the Champlain Society of Toronto published their letters, journals, and allied documents for its 500 subscribers.

Poor, old, illiterate Peter Pond's account of his invaluable explorations and achievements suffered the deepest ignominy of all. Written about 1800, its crude, homemade phonetics give it the flavor of a tale told by an amateur Chaucer:

It hapened that a parson [person] who was in trade himself to abuse me in a shameful maner knowing that if I resented he could shake me in peaces at the same time suposing that I dare not sea him at the pints or at leas would not but the abuse was to grate. We met the next morning eairley and discharged pistels in which the pore felow was unfortenat.

Largely lost or destroyed as worthless after Pond's death, its fragments were not assembled and published until 1930.

Who knows what proofs and records of Norse arrivals in Red River Valley in the fourteenth century or earlier were found and destroyed by Indians, fur traders and first settlers along the River? Little significance was given such weapons, equipment and other articles uncovered during the past fifty years until the controversial Kensington Rune Stone came to light in 1907.

One should remember too, that despite the "pure" aspects of science, scientists of eastern Canada and the United States hold adulterated opinions of anything that emerges from the "old" west. That those of the Old World still are reluctant to concede age to the New, whether it be North, Central or South America.

Fur trade journals, pioneer diaries, letters, and latter-day reminiscences exist in quantity in historical society collections and family archives of Manitoba and Upper Midwest States. But many of them, edited by relatives sensitive to "What will people say?" have been refined and purified. Hindsight often, and sometimes innocently, colors and embellishes others to a diffused and rosy glow.

For these and kindred reasons, the following Bibliography, selected from some 1,500 primary and secondary sources consulted, is offered merely as a reading list for those interested to know more on general subjects. With few exceptions, it must be said again, these should be read saltcellar in hand.

1) *Aborigines of Minnesota,* compiled by N. H. Winchell. Minnesota Historical Society, St. Paul, 1911

2) *Adventures of Zenas Leonard, Fur Trader and Trapper, 1831-36,* edited by W. F. Wagner. Burrows Brothers, Cleveland, 1904

3) *Agriculture in Minnesota,* by W. C. Coffee. Department of Agriculture, University of Minnesota, February, 1929

4) *Alexander Henry and David Thompson, 1799-1814, The Manuscript Journals of,* edited by Elliott Coues. Francis P. Harper, New York, 1897. 3 vols.

5) *America, 1355-1364; A New Chapter in Pre-Columbian History,* by Hjalmar R. Holand. Duell, Sloan, and Pearce, New York, 1946

6) *American Fur Trade in the Far West, The,* by H. M. Chittenden. Francis P. Harper, New York, 1902

7) *Astoria,* by Washington Irving. Putnam's, New York, 1859

8) *Birth of Western Canada, The,* by George F. G. Stanley. Longmans, Green and Company, New York, 1936

9) *Buffalo Hunters, The Last,* as told by Norbert Welsh to Mary Weekes. Thomas Nelson and Sons, New York, 1939

10) *Building of the Canadian West, The,* by James B. Hedges. The Macmillan Company, New York, 1939

11) *Caesars of the Wilderness,* by Grace Lee Nute. Appleton-Century Company, New York, 1943

12) *Canadian-American Relations, 1849-1874,* by Lester Burrell Shippee. Yale University Press, New Haven, 1939

13) *Canadian Northwest, The,* edited by E. H. Oliver. Government Printing Bureau, Ottawa, 1914. 2 vols.

14) *Canadian Red River Exploring Expedition of 1857 and the Assiniboine and Saskatchewan Exploring Expedition of 1858, Narrative of the,* by Henry Youle Hind. Longman, Green, Longman and Roberts, London, 1860. 2 vols.

15) *Canadian West, The Making of the,* by R. G. Macbeth. William Briggs, Toronto, 1898

16) *Canadian West to 1870-1, History of the,* by A. S. Morton. Thomas Nelson and Sons, New York, n.d.

17) *Cheadle's Journal of Trip Across Canada, 1862-1863,* by Walter Butler Cheadle. Graphic Publishers, Ltd., Ottawa, 1931

18) *Checkered Years, The,* by Mary Dodge Woodward. Caxton Printers, Ltd., Caldwell, Idaho, 1937

19) *Crisis of 1830-1842 in Canadian-American Relations, The,* by Albert B. Corey. Yale University Press, New Haven, 1941

20) *Dacotah or Sioux Indians, History of,* by Doane Robinson. State of South Dakota, Aberdeen, 1904

21) *Dakota,* by Edna LaMoore Waldo. Capital Publishing Company, Bismarck, N.D., 1932

22) *Dakota Territory, History of,* by George W. Kingsbury. S. J. Clarke Publishing Company, Chicago, 1915. 2 vols.

23) *David Thompson's Narrative of His Explorations in Western America, 1784-1812,* edited by J. B. Tyrell. The Champlain Society, Toronto, 1916

24) *Discoveries and Settlements of the French in the West and in the South Parts of North America, 1614-1754—Memoirs and Original Documents,* by Pierre Margry. Paris, 1886

25) *Earliest Fur Traders on the Upper Red River and Red Lake, 1783-1810,* by Charles Napier Bell. Historical and Scientific Society of Manitoba, New Series, No. 1, Winnipeg, 1926

26) *Early Bonanza Farming in Red River Valley,* by Harold E. Briggs. Vols. V-VII, Agricultural History, 1931-33

27) *Early Days and Ways in the Old Northwest,* by Maude L. Londquist and James W. Clark. Charles Scribner's Sons, New York, 1937

28) *Early Empire Builders of the Great West,* by Moses K. Armstrong. E. W. Porter, St. Paul, 1901

29) *Empire Builder, The* (James J. Hill), by Oscar M. Sullivan. Century Company, New York, 1928

30) *Expedition of Captains Lewis and Clark, 1804-5-6, History of the,* (Reprinted from 1814 edition). With Introduction and Index by James K. Hosmer. A. C. McClurg and Company, Chicago, 1902

31) *Expedition to the Source of St. Peter's* [the Minnesota] *River, Lake*

Winnepeek, Lake of the Woods, etc., Performed in the Year 1823 . . . under the Command of Stephen H. Long, Narrative of an, compiled by William H. Keating. G. B. Whittaker, London, 1825. 2 vols.

32) *Explorations of the Country Between Lake Superior and Red River Settlement, Report of the,* by S. J. Dawson. John Lovell, Toronto, 1859

33) *Explorers of North America, The,* by John Bartlett Brebner. The Macmillan Company, New York, 1933

34) *Five Fur Traders of the Northwest,* edited by Charles M. Gates. Minnesota Society of Colonial Dames of America, through the University of Minnesota Press, 1933

35) *Flood at Red River, Notes of,* by Reverend David Anderson. Hatchard's, London, 1852

36) *French Regime in Wisconsin, 1727-48, The,* edited by Reuben Goldthwaites. State Historical Society of Wisconsin, Madison, 1906

37) *French Regime in Wisconsin and the Northwest, The,* by Louise Phelps Kellogg. State Historical Society of Wisconsin, Madison, 1925

38) *Fur Trade and Empire; George Simpson's Journal,* edited by Frederick Merk. Harvard University Press, Cambridge, 1931

39) *Fur Trade in Canada, The,* by Harold A. Innis. Yale University Press, New Haven, 1930

40) *Glacial Lake Agassiz,* by Warren Upham. Government Printing Office, Washington, D.C., 1895

41) *Great American Land Bubble, The,* by A. M. Sakolski. Harper and Brothers, New York, 1932

42) *Great Lone Land, The,* by Colonel William Francis Butler. Sampson Low, Marston and Company, London, 1891

43) *James J. Hill, The Life of* (Authorized), by Joseph Gilpin Pyle. Doubleday, Page and Company, New York, 1917. 2 vols.

44) *Honorable Company, The,* by Douglas Mackay. Bobbs-Merrill, New York, 1936

45) *Hudson Bay, Documents Relating to the Early History of.* The Champlain Society, Toronto, 1943

46) *Hudson's Bay Company, A Few Words on,* by A. K. Isbister. London, 1846

47) *Hudson's Bay Company, 1670-1920,* by Sir William Schooling. Hudson's Bay Company, London, 1920

48) *Hudson's Bay Company, 1671-1674, Minutes of the.* The Champlain Society, Toronto, 1943

49) *Hudson's Bay Company's Land Tenures and the Occupation of Assiniboia by Lord Selkirk's Settlers,* by Archer Martin. William Clowes and Sons, London, 1896

50) *Hudson's Bay Company's Monopoly of the Fur Trade at Red River Settlement, 1821-1850,* by Chester Martin. Mississippi Valley Historical Association Proceedings, Cedar Rapids, Iowa, 1914

51) *Hunting of the Buffalo, The,* by E. Douglas Branch. Appleton and Company, New York, 1929

52) *Indians North of Mexico, Handbook of the American,* edited by Frederick Webb Hodge. Bureau of American Ethnology, Smithsonian Institute, Washington, D.C., 1907. 2 vols.

53) *John Jacob Astor, Business Man,* by Kenneth Wiggins Porter. Harvard University Press, Cambridge, 1931. 2 vols.

54) *Kelsey, The Journal of Henry, 1690-92,* with preface by Charles Napier Bell. Historical and Scientific Society of Manitoba, Winnipeg, 1928

55) *Kelsey Papers, The,* collected by Chester Martin. Public Archives of Canada and the Public Record Office of Northern Ireland, 1929

56) *Kensington Rune Stone, The,* by Hjalmar R. Holand. Privately printed, Ephraim, Wisconsin, 1932

57) *Lake Superior,* by Grace Lee Nute. Bobbs-Merrill, New York, 1944

58) *Lord Selkirk's Work in Canada,* by Chester Martin. Oxford University Press, Toronto, 1916

59) *Lord Strathcona and Mount Royal (Donald A. Smith), Life of,* by Beckles Willson. Houghton Mifflin, New York, 1915. 2 vols.

60) *Manitoba,* by George Bryce. London, 1882

61) *Manitoba, Creation of; A History of Red River Troubles,* by Alexander Begg. Hunter, Rose and Company, Toronto, 1871

62) *Manitoba, from the Earliest Settlement to 1835, History of,* by Donald Gunn. MacLean, Roger and Company, Ottawa, 1880

63) *Manitoba, History of Its Early Settlement,* by Robert B. Hill. William Briggs, Toronto, 1898

64) *Manitoba, Place Names of.* Geographic Board of the Department of the Interior, Ottawa, 1933

65) *Manitoba School Question, The (An Historical Acount of the Red River Outbreak in 1869 and 1870),* by John S. Ewart. Copp, Clark Company, Ltd., Toronto, 1894

66) *Manitoba, 1880-1881, A Year In,* by Captain Goodridge. W. & R. Chambers, London, 1882

67) *Massacre by the Sioux Indians in Minnesota, History of the Great,* by Charles S. Bryant. Hickey and Carroll, Cincinnati, 1864

68) *Minnesota, A History of,* by William Watts Folwell. Minnesota Historical Society, St. Paul, 1921. 4 vols.

69) *Minnesota and Dacotah in Letters Descriptive of a Tour Through the North West in the Autumn of 1856,* by Christopher C. Andrews. Robert Farnham, Washington, D.C., 1857

70) *Minnesota, Geography and Geology of,* by Christopher Webber Hall. H. H. Wilson Company, New York, 1903

71) *Minnesota and Its Resources,* by J. W. Bond. Redfield, New York, 1853

72) *Minnesota and Its People, and Early History of Minneapolis,* by John Harrington Stevens. Tribune Job Printing Company, Minneapolis, 1890

73) *Minnesota in Three Centuries, 1655-1908.* Publishing Society of Minnesota, 1908
Vol. I *Descriptions and Explorations,* by Warren Upham.
Vol. II *Early History,* by R. I. Holcombe
Vol. III *Minnesota As a State,* by Lucius F. Hubbard and R. I. Holcombe

74) *Minnesota: Its History and People (A Study Outline with Topics and References)* by Theodore C. Blegen. University of Minnesota Press, Minneapolis, 1937

75) *Minnesota, Report of an Exploration of the Territory of,* by John Pope. Sen. Exe. Doc. No. 42, 31st Congress, 1st Session, Serial No. 558

76) *Minnesota, The History of,* by Reverend Edward Duffield Neill. Johnson, Smith and Harrison, Minneapolis, 1878

77) *Mound Builders, The,* by Henry Clyde Shetrone. Appleton Company, New York, 1930

78) *Norse Discovery of America,* by Professor Andrew Fossum. Augsburg Publishing House, Minneapolis, 1918

79) *Northern Pacific Railway, History of the,* by E. V. Smalley. G. F. Putnam's Sons, New York, 1883

80) *North West Company, The,* by Gordon C. Davidson. University of California Press, Berkeley, 1918

81) *Northwest, History of the,* by Alexander Begg. Hunter, Rose and Company, Toronto, 1895

82) *Northwest Minnesota.* Minnesota State Board of Immigration, St. Paul, 1925

83) *Norwegian Emigrant Songs and Ballads,* by Blegen and Ruud. University of Minnesota Press, Minneapolis, 1936

84) *Not By Bread Alone,* by Vilhjalmur Stefansson. The Macmillan Company, New York, 1946

85) *Pacific Railways and Nationalism in the Canadian-American Northwest, 1845-73,* by Leonard Bertram Irwin. University of Pennsylvania, Philadelphia, 1939

86) *Pembina Settlement; Samuel Woods' Report Relative to His Expedition to.* Sen. Exe. Doc. No. 42, 31st Congress, 1st Session, Serial No. 558

87) *Peter Pond, Fur Trader and Adventurer,* by H. A. Innis. Irwin and Gordon, Ltd., Toronto, 1930

88) *Pilgrimage in Europe and America Leading to the Discovery of the Sources of the Mississippi and Bloody Rivers,* by G. C. Beltrami. Hunt and Clark, London, 1828. 2 vols.

89) *Pleistocene Man in Minnesota,* by Albert Ernest Jenks. University of Minnesota Press, Minneapolis, 1936

90) *Prairie, Death on the, (The 30 Years Struggle for the Western Plains),* by Paul I. Wellman. The Macmillan Company, New York, 1934

91) *Prairie Frontier, Following the,* by Seth King Humphrey. University of Minnesota Press, Minneapolis, 1931

92) *Prairie Provinces of Canada,* compiled by Henry J. Boan. Sells, Ltd., London, 1914

93) *Prairie Provinces, Romance of the,* by A. L. Burt. W. J. Gage and Company, Ltd., Toronto, 1942

94) *Prairie Settlement, the Geographical Setting,* by William A. Mackintosh. (Vol. I of the IX-volume series on *Canadian Frontiers of Settlement.*) Macmillan Company, Ltd., Toronto, 1934

95) *Prairies, Thirteen Years on the,* by John Pennefather. Kegan, Paul, Trench, Trubner, London, 1892

96) *Red River,* by Joseph James Hargrave. John Lovell, Montreal, 1871

97) *Red River Colony,* by Louis Aubrey Wood. Chronicles of Canada, Vol. XXI. Glasgow, Brook and Company, Toronto, 1915

98) *Red River Colony, British North America, Substance of a Journal, During a Residence at,* by John West. L. B. Seeley and Son, London, 1824

99) *Red River Country, Hudson's Bay and Northwest Territories,* by Alexander J. Russell. G. R. Desbarats, Montreal, 1870. 3rd edition.

100) *Red River Expedition, The,* by Captain G. L. Huyshe. The Macmillan Company, New York, 1871

101) *Red River of the North, Minnesota and North Dakota.* Doc. No. 616, 62nd Congress House of Representatives, 2nd Session

102) *Red River Rebellion, In the Days of,* by John McDougall. William Briggs, Toronto, 1903

103) *Red River Settlement; Its Rise, Progress and Present State,* by Alexander Ross. Smith, Elder and Company, London, 1856

104) *Red River Valley, 1811-1849, The,* by John Perry Pritchett. Yale University Press, New Haven, 1942

105) *Romantic Settlement of Lord Selkirk's Colonists,* by George Bryce. Musson Book Company, Ltd., Toronto, 1906

106) *Saskatchewan and the Rocky Mountains, a Diary and Narrative of Travel . . . during a journey through the Hudson's Bay Company's Territories, in 1859 and 1860,* by James Carnegie, Earl of Southesk. Edmonston and Douglas, Edinburgh, 1875

107) *Scotch Grove Trail, The,* by Bruce E. Makan. *The Palimpsest,* November, 1922

108) *Seat of Empire, The,* by Charles Carleton Coffin. Fields, Osgood and Company, Boston, 1870

109) *Selkirk Settlers in Real Life, The,* by R. G. Macbeth. William Briggs, Toronto, 1897

110) *Selkirk's Settlement Upon Red River in North America; Its Destruction in 1815 and 1816; and the Massacre of Governor Semple and His Party, Statement Respecting the Earl of,* by John Halkett. John Murray, London, 1817

111) *Sir Alexander Mackenzie, Explorer and Fur Trader,* by Hume Wrong. Macmillan Company, Ltd., Toronto, 1927

112) *Sir George Simpson, Overseas Governor of the Hudson's Bay Company,* by A. S. Morton. Oregon Historical Society, Portland, 1944

113) *Social Economics of North Dakota,* by J. M. Gillette. Burgess Publishing Company, Minneapolis, 1942

114) *Sod House Frontier, The, 1854-1890,* by Everett Dick. Appleton-Century Company, New York, 1937

115) *St. Paul, A History of the City of,* by J. Fletcher Williams. Minnesota Historical Society, St. Paul, 1876

116) *Steamboating on the Red River,* by Marion H. Herriot. Clipping Collection, Minneapolis Public Library.

117) *Steel of Empire, The Romantic History of the CPR,* by John Murray Gibbon. Bobbs-Merrill, New York, 1935

118) *Trail of an Artist-Naturalist; the Autobiography of Ernest Thompson Seton.* Charles Scribner's Sons, New York, 1940

119) *Unguarded Frontier—A History of American Canadian Relations, The,* by Edgar W. McInnes. Doubleday and Company, New York, 1942

120) *Verendrye and His Sons, Journals and Letters of Pierre Gaultier de la.* The Champlain Society, Toronto, 1927

121) *Voyages from Montreal Through the Continent of North America*

to the Frozen (Arctic) and Pacific Oceans in 1789 and 1793, by
Alexander Mackenzie. A. S. Barnes and Company, New York,
1903. 2 vols.

122) *Voyages of Peter Esprit Radisson, Being an Account of His Travels
and Experiences Among the North American Indians from 1652
to 1684.* Prince Society of Boston, 1880

123) *Voyageur's Highway, The,* by Grace Lee Nute. Minnesota Historical Society, St. Paul, 1941

124) *Westward from Vinland,* by Hjalmar R. Holand. Duell, Sloan and
Pearce, New York, 1940

125) *Westward Movement, The,* by Ina Faye Woestemeyer. Appleton-
Century Company, New York, 1939

126) *Wheat Market and the Farmer in Minnesota, 1858-1900, The,* by
Henrietta M. Larson. Columbia University Press, New York,
1926

127) *Wild Northland, The,* by General Sir William Francis Butler. A. S.
Barnes and Company, New York, 1904

128) *Windmill and Its Times, The,* by E. B. Shuttleworth. Edward A.
Apted, Toronto, 1924

129) *Winnipeg, Old Forts of,* by Charles Napier Bell. Winnipeg, 1927

130) *Winnipeg, Sketch of the History of the City of,* by George Bryce.
Winnipeg, 1909

131) *Women of Red River,* by W. J. Healy. Russell, Lang and Company,
Ltd., Winnipeg, 1923

FICTION

132) *Mine Inheritance,* by Frederick Niven. The Macmillan Company,
New York, 1940

133) *Mystery of Metropolisville, The,* by Edward Eggleston. Orange
Judd Company, New York, 1905

134) *Ojibway, The; a novel of Indian life of the Period of the Early Advance of Civilization in the Great Northwest,* by Joseph A. Gil-
fallan. The Neale Publishing Company, New York, 1904

135) *O River, Remember,* by Martha Ostenso. Bobbs-Merrill, New York,
1943

136) *Red River Shadows,* by Olive Knox. The Macmillan Company, New
York, 1948

137) *Threshers, The,* by Herbert Krause. Bobbs-Merrill, New York, 1947

138) *Wind Without Rain,* by Herbert Krause. Bobbs-Merrill, New York,
1938

Endlessly suggestive material on every phase of Red River history
can be found in archives and publications of the State Historical Soci-

eties of Minnesota, North and South Dakota, the Mississippi Valley Historical Association, and in the Historical and Scientific Society of the Province of Manitoba. Many of the State University libraries from Michigan and Wisconsin to Washington and Oregon have made books and other material on the Old Northwest, of which Red River Valley is a part, important to their collections on the entire Northwest.

Public libraries of Minneapolis and St. Paul, the James J. Hill Library, also in St. Paul, the Provincial Government Library in Winnipeg, the Carnegie Public Library in Sioux Falls, have built and are continuing to enlarge their collections of primary and secondary sources on the Old Northwest. Anyone with the eyesight of an eagle, the tenacity of a beagle, can find both information and entertainment in pioneer issues of the *Winnipeg Free Press, St. Paul Pioneer Press, Minneapolis Tribune, Grand Forks Herald, Fargo Forum, Sioux Falls Argus Leader.*

INDEX